SATURDAY NIGHT LIVE AND PHILOSOPHY

The Blackwell Philosophy and Pop Culture Series
Series editor William Irwin

A spoonful of sugar helps the medicine go down, and a healthy helping of popular culture clears the cobwebs from Kant. Philosophy has had a public relations problem for a few centuries now. This series aims to change that, showing that philosophy is relevant to your life—and not just for answering the big questions like "To be or not to be?" but for answering the little questions: "To watch or not to watch *South Park*?" Thinking deeply about TV, movies, and music doesn't make you a "complete idiot." In fact it might make you a philosopher, someone who believes the unexamined life is not worth living and the unexamined cartoon is not worth watching.

Already published in the series:

SATURDAY NIGHT LIVE AND PHILOSOPHY

Deep Thoughts Through the Decades

Edited by

Jason Southworth
Ruth Tallman

WILEY Blackwell

This edition first published 2020
© 2020 John Wiley & Sons Ltd

The right of Jason Southworth, Ruth Tallman, and William Irwin to be identified as the authors of this editorial material in this work has been asserted in accordance with law.

Registered Offices
John Wiley & Sons, Inc., 111 River Street, Hoboken, NJ 07030, USA
John Wiley & Sons Ltd, The Atrium, Southern Gate, Chichester, West Sussex, PO19 8SQ, UK

Editorial Office
111 River Street, Hoboken, NJ 07030, USA

For details of our global editorial offices, customer services, and more information about Wiley products visit us at www.wiley.com.

Wiley also publishes its books in a variety of electronic formats and by print-on-demand. Some content that appears in standard print versions of this book may not be available in other formats.

Library of Congress Cataloging-in-Publication Data

Names: Southworth, Jason, editor. | Tallman, Ruth, editor.
Title: Saturday night live and philosophy : deep thoughts through the decades / edited by Jason Southworth, Ruth Tallman.
Description: Hoboken : Wiley-Blackwell 2020. | Series: The Blackwell philosophy and pop culture series | Includes bibliographical references and index.
Identifiers: LCCN 2019052001 (print) | LCCN 2019052002 (ebook) | ISBN 9781119538554 (paperback) | ISBN 9781119538578 (adobe pdf) | ISBN 9781119538684 (epub)
Subjects: LCSH: Saturday night live (Television program)
Classification: LCC PN1992.77.S273 S225 2020 (print) | LCC PN1992.77.S273 (ebook) | DDC 791.45/72–dc23

LC record available at https://lccn.loc.gov/2019052001
LC ebook record available at https://lccn.loc.gov/2019052002

Cover Design: Wiley
Cover Image: © Philippe LEJEANVRE/Getty Images

Set in 10.5/13pt Sabon by SPi Global, Pondicherry, India

Printed in the United States of America.

VF3B45D51-DE91-444C-915E-B5932083D2E5_011320

Contents

Cast Members

Robin Barrett is a Ph.D. candidate at Faulkner University, and an online faculty member with Likewise College. Robin is currently focusing his research on divine revelation as it relates to epistemology for his upcoming dissertation. Other areas of interest are metaethics and philosophy of religion. Robin resides in the Pacific Northwest with his wife and three children, and they are all Superfans of da Seattle Seahawks.

Erich Christiansen is a Ph.D. candidate at the University of Georgia. He is writing a dissertation on the ethical and political problems with military drones. His article "Wicked world: the politics of the supernatural in Black Sabbath" was included in *Black Sabbath and Philosophy: Mastering Reality*. He has covered jazz for *A Gathering of the Tribes* and jazz and comics for *Pulse: Berlin*. His poetry has appeared in *Bad Newz* and *Maintenant*. Erich's other research interests include Greek diners with extremely limited menus, sibling blues musicians, and "French immigrants" with questionable craniums.

Gerald J. Erion is Professor of Philosophy at Medaille College in Buffalo, New York. His research interests include ethics, philosophy of mind, communication theory, and cities; he also writes on critical thinking and the teaching of philosophy. Buffalo's hottest club is Erion's office. This place has *everything*: books, stacks of paper, Fisher-Price toys, a Labrador retriever, X Day cards, and temporary tattoos. And if you ask about utilitarianism, you might get to see photographs of Jeremy Bentham's body.

Kimberly S. Engels is Assistant Professor of Philosophy at Molloy College. Her research focuses on existentialism as a contemporary living philosophy, applicable to all domains of modern life. She is co-editor of

Westworld and Philosophy: If You Go Looking for the Truth, Get the Whole Thing, and has published articles relating existentialism to issues in environmental ethics, medical ethics, and public policy. Though she hates to be a Debbie Downer, she feels obligated to remind the reader that feline AIDS is the # 1 killer of domestic cats.

Jeremy Fried is a Ph.D. candidate in philosophy at the University of Oklahoma and also received his J.D. from UC-Berkeley. His current research focuses on the intersection between aesthetics and legal rights, particularly regarding intellectual property. He also does work in philosophy of sport and philosophy of race. Jeremy's favorite *SNL* sketch is The Polar Bear Cage and he can objectively claim that his cat Risky Biscuits is the best cat in the whole entire world even if she isn't quite the driver Toonces was.

Erik Garrett is Associate Professor in the Department of Communication and Rhetorical Studies at Duquesne University. He received a dual doctorate in philosophy and communication from Purdue University. His books and monographs include *Why Do We Go to The Zoo? Communication, Animals, and the Cultural-historical Experience of Zoos* and *El barrio de la colina: Dos estudios de fenomenologia urbana.* He currently is working on a book about urban phenomenology and communication. He is chair of the Society for Phenomenology and the Human Sciences and the North American Levinas Society. No Really!?! This has been Really with Erik and Kati.

Theodore Gracyk is Professor of Philosophy at Minnesota State University Moorhead and (since 2013) the co-editor of *The Journal of Aesthetics and Art Criticism.* He is the author of several philosophical books on music, including *Rhythm and Noise: An Aesthetics of Rock Music* (Duke University Press, 1996); *Listening to Popular Music* (University of Michigan Press, 2007); *On Music* (Routledge, 2013); and co-author of *Jazz and the Philosophy of Art* (Routledge, 2018). He has authored numerous articles on the aesthetics of music and the history of aesthetics. He was co-recipient of the 2002 Woody Guthrie Award (the 2002 IASPM/US Book Award). With Andrew Kania, he co-edited *The Routledge Companion to Philosophy and Music* (2011).

John Scott Gray is Distinguished Teacher and Professor of Philosophy at Ferris State University in Big Rapids, MI. He earned degrees at Furman University (B.A.), Baylor University (M.A.), and Southern

Illinois University, Carbondale (Ph.D.). His research interests focus on areas of applied philosophy, including the Philosophy of Sports, Sex and Love, Bioethics, and numerous publications in the Philosophy of Popular Culture. Dr. Gray co-authored *Introduction to Popular Culture: Theories, Applications, and Global Perspectives* (2013). He is currently working on his next book, *An Atheist's Guide to Sacred Space*. His hobbies include playing hockey and collecting vintage sports cards. He and his wife, Jo, and his son, Oscar, live in Canadian Lakes, MI.

Jason Holt is Professor in the School of Kinesiology at Acadia University. His current research areas are aesthetics, philosophy of sport, and philosophy and popular culture. His books include *Meanings of Art: Essays in Aesthetics* and *Blindsight and the Nature of Consciousness*, which was shortlisted for the Canadian Philosophical Association Book Prize, and as editor, *Leonard Cohen and Philosophy: Various Positions*, *Philosophy of Sport: Core Readings*, and *The Daily Show and Philosophy: Moments of Zen in the Art of Fake News*. His literary work includes the recent *Up Against Beyond: Selected Poems, 1994–2017*. He aspires one day to affirm that he's good enough, he's smart enough, and doggone it, people like him.

William Irwin is Hervé A. LeBlanc Distinguished Service Professor and Chair of Philosophy at King's College in Pennsylvania. He is the general editor of the Blackwell and Philosophy Pop Culture Series in addition to being the volume editor for *Metallica and Philosophy* and *Black Sabbath and Philosophy*. Irwin's most recent books include *God Is a Question, Not an Answer: Finding Common Ground in Our Uncertainty* and the novel *Little Siddhartha*. Bill has always thought that philosophy needs more cowbell.

David Kyle Johnson is Professor of Philosophy at King's College, in Wilkes-Barre. Pennsylvania. His specializations include metaphysics, logic, and philosophy of religion. His recording for "The Great Courses" include *Sci-Phi: Science Fiction as Philosophy*, *The Big Questions of Philosophy*, and *Exploring Metaphysics*. Kyle is the editor-in-chief of *The Palgrave Handbook of Popular Culture as Philosophy* (forthcoming) and has also edited *Black Mirror and Philosophy: Dark Reflections* and *Inception and Philosophy: Because It's Never Just a Dream*. A fan of SNL since his youth, Kyle grew up in an evangelical household and coined the phrase "SNL Hangover."

It's the exhaustion and frustration a person feels when they have to get up early go to church after having secretly stayed up to watch SNL the night before.

J.R. Lombardo is a social worker and addictions specialist in private practice in White Plains NY. He teaches classes on various mental health and addictions topics and presents workshops to both helping professionals as well as the general public. He has a particular interest in the correlation between early attachment patterns and addictive behaviors. J.R. is a caring nurturer, a member of several 12-step programs, **and** *a licensed therapist.*

Michael McGowan is Professor of Philosophy and Religion at Florida Southwestern State College. He earned graduate degrees from Yale University, University of South Florida, Claremont Graduate University, and Malone University. He is the editor of *David Foster Wallace and Religion: Essays on Faith and Fiction* (Bloomsbury, 2019) and author of *The Bridge: Revelation and its Implications* (Pickwick, 2015). He has written for the *Journal of Human Rights, Teaching Ethics, Christianity Today, Journal of Religion and Film, Christian Scholar's Review, Theological Book Review, International Journal of Systematic Theology,* and the *Journal of Religion and Film.* Find him online at www.loveofwisdom.org.

Edwardo Pérez spent his formative, middle-school years, staying up late at friends' houses during sleep-overs to watch *SNL,* feeling like the little brother of Yortuk and Georg Festrunk (absolutely clueless when it came to dating). Inspired by the Blues Brothers (and Tom "Bones" Malone), Edwardo spent many years playing trombone and trumpet in jazz venues across the country before becoming a professor of English, contributing essays to *1984 and Philosophy, Doctor Strange and Philosophy, The Handmaid's Tale and Philosophy, Disney and Philosophy,* and *Black Mirror and Philosophy.* He is currently co-editing *Black Panther and Philosophy* with Timothy Brown, writing philosophical blogs on andphilosophy.com, and managing the website lightsabertoss.com. Edwardo's wife, whom he lovingly refers to as his "Wild-American Fox," keeps him grounded in reality.

Joshua J. Reynolds is an unaffiliated guy who lives somewhere in the United States. He's got a Ph.D. from Princeton (framed and propping up a stack of articles on the metaphysics of fidget spinning), as well as a B.A. from Arizona State. The author of several soporific master-pieces on Plato, Thucydides, and Aeschylus, this guy eventually aban-doned the life of library research and education to offer a more fitting response to existence: smartassery. His book, *In the Beginning: A Serious Satire on Myth, Philosophy, and Belief*, is available on Amazon and selling like hotcakes (well, maybe more like gluten-free porridge). Joshua dislikes leaf blowers, Harleys, and HID headlights. He enjoys breathing, sounds of nature, and vision.

Tadd Ruetenik is Professor of Philosophy at St. Ambrose University. He is the author of *The Demons of William James: Religious Pragmatism Explores Unusual Mental States*, and has published arti-cles on a wide variety of subjects, including psychical research, reli-gious philosophy, animal ethics, and non-violence. As a child, he was sometimes allowed to watch *SNL* with his parents and pretended he didn't already know the meaning of the raunchy jokes that they were explaining to him.

Jason Southworth is an adjunct philosopher at a number of schools. He no longer feels it's appropriate to give them free advertising if they're unwilling to pay a living wage and provide health insurance. He has contributed to many Popular Culture and Philosophy volumes, includ-ing *House of Cards and Philosophy*, *Green Lantern and Philosophy*, and *Stephen Colbert and Philosophy*. And that's the way it is.

Kati Sudnick is a Ph.D. candidate in the Department of Communication and Rhetorical Studies at Duquesne University. Her research interests include the media ecological foundations of social media, applied communication and philosophy, and communication ethics and pop-ular culture. She currently serves as editorial assistant for the *Journal of Communication and Religion* and has previously published in *In Media Res* with her contribution "Harry Potter, World War II, and the Banality of Evil." She gives special thanks to the philosophy depart-ment at King's College in Wilkes-Barre, PA for cultivating a love of all things philosophy and popular culture during her undergraduate studies. Really!?!

Ruth Tallman teaches philosophy at Hillsborough Community College. Her research area is biomedical ethics, with a particular focus, of late, on moral issues arising within the physician-patient relationship. Her safe word is "popcorn."

J. Jeremy Wisnewski earns his keep as a Professor of Philosophy at Hartwick College. He has authored or edited twelve allegedly non-fiction books, all of which seem suspicious in retrospect. These include: *Wittgenstein and Ethical Inquiry* (Continuum, 2007), *Understanding Torture* (Edinburgh University Press, 2010), *Heidegger: An Introduction* (Rowman & Littlefield, 2013*)*, and *The Politics of Agency: Toward a Pragmatic Philosophical Anthropology* (Routledge, 2016). He has also edited six books in Blackwell's Philosophy and Pop Culture series. His delusions include the belief that telling you about these books will help get him on *SNL*'s Celebrity Jeopardy (he really wants to meet Sean Connery).

Cold Open
The Introduction

Most of us can identify television programs that shaped and defined us as we grew up. They were the backdrop of our experiences of first loves, first apartments, minimum wage jobs, and bad break ups. In addition to being personally meaningful, pop cultural artworks such as TV shows often contribute to the collective consciousness of a generation, helping us understand our peers as set apart from those older and younger than ourselves. Owing to its exceptional longevity, *Saturday Night Live (SNL)* has helped define not *a* generation, but multiple generations of viewers. The young fans who stayed up late to see the Land Shark and the Killer Bees went on to share the joys of the Spartan Cheerleaders and the Ambiguously Gay Duo with their own children. Now, those same fans are watching Morning Joe and Eric and Donald Trump Jr. with their grandkids. We can date ourselves based on who we consider "our" Update hosts, and most of us see the decade of our own adolescence as the golden age of the show. Despite our disagreements, we're unified in that none of us can recall the major news events of our lives without also thinking about the ways we saw them lampooned on Saturday nights.

We sit down to watch (and keep coming back) for the laughs, but *SNL* has done more than just entertain us for the past four and a half decades. Like philosophy itself, *SNL* has challenged us to view our world with a critical and questioning eye. Kids can laugh long before they're capable of engaging in critical analysis. Thanks to *SNL's* use of parody and satire, those of us who grew up watching the show

Saturday Night Live and Philosophy: Deep Thoughts Through the Decades,
First Edition. Edited by Jason Southworth and Ruth Tallman.

were wired to think philosophically by the time our brains caught up to the task. This book takes us further down that road with a careful, deliberate look at the philosophy that is laced throughout four and a half decades of *SNL* sketches, impressions, and fake news. Happy reading, and have a pleasant tomorrow!

Part I
THE OPENING MONOLOGUE

Chase's Ford vs. Belushi's Samurai

Why Is it OK to Punch Up But Not Down?

Ruth Tallman

Since its inception, *SNL* has displayed a willingness – even eager-ness – to take comedic shots at public figures – and it seems no status is so exalted as to earn someone a pass. No sitting president has been immune from *SNL*'s mockery – and in recent election cycles all major contenders for the White House have been lampooned as well. Supreme Court justices have taken their turns, as have senators and congress people. Popes – heck, even Jesus Christ himself – have been the subject of *SNL*'s playful mirth. The question we'll consider in this chapter is – why do we find this acceptable? Why does no one mind that irreverent young comedians don funny wigs and make up to poke fun at political and religious leaders on national television? Where's the respect? We'll also consider how it could be that sometimes, a joke that targets people who aren't that powerful at all seems to violate moral norms in a way that jokes targeting the most powerful among us do not.

Radical Autonomism

Ethical comedy might sound like an oxymoron – many people hold the belief that, if it's part of a comedic act, it's somehow immune to moral criticism. This view has deep roots in aesthetics, or the philosophy of art. Radical autonomism is the position that moral categories simply do not apply to works of art – and that only aesthetic categories are

Saturday Night Live and Philosophy: Deep Thoughts Through the Decades, First Edition. Edited by Jason Southworth and Ruth Tallman.
© 2020 John Wiley & Sons Ltd. Published 2020 by John Wiley & Sons Ltd.

appropriate. The British art critic Clive Bell (1881–1964) was a strong proponent of autonomism. On this view, the purpose of a work of art is to stimulate aesthetic responses in the audience. Aesthetic emotions are necessarily good, on this view, so a work of art is good or bad to the extent that it does or does not produce aesthetic emotions in the audience. Generally, the aesthetic emotion a work of comedic art is aimed at producing is humor. Thus, the grounds by which it would be appropriate to judge the work would simply be, "is it funny?" On the other hand, "is it mean, hurtful, or disrespectful?" are inappropriate questions to ask about a work of art. Autonomism sees art as set apart from ordinary life, and its rules. What might be negatively judged in the real world due to moral considerations gets a pass when it's presented as part of a work of art. While this may sound a bit strange, consider how different our reaction might have been if, in an interview, Chevy Chase described sitting president Gerald Ford as a bumbling idiot who couldn't walk across a room without tripping over his own feet. This sounds harsh and disrespectful, particularly when said of a president while in office. Yet, isn't that exactly the sentiment Chase conveyed each Saturday night as he stumbled across the stage in the character of President Ford?

Autonomism stems from the belief that there is something very valuable – even sacred – about art and its role in our lives. Works of art provide us with a space where we can play imaginatively with ideas that might be better shied away from in real life. Placing art in a realm in which it may remain immune from moral criticism allows artists to fully develop their creativity. Art thereby creates a safe space in which both artist and audience can explore radical ideas without causing harm in the real world. We can engage in imaginative exploration in fiction without carrying those ideas into reality, where they might cause harm. Because art is, by its very nature, *not* reality, we can allow what would be morally reprehensible in real life to simply be awesome aesthetic fun in a work of art. It's a mindset of radical autonomism that allows us to evaluate, for instance, Debbie as a great comedic character, while recognizing that were she to exist in real life she would be, well, a downer.

Radical Moralism

The flip side of radical autonomism is known as radical moralism. The Russian author Leo Tolstoy (1828–1910) was a proponent of this view, which holds that art is good insofar as it promotes good values,

and bad to the extent that it promotes bad values. Unlike autonomism, which says aesthetic evaluations are entirely distinct from
moral evaluations, radical moralism holds that it's impossible to separate the two. So, an artwork that promotes immoral beliefs would
necessarily be a bad work of art – there's no way for its aesthetic
qualities to redeem it, because radical moralists hold that moral values supersede aesthetic ones. An obvious complication of this view is
that we don't all agree about what constitutes a moral or an immoral
belief. Tolstoy had some ideas about this – he saw social inclusivity as
good, and elitism and social division as bad. To the extent that high
presidential approval ratings promote social unity, then, depictions of
the two Presidents Bush by Dana Carvey and Will Ferrell – by most
accounts far more lovable in their comedic hands than in real
life – would arguably receive high moralist marks from Tolstoy.

Radical moralism traces its roots back to Plato, who was all too
aware of art's power to sway the hearts of its audience. It was the very
power of art that scared Plato silly, as he saw art working through
emotion (paving the way for Bell and Tolstoy), rather than reason,
making it much less controllable or dependable than Plato would like.
Plato worried that a rousing work of art could prompt a riot, or give
credence to a view or a leader not worthy of rational endorsement (an
accusation that has been leveled against the role of Ferrell's Bush
character in the reelection of George W. Bush).[1] Tolstoy seemed to
share this worry with Plato, although he was happy to use the emotional efficacy of art to noble advantage, seeing art as having great
power to bring about social good.

Moderate Moralism

Splitting the difference between radical autonomism and radical moralism is the view known as moderate moralism, endorsed by contemporary aesthetician Noël Carrol. On this view, moral considerations
ought to be applied when evaluating a work of art, but so too should
aesthetic considerations, and the significant weight of either could
override the other. For instance, a work with troubling moral implications could be so aesthetically captivating that it causes us to forgive,
or look past, its moral failings. A work with particularly weighty moral
sins might be unable to muster the aesthetic wherewithal to overcome
its morally complicating elements. Moderate moralistic considerations
are probably in the background when we allow ourselves to snicker at

morally questionable jokes on the grounds that they are, in fact, quite funny, while being unwilling to extend the same generosity to a morally questionable joke that is hack or otherwise unfunny.

Who is the Butt of the Joke?

Although there are plenty of radical autonomists in the world today, it's hard for many people to engage with a work of art such as *Saturday Night Live* without considering the moral dimensions of its sketches, particularly when those sketches portray characters who have real life counterparts (who are, presumably, subject to moral evaluation, even if the art that portrays them might not be, according to an autonomist). How would a moralist, particularly a moderate moralist, go about evaluating the aesthetic and moral elements of a work of art – in this case, in an *SNL* sketch? A good starting point is to ask, is there a butt of the joke? Not all jokes have butts. Sketches such as Toonces the Driving Cat do not obviously target anyone; they're just absurd. To determine if the joke has a butt, ask, is there someone we're laughing *at*? Let's think about some examples. The butt of an impressionist's joke is usually, pretty straightforwardly, whoever they are doing an impression of. So, the butt of a typical Chase-as-Ford pratfall is Gerald Ford, and the butt of Carvey's famous "read my lips" antics is George H.W. Bush.

When we talk about "punching up" and "punching down," the person who's being "punched" is the butt of the joke. So, who is it OK to punch? To answer this question, we need to think about the various individuals and groups involved. We need to ask not just, who is the butt, but also, who is the butt in relation to the audience and to society. And, as we learned on the playground as kids, we should pick on someone our own size. Only bullies (who are actually weak cowards) pick on people who are smaller than them. This is what it means to punch down. But this isn't about physical size (otherwise way more people would be fair game for Jane Curtin's jokes (as she's only 5′ 4″), than would be for Chevy Chase (who comes in at 6′ 4″). No, the real issue is something more like social status. Let's think about this first in terms of individuals and their social status (generally, celebrities versus the rest of us), and then in terms of members of groups that hold varying levels of social status.

Public Figures: The Clintons

There seems to be something in our nature that renders us fascinated with celebrity. We love to observe (and judge) the lives of public figures. Perhaps it's our (often false) understanding of their lives as easy, glamorous, and exciting in ways that we wish our own were. Maybe it's a craving for the fame the celebrities themselves often seem to want to escape. Or maybe it's simply that we wish we had the wealth that fame often carries with it. *SNL* impressions are generally of celebrities, if for no other reason than that, for an impression to succeed, the audience must be familiar with its subject, and celebrities can serve as cultural touchstones.

Celebrities are usually understood as fair game for comedians, for a couple of reasons. First, there's the view that, since they chose their role as public figures (by seeking public office, or by pursuing careers as entertainers or in other high profile professions), they in some sense "asked for it," or at the very least, chose to accept a life that would include it. Additionally, there is the belief that most celebrities can take it. Because celebrities are famous, rich, and powerful, targeting a celebrity with a joke is usually "punching up." Comedians, while sometimes holding celebrity status themselves, do not hold anywhere near the status of, say, the president. So the comedian, holding a subordinate position in society, relative to the butt of the joke, punches up – taking a shot at the person in power. And when that happens, the audience – comprised of individuals who share that subordinate position – cheers. It's not about hating the butt of the joke, or wishing that person harm. There is simply something deeply psychologically satisfying about seeing a powerful person "brought down" through laughter. It reduces the gap between them and us. The joke slightly depowers the powerful person, by transferring that power to the audience who laughs.

Punching up can be affectionate. Comedians enjoy lampooning their heroes – that's the whole idea behind a roast, for instance. Public figures often tacitly acknowledge that they understand their role as comedic fodder to be friendly, accepting offers to appear on the show alongside their *SNL* doppelgangers. (There are many examples of this – some particularly memorable ones are Hillary Clinton joining Amy Poehler onstage in matching pantsuits, and Sarah Palin coming face to face with her double played by Tina Fey). But at other times the comedy is intended to question or even condemn the behavior of its target. When that target holds a powerful position, however, they are arguably not harmed by this comedic calling out. It makes us feel better about situations we don't like, and have relatively little power to change, and the butt of the joke remains unharmed. Moralists – radical and moderate – will have little objection to comedy such as this, that punches up.

Not all public figures meet the criteria outlined above, however. Some do not choose to be public figures, and they're not all powerful. Prime examples of this are the children of celebrities – thrust into the limelight by the decisions of their parents, and, as kids, necessarily pretty vulnerable in an adult world. When her father decided to run for president, pre-teen Chelsea Clinton became a household name. Young Clinton (twelve years old at the time) was the butt of a 1992 Wayne's World sketch (Season 18, Episode 8) that was subsequently removed from rebroadcasts of the show, with apologies from Lorne Michaels and Mike Myers. *SNL* had punched down, targeting a child who, while a public figure, had not chosen the role, and who certainly stood to be harmed, as a shy teen whose appearance was being scrutinized on national television by two of the most famous men in comedy at the time. *SNL* seemed to realize (after the fact, unfortunately), that there's a big difference between punching up at an adult Clinton who has chosen to be a powerful public figure, and punching down at a teenage Clinton, who is neither powerful not purposely public.

Group Membership: The Delicious Dish and Samurai Futaba

While *SNL* impressions focus on individuals – public figures who are recognizable to the audience – sketches featuring *SNL* original characters often appeal based on their ability to capture the essence of a type of person, or a group of people. Often, the type of person targeted by these kinds of characters is innocuous. Sketches featuring Bill Swerski's Super Fans poke fun at sports fanatics, while the sweater-wearing hosts of the Delicious Dish nail what it means to be on Team Public Radio. Targeting these "types" seems relatively unobjectionable, due partly to the fact that membership in fan groups and interest groups is optional – people *choose* to be fans, and public radio listeners.

More problematic are characters that target based on group membership that is unchosen – groups based on race, ethnicity, country of origin, sexual orientation, gender identification, disability, and (sometimes) religion[2] – and that is deeply connected with one's identity. John Belushi's Samurai Futaba sketches are more cringy than funny to modern sensibilities, because the butt of the joke is Belushi's fictitious Futaba – a stand-in for a stereotypical 1970s American understanding of a Japanese person. There's no social commentary or deeper meaning – just a white guy in a bathrobe swinging a katana and making fun of the sound of the Japanese language.

Targeting members of groups based on unchosen, identity-forming inclusion in those groups is morally objectionable partially for the same reason it's ethically suspect to target children based on who their parents are. In both cases, a person becomes the subject of attack (even if it's a lighthearted comedic attack) without any sort of choice that led them to be in that spotlight. When the comedy stems from stereotypes surrounding language, clothing, and behavior, life for members of that group becomes a little harder. It is doubtful that Belushi and the writers of the Samurai sketches intended any harm to Japanese or Japanese American people with the sketches. And it's unlikely that great harm occurred. But this is still an example of punching down, as individuals from a minority group in this country – probably already hassled for their accents and other differences – were the butt of a joke made by and predominantly for members of the dominant group (white Americans).

Targeting as a Means of Elevating: Lunch Lady Land

Part of the beauty and genius of art generally, and comedy in particular, is that it's not always straightforward. Great comedy is capable of remarkable nuance, and sometimes the intended message is not what one might think at first glance. There's a certain kind of comedian, who recognizes the power that comes from their platform, and chooses to use that platform to elevate those who have less social status, or less power in society – to lift them up, rather than to punch them down. Chris Farley's Lunch Lady character (with Adam Sandler's accompanying song) is a prime example of comedic targeting as a way of elevating, and celebrating, members of a group that have little social status or power, and who receive far less respect than they deserve.

School cafeteria workers are underpaid, underappreciated, and put up with plenty of crap from ill-mannered school kids. Farley and

Sandler, rather than taking cheap shots at members of a group who already get plenty of grief, pay tribute to these (previously) unsung individuals, who play a really important role in the daily lives of children. Amidst the psychedelic imagery of "Clouds made of carrots and peas/Mountains built of shepherds pie/And rivers made of macaroni and cheese," we're reminded that these workers provide children who might otherwise be having a hard, lonely day with food served, "with a little slice of love." In a world where many children face food insecurity at home, "everybody gets enough food/down here in Lunchlady Land."[3] Farley and Sandler's sketch calls us to reflect on the value of the individuals who kept our bellies full during what may have been some very hard years in our own young lives, and reminds us to appreciate the role these workers currently play in the lives of our own children. The lives of lunch ladies get better, not worse, as a result of this sketch. Moralists would approve.

When the Subject is Not the Butt: Schmitts Gay Beer

The subject of a joke is not always the butt of a joke. Remember, a joke with a butt is at the butt's expense – it's who we're laughing *at*. But sometimes – remember good jokes are often subtle – the butt of the joke is not seen or directly referenced. And what's more, the butt doesn't have to be a person or a group of people. Societal norms can also be the target of jokes, as is the case in this next example. The faux commercial for Schmitts Gay beer once again features the Farley and Sandler duo, along with a handful of hot, dripping wet beefcakes.[4] But the butt of this sketch is not gay people. Rather, the sketch is full of standard beer commercial tropes – Farley and Sandler are two impossibly lucky guys. Because the beer is so great, it turns a dirty, dry swimming pool into a sexual mecca, with close ups on gorgeous, near-naked bodies, all there for these men's enjoyment. Drink this beer, the message seems to be, and you too will become irresistible to human beings who are being portrayed as sex objects. This was a standard commercial message at the time (and today, for that matter), but viewers were (and are) so numb to it that the exploitation doesn't even register for a lot of people.

The Schmitts Gay sketch jolts viewers out of their complacency by replacing the usual (socially acceptable) sex objects – large-breasted women in bikinis – with large-penised men in speedos – not to ridicule gay people, but to point out that the shock we feel in seeing the blatant objectification of male bodies is a shock that we *ought* to feel when we see the same level of objectification of female bodies. The butt of the joke, then, is not gay people at all, but the advertising industry, as well as all of us who buy into it without questioning its heteronormativity and sexually exploitive tactics. Schmitts Gay thus punches up, not down. Once again, moralists would approve.

With these concepts in hand, the next time you watch *SNL*, take a moment to reflect. Who is the butt of the joke (if there is one)? Does that person hold a position of power in society, or is that person a member of a dominant societal group? Does the answer to those questions affect your response to the joke? If so, you're probably a radical or moderate moralist. If not, you just might be a radical autonomist. Either way, having the tools to engage in an ethical analysis of your meta-response to the art can enrich your ability to engage with the material in a more philosophical way.[5]

Notes

1. *THR* Staff. "Horatio Sanz: "Conservative" 'SNL' May Have Helped George W. Bush Get Elected," *The Hollywood Reporter*, March 20, 2015.
2. Religion is complicated because, while membership in a religious group can often be chosen and rejected, it can also be closely tied with non-chosen factors such as ethnicity (a person who is ethnically Jewish will remain so even if they chose to reject religious Judaism). Additionally, religion is seen by many to be an integral part of their identity since birth, and thus not chosen in the way one's allegiance, for instance, to Da Bears is chosen.
3. *Saturday Night Live*, Season 19, Episode 11, 1994. "Lunchlady Land" by Adam Sandler.
4. *Saturday Night Live*, Season 17, Episode 1, 1991.
5. I would like to thank my partner, Jason Southworth, for his help on this chapter, and in life.

Mr. Mike
The Dark, Existentialist Vision of Michael O'Donoghue

Erich Christiansen

Known for his dark, disturbing brand of comedy, which he had perfected at *National Lampoon*, Michael O'Donoghue was the first head writer for *Saturday Night Live*. He wasn't just a writer, though. In front of the *SNL* camera, as "Mr. Mike," he told "Least-Loved Bedtime Tales," that reflected themes of meaninglessness, suffering, and death from the existentialist philosophy of Jean-Paul Sartre (1905–1980). As we'll see, despite the darkness, O'Donoghue and Sartre ultimately offer hope.

Absurdity

In a 1945 lecture, Sartre gave a short, programmatic statement defining existentialism – or at least his version of existentialism. He said that, for human beings, "Existence precedes essence." The "essence" of something is the trait that makes it what it is. It's whatever makes something, for example, a rock, rather than a plant or an animal. But for conscious beings, like humans, essence isn't something we're born with. This is why, "subjectivity must be our point of departure."[1] Subjective beings like us are always making decisions about what we're going to do – which end up being decisions about what we will be. Thus, we are always being formed by our individual and collective choices.[2]

For Sartre, this is the logical consequence of atheism. If God made me, then I already know what I am, and therefore what my life means. This is because, in order to create me, God had to already have had an

Saturday Night Live and Philosophy: Deep Thoughts Through the Decades, First Edition. Edited by Jason Southworth and Ruth Tallman.

idea of what I am, and what my purpose would be. This is true of anything that is created: the person who made the coffee cup that I'm drinking out of had to have an idea of what it was, and what it was for, in order to have made it at all.[3]

But if the world wasn't created by God, then the world doesn't come equipped with purpose, values, and meaning. Things in the universe just exist, without being part of a grand plan that would make them meaningful. For Sartre, and for atheistic existentialists in general, this idea is very liberating. It means that I get to decide what my life is going to mean, rather than be told by some supernatural being – or His purported human representative. Rather than needing to *discover* values, we get to *create* them, like an artist creating her work. For Sartre, just because the universe has no *inherent* meaning doesn't imply that it's meaningless. Rather, it's up to us to create meaning.[4]

But for many people, the prospect of a universe of bare existence, with no purpose or values built into it, isn't a liberating chance for creation, but a bleak and terrifying nightmare. This is the nightmare that O'Donoghue tapped into with his "Least-Loved Bedtime Tales," which subvert narrative conventions to show the breakdown of meaning through the breakdown of language. Parents tell bedtime stories to pacify children with entertaining, happy thoughts. But a "fairy tale" or "bedtime story" isn't real – it's a comforting lie told to children. And indeed, we often do tell children lies, not just in bedtime stories, but in all kinds of ways – because we don't want them to despair over the harsh realities of the world. We want them to think that life has a point.

In contrast to traditional bedtime stories, O'Donoghue's tales emphasize the meaninglessness – even the violent meaninglessness – of existence. Mr. Mike tells disturbing, pointless stories, not to comfort children, but to make them aware of the darkness of the human condition. As O'Donoghue's biographer, Dennis Perrin, explains, "His character would enjoy relating in full detail the brutality and nastiness of a world in which 'innocence' is routinely shot in the face and tossed into a ditch. Why lie to the kids and give them hope that somewhere an answer exists? Better to spell out the savagery simply and directly and trust that those listening get the point."[5]

Rather than speaking to children with a reassuring parental visage, Mr. Mike looks into the camera with dark glasses. O'Donoghue had acquired the dark lenses as a way of hiding; they were "portable two-way mirrors behind which he could watch the diseased human carnival…" They were Mike's real glasses, but they perfectly suited the character he was playing. "His eyes effectively blacked out, his 'death stare' resembled that of an insect – cold, calculated, indifferent to the misery of 'others.' What began as a defense mechanism soon became the finishing touch on the costume. Mr. Mike was born."[6]

Mr. Mike's dark vision was particularly disturbing in his encounter with the famous storytelling character, Uncle Remus. The portrayal of Uncle Remus was based on his depiction in the Disney movie *Song of the South*, which is now widely recognized as a racist caricature. O'Donoghue's writing satirizes racism, but these kinds of parodies of racism are uncomfortable and disturbing, especially when written by white people for black actors. After all, the line between portraying racism and espousing racism can be exceedingly thin.

In any case, Mr. Mike drops in to Uncle Remus' cabin to tell him a Least-Loved Bedtime Tale, about "your old buddy, Brer Rabbit." But in this version, Brer Rabbit is simply stopped on the road by Brer Fox and Brer Bear, who threaten to skin him alive. He tries his legendary tactic of saying "Skin me alive; do anything you want, but don't throw me in the briar patch." But O'Donoghue's version turns out differently from the classic one. "In my story," Mr. Mike says, "they respect his wishes and skin him alive." Reaching a crescendo of dark demystification, Mr. Mike says, "I mean, it's all very amusing to talk about being skinned alive in some children's book, but can you imagine it actually going down? Toward the end, when they were cutting the ears away from the side of the skull" – you can hear the studio audience gasp at this point – "he was screaming: 'Throw me in the briar patch! Throw me in the molten glass furnace, anything but this!'"

Uncle Remus is aghast. "But, but, Mr. Mike, what am de moral of your fable?"

"There's no moral, Uncle Remus, just random acts of meaningless violence." This line concisely sums up O'Donoghue's view of sense-making narratives, and his view of the world. The storytellers of the world are lying to us, because the very form of the narrative, maybe the very use of language itself, tries to establish a meaning where there just isn't one.

O'Donoghue portrays the absurd not only in the breakdown of language, but in the failure of action. In "Sartresky and Hutch," a parody of *Starsky and Hutch*, O'Donoghue gives us "two cops. One tough; the other existential!" John Belushi plays Hutch, and Dan Aykroyd portrays Jean-Paul Sartre, with his signature thick glasses and pipe.

The partners are called in because "another freaked-out Vietnam veteran" is strapped with explosives and threatening to blow himself up at the Sunshine National Bank. The perpetrator is Rusty, a childhood friend of Hutch's. Jean-Paul offers philosophical observations, such as "He is trying to destroy the bank. Therefore, destruction is to be given a place among this man's appropriated mode of behavior." Which means...nothing. The statement is a tautology; it only means that if he destroys the bank, then destroying the bank is one of the things that he does. O'Donoghue puts similarly unhelpful gobbledygook in "Sartre's" mouth throughout the sketch. The philosopher-cop's statements take key words of existentialist philosophy – being, action, human reality, consciousness – and fling them together into a meaningless "word salad."

The absurdity isn't limited to language in this sketch or anywhere else. To get more information, Hutch asks Tanya, a prostitute and informant, where the Sunshine National Bank is. She says it's right across the street from his office, and Jean-Paul interjects, "C'est l'absurd!" Indeed it is. The answer is something that Hutch could have discovered with his own eyes by looking out the window. The whole trip to see Tanya was pointless, meaningless. But before they leave, Jean-Paul observes that "Rusty is desperate because he's in a state of need, you see, and scarcity and need are human conditions that often result in violence." The real Sartre would agree, and Jean-Paul turns out to be right. When they go to the bank and talk to Rusty (Bill Murray), they find out that, as the captain had alluded to, his condition is the result of fighting in the Vietnam War – an imperialist war to retain control over the resources of another country, which the real Sartre militantly and publicly opposed. As a result of this brutal and unethical war, Rusty suffers from what would today be called PTSD.

When Hutch asks Rusty why he has strapped explosives to himself and taken hostages, he answers, "When you were in the police academy, I was in 'Nam, fighting for what I thought – what they told me – was right. I gave them five years and I got back here wounded, shell-shocked and defeated. Then I met this girl." He introduces his wife, Gwen (Jane Curtin), whom he has taken hostage. Meeting her gave him enough hope to try to start over. He wanted a loan, but the bank wouldn't give him one. They said he was crazy. His investment? He wanted to buy Vermont.

Jean-Paul says, "Rusty, do you realize that death is the highest form of human self-negation? In death, there is no being and no consciousness. There is only life's most beautiful element – nothingness."

RUSTY: "You think he's bluffing, dear?"
GWEN: "Oh no, I think it sounds wonderful."

The real Jean-Paul Sartre would not have said this. Yes, he did see nothingness as the ability to negate. This is what human freedom is all about – we can always negate the circumstances we find ourselves in; we can always change things in a certain way. But this freedom comes from the fact that we are conscious beings. Our ability to think about something that isn't the reality right in front of us – whether remembering the past or imagining the future – "negates" that reality by allowing us to see that there are other possibilities.[7] This is the only sense in which Sartre would have ever called nothingness "beautiful."

Nonetheless, this utterance is just what is needed for the ultimate outcome of the story. These struggling people are attracted to nihilism, and they are convinced to set off the bomb and thus kill themselves. Rusty says, "We've been looking for a new start, and death sounds like the life for us. Thanks, guys."

Jean-Paul exclaims, "It's absurd!" several times through the sketch, and with good reason. Every action that's taken is a failure, a waste of time, ultimately meaningless. Hutch seeks out Tanya for information he should have had already. Rusty fails to have his demands met. Jean-Paul and Hutch fail to save the bank or the hostages. At the end of the sketch, as one last cry against the absurd, Hutch asks, "But what does it all mean?" Jean-Paul answers, "What does it mean? It means we can take the rest of the day off!" There is no point, no meaning, no justification – only the next thing that happens that day.

Death

Michael O'Donoghue was sometimes called "the Mayor of Death," and the confrontation with death is a key aspect of existentialist philosophy. For existentialists, mortality is one of the defining characteristics of human existence. The fact that we are finite beings affects everything else that's true about us. When we refuse to face up to this fact, we fundamentally misunderstand ourselves. We do not always know when to expect death, and even when we think we know the time of our demise our expectation may be thwarted. For Sartre, it's as if you were a condemned prisoner, and while you were waiting to be executed, you died of a flu epidemic.[8] Far from death allowing us to realize the meaning of our lives, death is always absurd. Our projects, our free choices of what we want out of life, are what make our lives meaningful, but death always interrupts the project. Therefore, death isn't one of our possibilities, but rather the annihilation of our possibilities. It's not the logical resolution of a life in a way that gives that life meaning, like the chord resolves the melody to give it meaning. Rather, death comes from outside life, and ruins whatever we want to do.[9]

The Look and the Other

It's not just our mortality that makes humans what they are, but short of that, our ability to suffer: our vulnerability to each other. This is captured in what Sartre called "the look." Sartre says that when I encounter another conscious being like myself, the whole world gets reorganized.[10] I can't just automatically use this being for my own purposes, the way I can with non-conscious beings like rocks and plants. That's because this other conscious being is free and has his or her own goals and needs. How do I know that I'm encountering another self-aware being? Because they are *looking back* at me. I can see from the "look" or the "gaze" that there is a subjectivity that sees me, just as I see them.[11]

That's also where the danger lies. Each of us is not just a subjective consciousness, but also a physical being. [12] Therefore, *I* can be used, just like any of the physical things that I use to serve my needs. I know I'm free and therefore shouldn't be treated like an object, because I know all my own goals, my own possibilities. But the person looking at me doesn't. He might very well see me as just another object to be used. In fact, this ability to objectify me is one of the ways that I know that I'm dealing with another consciousness. A tree or a rock can't objectify me – but the gaze of a person can.[13] In short, the act of being seen lets me know that there is another being with personhood – but it also lets me know that I am vulnerable. If somebody sees me, then they can also hurt me.[14] Thus, the existence of other people constitutes a permanent threat to my body, and to my freedom. With the Other, there is always the possibility of violence, and the possibility of domination. Because of this, Sartre, at least in his early work, saw human relations as fundamentally hostile. In line with this Sartrean insight, Michael O'Donoghue shows us a cruel, exploitative world in which people are constantly trying to harm each other, constantly in danger of violence. Thus, the sadistic Mr. Mike character wears dark glasses to avoid making contact with the gaze that would humanize.

O'Donoghue captures our common mortality/vulnerability in a series of sketches in which he appears as an "impressionist." In this series, he starts out with the usual insincere sounding "showbiz" banter, introducing his impression of a celebrity. But no matter who the celebrity turns out to be, the impression always goes the same. For example, in the first one, about talk show host Mike Douglas: "You know, I was home the other day and I happened to catch Mike's show, and a funny thought occurred to me. I wondered: what if someone took very large steel needles, say fifteen, eighteen inches long; large steel needles with real sharp points, and plunged them into Mike's eyes. What, what would his reaction be, huh? I think it might go something like this." At which point, he screams, his hands on his eyes, falls to the floor, and thrashes violently around, screaming and twitching, until he falls off the stage.[15]

This sketch grew out of O'Donoghue's own embodied mortality. He suffered from tremendous migraines, and the symptoms could sometimes be like the ones he portrayed in these impressions. "In this O'Donoghue was a method comic: His migraines were so intense...it felt as though needles were indeed being thrust in his sockets. He expressed this by wishing the pain on others – preferably showbiz figures he despised – but in the end it was he who acted out the pain, for he alone knew how profound it could be."[16]

The point is more general, though. No matter who we are, TV personality or pop star, no matter how much money or fame we have, or how well thought-of we are – we all respond the same way to torture. Humans come equipped with, basically, the same kinds of bodies, all of which feel pain, all of which are vulnerable, and all of which will die. Our embodiment, and the mortality that results from that, is the great equalizer.

Responsibility

O'Donoghue's emphasis on violence, cruelty, and death wasn't limited to the natural end of life and the body's natural vulnerabilities, or even to everyday cruelties between people. Rather, he was especially concerned with social structures of organized violence – just like Sartre was. One of the clearest examples of this concern was his first-season sketch, "Police State."

A parody of 1970s cop shows, "Police State" features the partners Aramis McCord (Chevy Chase) and Kevin Brut (Dan Aykroyd). Throughout the sketch, they discuss where, of many possible ethnic restaurants, they will have dinner. When McCord suggests they have Chinese, Brut answers that they just had Chinese recently.

MCCORD: That wasn't Chinese. That was Polynesian.
BRUT: Same difference, pal, same difference.

They take police calls – always shooting and killing a harmless person as soon as they arrive – and then immediately resume the restaurant discussion. On one call, they burst into the apartment of a man who has apparently just hung a painting. Brut yells, "Okay! Hold it right there!" – but without hesitation, they shoot him and kill him. Still, they point their guns at the dead body, Brut instructing it to "Freeze!" He then proceeds to recite to the dead man his Miranda rights, after which, the restaurant discussion continues.

A kind of climax occurs when they are chasing a black man (Garrett Morris, of course) down a stairway, and shoot from behind, killing him. Brut yells "Stop or I'll shoot!" afterwards – and, as the stage directions put it, "fires an extra shot into the dead man just to make sure." The restaurant conversation seems to continue, but we actually get the dark punchline to it, in a callback to the beginning:

MCCORD: Hey, champ. How would you feel about Mexican? You'd like to, uh, kill Mexican tonight?
BRUT: Didn't we, uh, kill Mexican last night?
MCCORD: That wasn't Mexican. That was Filipino.
BRUT: Six o' one, amigo, six o' one.

This sketch presaged the kind of things that would later be publicly revealed to be true: "the racist musings of detectives such as Mark Fuhrman and those L.A. patrolmen who referred to the Rodney King beating as 'monkey-slapping time.'"[17]

Despite the darkness, Michael O'Donoghue's vision of the world is not really without hope. Sketches of biting and angry protest, like "Police State," point us in the direction Sartre took. Sartre regarded the universe as lacking inherent meaning, but he also thought we could overcome meaninglessness through creative, meaning-giving action. What kind of action? Artistic creation is one possibility, as in the novels and plays that Sartre himself wrote. Creative political activity is another possibility. After World War II, Sartre became more and more influenced by Marxism – and more and more publicly political. In later works like *The Critique of Dialectical Reason*, he got away from the phenomenological study of consciousness, and got more interested in human material existence. In other words, he examined the ways that humans produce what they need, and the technological and social structures that they fashion at different times in history in order to make that happen. Thus, he came to see that the kind of hostility between humans that he described in *Being and Nothingness* wasn't the inevitable result of conscious beings encountering each other. Rather, it was the result of a society in which people were forced to compete over scarce resources.

For Sartre, the fact that there aren't enough resources to provide for everyone is "contingent." It's not a necessary part of existence, but rather is created by specific natural conditions like famine, or by social conditions, like an oppressive system that lets a few people have most of the resources, leaving everybody else to struggle for what's left. When there isn't enough to go around, another person with his needs poses a threat to me. In order to get what I need, I have to deny his humanity, and his right to his needs, in order to satisfy mine.[18] Not only does this lead to violence between people, but such an unjust social system uses organized violence in order for the ruling class to keep its power.[19]

The kind of vulnerability to the Other that Sartre spoke of in *Being and Nothingness* wasn't the result of the clash of two consciousnesses, but rather the clash of material needs within an alienated society. Ultimately, one could change those conditions by working to change the society. O'Donoghue alludes to this argument in "Sartresky and Hutch" with the depiction of the damaged Vietnam veteran.

Sartre opted for political struggle as a way of overcoming meaninglessness and violence, and we can say something similar about Michael O'Donoghue. Despite his apparent cynicism, the fact that he bothered to point out, and be enraged by, systemic injustice and oppression shows that O'Donoghue wasn't willing to take the violence of the world as an unavoidable given. It is that protest that shows that Mr. Mike held out the possibility that some kind of meaning in the world was worth at least fighting for.

Most of Michael O'Donoghue's work was the darkest of dark comedy. As such, it illustrates the absurdity and violence that we are always at risk of in the kind of universe that Jean-Paul Sartre described. But Sartre also said that these conditions were the result of our freedom. And if we're free, we are able to rebel against the injustice of some of those conditions. That means we can have some hope. O'Donoghue's sense of injustice shines through at certain times in his work, showing us that he wasn't devoid of that kind of hope, either.

Notes

1. Jean-Paul Sartre, *Existentialism is a Humanism*. Tr. Carol Macomb (New Haven, CA and London: Yale University Press, 1947/2007), 20.
2. Ibid., 22.
3. Ibid., 21.
4. Ibid., 23–24.
5. Dennis Perrin, *Mr. Mike: The Life and Work of Michael O'Donoghue* (New York: Avon Books, 1998), 322–323.
6. Ibid., 321.
7. Jean-Paul Sartre, *Being and Nothingness*. Tr. Hazel Barnes (New York: Washington Square Press, 1943/1956), 62–64.
8. Ibid.
9. Ibid., 687.
10. Ibid., 341.
11. Ibid., 344.
12. Ibid., 343.
13. Ibid., 344–345.
14. Ibid., 347.
15. Saturday Night Live Transcripts, Season One, Episode 10, "Mike Douglas Impression." Retrieved from http://snltranscripts.jt.org/75/75jmrmike.phtml on July 6, 2019.
16. Perrin, 250.
17. Perrin, 306.
18. Jean-Paul Sartre, *Critique of Dialectical Reason*. Tr. Alan Sheridan-Smith (London & New York: Verso, 1960/2004), 735–736.
19. Ibid., 739.

3

How Do They Get Away with It?

Pushing Boundaries with Offensive Material on *Saturday Night Live*

Michael McGowan

Curb Your Enthusiasm is one of my favorite shows of the past two decades because of Larry David's ability to capture awkward human interactions that put his perceptions and behaviors at odds with social conventions. When I heard he would host *Saturday Night Live* in November 2017, I had high expectations. David is a former standup comedian, and I hoped he would bring his cantankerous, curmudgeonly persona and self-deprecating humor to his opening monologue. David started well, responding to the crowd's applause not with "You Flatter Me!" but rather, "You tolerate me." Then it got weird. David joked about homelessness and disabled persons. He also insulted the blind community by joking about how easy it was to "get away with murder" when he chauffeured an elderly blind woman New York. The audience did not give him the reaction he was hoping for, and David said, "I think I'm doing quite well. Shut up." Then he went further off the rails by acting out how dating might have looked in a concentration camp. "There are no good opening lines in a concentration camp," he said. "'How's it going? They treating you okay?'" Anticipating the hypothetical blowback from a non-interested concentration camp prisoner, he asked, "What?! What'd I say? Is it me, or is it the whole [concentration camp] thing?"

SNL is no stranger to comedically going where others dare not go.[1] In the first season, for example, Chevy Chase confronts Richard Pryor with the "n-word" in a job-interview sketch. In 1988's "Nude Beach" sketch, a group of naked men and women use the word "penis" over

Saturday Night Live and Philosophy: Deep Thoughts Through the Decades,
First Edition. Edited by Jason Southworth and Ruth Tallman.
© 2020 John Wiley & Sons Ltd. Published 2020 by John Wiley & Sons Ltd.

three dozen times in less than five minutes, seemingly for shock value alone.[2] It doesn't stop there: *SNL* has been criticized for trivializing domestic/spousal abuse ("Tiger Woods") and the sex-trade industry ("Rosetta Stone"). They have poked fun at religion and the people who take it seriously ("Jesus and Tebow"). *SNL* has exploited sexual power differentials ("Canteen Boy"), pedophilia and molestation (Louis CK's monologue), and produced "Digital Shorts" that use women for sexual ends ("D*ck in a Box"). *SNL* has even made light of slavery ("Slave Draft Pick") and mass shootings ("Guns"). A month before the 2016 Presidential Election, Alec Baldwin's candidate Trump used the word "p*ssy" on live television and bragged about his sexual prowess. Baldwin was, of course, simply repeating what Trump actually said in the *Access Hollywood* tape, but Baldwin went further – "I can do a whole lot more than just grab it," he said, along with wildly inappropriate hand gestures. The list could go on and, in fact, does: at the end of each season, "Weekend Update" hosts trot out jokes too offensive or racy to be delivered in regular episodes during the season. Suffice it to say, *SNL's* producers, writers, and actors are unafraid to push the boundaries of what is considered socially acceptable on network television.

What gives? Sketches like these raise a very serious, yet simple question: how do they get away with it? Ours is an era in which public officials are fired or resign, college students are expelled, and faculty members lose their teaching positions for much less.[3] Why do we, as a society, tolerate *SNL's* offensive behavior? Shouldn't jokes that cause outrage be silenced or censored? Why do they go unchecked, and how has *SNL* gotten away with it for so many years? Why have we permitted rude, insensitive, and offensive material to be broadcasted? Should there be stricter laws to limit what can be said on air? If so, how would we construct such laws and on what philosophical or moral bases? Are there any benefits to jokes that cause outrage?

Censorship and its Problems

In response to the question of how *SNL* gets away with offensive material, we can group the potential answers into three broad categories. The first answer, simply put, is that they *shouldn't*; the second, that they *can* because they are protected by the First Amendment; and the third is that they *should*. In what follows, I will elaborate the logic behind each response.

The first response is to argue that we should not permit offensive material to be aired. Some of the responses to Larry David's monologue seemed to lean in this direction, suggesting that either he should not have been asked to host or that he shouldn't have made the kind of jokes he did. Despite David's protestation that he doesn't like Jews being in headlines for the wrong reasons, his monologue was met with serious criticism by Jonathan Greenblatt, CEO of the Anti-Defamation League, who said that David "managed to be offensive, insensitive, and unfunny all at the same time. Quite a feat." Writing for the *New York Times*, Dave Itzkoff called the performance a "discomforting monologue that even his cable-TV alter ego would have had trouble getting away with."[4] *The Washington Post's* Avi Selk questioned David's choices, wondering if it was "Bad taste, or just bad comedy?"[5] Jeremy Dauber writes in *The Atlantic* that David has a history of this type of humor. He "thrives on presenting himself as deeply unlikeable, a magnet for hostility ... Watching these antics is often supremely cringeworthy for viewers, if not for the character himself."[6] David was no stranger to Holocaust jokes, having made them in both *Seinfeld* and *Curb Your Enthusiasm*, but the situation now is very different: "That thought-provoking *Curb* episode aired in 2004, and this is 2017, and after Charlottesville," when jokes like these "might ring particularly hollow in an America where neo-Nazis march openly on the streets and white-nationalist memes proliferate online."[7] Simply put, times have changed.

This brings us to the major reason why some would support censorship of offensive media: we don't want people to be marginalized by being exposed to material that may give rise to the feeling that they are not full members of our community. Those about whom the jokes are made (or on whose backs the jokes fall) have dignity, and they deserve respect by virtue of their personhood. Thus, they should not be spoken about in offensive ways. On this much, there is overlap between conversations about offensive speech and discussions of "hate speech." The latter can have real – mental, emotional, *and* physical – effects in the lives of its victims.

Critical Race Theorist Richard Delgado suggests that hate speech causes serious psychological harms, which result in fragmentation and polarization based on (among other things) racial categories: "In addition to the harms of immediate emotional distress and infringement of dignity, racial insults inflict psychological harm upon the victim. Racial slurs may cause long-term emotional pain because they draw upon and intensify the effects of the stigmatization, labeling, and disrespectful treatment that the victim has previously undergone."[8] Not only are there psychological impacts of hate speech, but these psychological damages produce physical effects. Mari Matsuda says, "Victims of vicious hate propaganda experience psychological symptoms and emotional distress ranging from fear in the gut to rapid pulse rate and difficulty in breathing, nightmares, post-traumatic stress syndrome, stress disorder, hypertension, psychosis, and suicide."[9] Clearly, these are serious consequences. Insofar as offensive speech mirrors the effects of hate speech, it demands a response.

So, what do we do about it? Delgado partnered with Jean Stefancic to write *Critical Race Theory*, arguing that the only way to minimize these negative effects is through legislation, that is, censorship. As they discuss the potential responses to critical race theory, they argue that "the status quo is inherently racist, rather than merely sporadically and accidentally so... The need for regulation of hate crime and speech will probably eventually become evident [in the United States], as it has to dozens of European and Commonwealth nations."[10] We stop offensive speech by making it illegal, they say. After that, they argue, we will make progress toward limiting offense felt by innocent victims. If offensive or hateful speech is harmful, then the state is justified in getting involved to limit what people can and cannot say.

This argument – that the government should prevent that which is *harmful* – is not a new idea. For centuries, philosophers have been exploring the extent to which societies should limit the liberty of their citizens. John Stuart Mill's (1806–1873) landmark classic, *On Liberty*, has one very simple goal: to present the only justifiable reason why a state can limit the liberty of its citizens.[11] According to Mill, one justifiable reason is to prevent harm to others.[12]

But not so fast. "That's crazy," you say, "to put *SNL* writers in the same category as those who speak hate." Indeed, I could not agree more. Insofar as *SNL* is entertainment and thus its intent is to entertain, common sense tells us that *SNL* shouldn't be placed in the same "hate speech" category as the white nationalists who marched in Charlottesville. There's something *different* that they're up to. To figure it out, though, we will need to consider some arguments against censorship of offensive speech on *SNL* and elsewhere.

Consider what type of speech enables society to learn about injustices. Sure, we *could* limit speech to prevent offense to others, but *should* we? The "first freedoms" argument says that some freedoms are necessary in order to wake society up to situations that need addressing. A near absolute freedom of speech will allow, for example, a wider audience of voting citizens, activists, and politicians to be aware of problems they would not have known about otherwise.

Offense is a relative concept: what offends one person will not offend another. The relativity of the "offense concept" is seen by looking at the ways in which the passing of time brings major changes in what offends people. It is simply not the case that what offended people at the beginning of the twenty-first century had the same offensive reactions even fifty or sixty years ago. The Rev. Dr. Martin Luther King, Jr., for example, used the word "negro" and "colored" to describe the African American citizen and his/her struggle for equality and civil rights. In his "I Have a Dream" speech alone, he used "negro" well over a dozen times.[13]

But what reaction would a public figure get if the word "negro" were uttered today, not to mention the other "n-word"? Needless to say, the response would be swift and would likely lead to an embarrassing resignation, several days of media coverage, and the humiliation of the utterer's friends and family. Recently, for example, comedian and political host Bill Maher used the "n-word" on his show and was widely criticized for it. Ours is an unquestionably different world than when Chevy Chase played a character who used the "n-word" on *SNL* in the late 1970s. The evil of the word has not changed, nor has the nefarious motivation behind racial insensitivity, but the fallout from its use has been drastically increased. This is not to argue that Dr. King should have used a different word than "negro" or "colored." He was, of course, free to refer to himself and African Americans using whatever word he pleased, because we know his motivation was good. Rather, it is simply to underscore the point that what offends people changes over time. If we were to develop strict and unbending guidelines or laws making certain words, phrases, or ideas the subject of criminal prosecution, what would do we do when those expressions no longer offend and were replaced by new offensive expressions? The point of this argument against censorship is that if Congress were to make a law saying which sorts of things were offensive and criminalized people who said those things, we would end up with an overly rigid set of prohibitions that could not keep pace with the rate at which society changes. People get offended at all sorts of things, and the things that offend change, even among members of groups that were historically discriminated against.

Moreover, censorship faces a serious criticism in the form of a slippery slope argument, which should give us pause when seeking to silence even the most disturbing or hateful messages. Again,

Charlottesville is helpful here. It is entirely reasonable to want to silence white supremacists from speaking in public, and I find racists morally repugnant. But free speech advocates ask the hard follow-up question: if we were to prevent racists from uttering hateful ideology, what's next? Are jokes that cause outrage on *SNL* to follow? If so, what's after that? The silencing of any ideas we find uncomfortable? The permission of only those political or social ideas the masses find acceptable? Wouldn't we then have something of a "tyranny of the majority"? Where do we draw the line? Certainly not with public officials. If we permit lawmakers to decide what we can and cannot say, then who's to stop them from outlawing a word we *do* believe is necessary to make a social, political, ethical, moral, or religious point? And what's to stop them from going further, say, to outlawing not only certain expressions, but also certain ideas or states of mind or concepts? On the slippery slope's telling, the censorship story ends in a state with nearly unlimited power, a totalitarian regime of Orwellian proportions and the "thought police." Would we not then be dangerously close to a *Handmaid's Tale* sort of society at that point? What then separates the way the United States handles sensitive subjects from China, or worse, North Korea?

Now, this criticism of censorship is not without its rejoinder by those seeking to limit offense. They point out that we are, in some sense, already on the slope. That is, there is a false dichotomy at work in some of our political discourse that says there are only two options: we can choose either (a) absolutely no restrictions on speech, or (b) total restrictions. Anyone who has been in a conversation in which everyone is talking over everyone else knows that some restrictions on speech are necessary so that everyone can be heard. Insofar as we expect others to follow widely accepted rules of discourse in our courts, debates, and conversations, we limit the speech of others. However, we limit speech at certain times or in certain places in order to *increase* speech by giving everyone a turn, not decrease it by silencing some of the speakers.

In addition to selectively limiting speech for the purpose of hearing all voices, are there other justifiable restrictions? In an early twentieth-century Supreme Court case, Justice Oliver Wendell Holmes, Jr. opined that people should not be permitted to yell "Fire!" in a crowded theater because it would create a panic. The operative principle here is harm to others, literal physical harm from the "clear and present danger" of a stampede. In the case of the conversation, the limitation of liberty was necessary to hear *more* voices and ideas, and in the case of the theater it is to prevent physical danger. It is worth pointing out that these limitations are relevant to *context*, not content. If the state were to prevent a specific word or phrase from being uttered in *any* context, this would legislate the *content* of speech, which was not the problem in either of the two cases above. Therefore, the slippery slope concern on behalf of free speech advocates is not overturned by either case.

In sum, then, the answer to "why let *SNL* get away with it?" that says, "they shouldn't," is a non-starter. Without freedom of speech, injustices that demand a response may not be heard by a wider audience. Moreover, censorship risks too much and the standards for what offends are far too relative to justify legislation that limits speech in this way. This, naturally, leads to the second answer.

The First Amendment and its Applicability

The second answer goes something like this: "We allow *SNL* to write and perform offensive sketches because they are protected by the First Amendment." As any elementary school child will have learned, the First Amendment to the U.S. Constitution reads as follows: "Congress shall make no law respecting an establishment of religion, or prohibiting the free exercise thereof; or abridging the *freedom of speech*, or of the press; or the right of the people peaceably to assemble, and to petition the Government for a redress of grievances." *SNL's* First Amendment response to the problem of offensive material is basically this: "because we can."

As a corollary to the "We can say what we want because of the First Amendment" argument, one notices no such provision in the Constitution stating the opposite. There is no such enumerated "right to *not* be offended." But why? What might the founders have been thinking?

I will spare the reader a lengthy discussion of the history of "rights" language in U.S. or global political philosophy, but it is worth exploring the spirit in which the First Amendment was written. The First Amendment provides the citizens of the United States the "right" to speak their minds, and the founders anticipated that people would use that freedom in all sorts of ways: some bad, some good. Though some will use freedom poorly, that does not make giving them the freedom a bad thing. The worse thing, proponents of maximizing liberty would say, is forcing a person to do or say or believe something. Liberty was seen by the founders of the United States, and Madison in particular (who wrote the Bill of Rights), as a *first freedom* of paramount importance. It is so important, in fact, that we are willing to countenance evil remarks and offensive uses of it. We put up with offensive speech, the argument goes, because that state of affairs in which people are occasionally offended is preferable to living without freedom.

Mill said that negative "other-regarding" behavior was within the legitimate purview of a government. The state may use force to interfere with the liberty of the individual if a person is going to harm someone else. Note, however, that Mill views speech *not* as "other-regarding" behavior, but rather as "self-regarding." And on matters of self-regarding behavior, for Mill, the state should not be involved. The state may not interfere in the speech and thought of others, says Mill, for any reason, up to and including offense and even harm to self. The state cannot interfere in the lives of its citizens if their behavior impacts only themselves: not to increase their happiness, not for their betterment, and certainly not because others may find their actions immoral or offensive. Mill says that immoral actions, self-harm, and offense to others are good reasons for protest and persuasion through argumentation, but not for officially-sanctioned coercion or compulsion. Mill insists on free speech because people have absolute autonomy concerning matters pertaining to their own selves. He says, "in the part which merely concerns himself, his independence is, of right, absolute. Over himself, over his own body and mind, *the individual is sovereign.*"[14]

What does this have to do with *Saturday Night Live*? The answer is that the freedom argument cuts both ways. No one compels *SNL* to create socially acceptable sketches, but similarly, no one compels people to watch *SNL*. Just as *SNL* producers, writers, and actors are free to create and broadcast offensive content if they find a network that, acting in its own freedom, is willing to air the material – a right to speech is not a right to a platform – so too is the viewer free to change the channel, or not turn on the television at all, or even not own a television. This is the sort of freedom the philosopher Joel Feinberg (1926–2004) talks about in his book, *Offense to Others*.[15] Feinberg considers himself a member of the "liberal" tradition, as in, "promoting liberty" (which is distinct from the understanding of the word "liberal" in contemporary, American political discourse). In Feinberg's view, the state is justified in protecting people from profound and extreme offense when they are not free to protect themselves or remove themselves from the situation.[16] The state's involvement is dependent on an individual's ability to *voluntarily* withdraw from the situation. Feinberg calls it the *Volenti maxim*.

SNL passes Feinberg's test: no one is forced to watch. The same *Volenti maxim* can be applied widely in our society: no one is forced to view television or read Facebook posts, Twitter tweets, Instagram updates, or Snapchat messages. If a viewer becomes offended, she has the freedom to turn away. The ability to voluntarily remove oneself from the offensive situation is what separates the "harm principle," from the "offense principle." Feinberg says, "Not everything that we dislike or resent, and wish to avoid, is harmful to us"[17] and "It is not a necessary truth that we are personally wronged by everything at which we are morally outraged."[18] Offense only becomes harmful when a person is unable to avoid the offender.

Those of us who followed the Charlottesville incident and its fallout can see that this is what Tina Fey had in mind in *SNL's* "Weekend Update: Summer Edition" of 2017. A University of Virginia graduate, Fey said, "I don't want any more good people to get hurt... I know a lot of us are feeling anxious and are asking ourselves, 'What can I do?' I would urge people, instead of participating in the screaming matches and potential violence... Don't yell at the Klan," she said. Rather, "I want to encourage all sane Americans to treat these rallies like the opening of a thoughtful movie with two female leads: don't show up! Let these morons scream into the empty air."[19] Turn off the television. Back away from the hater. They have the legal right to say what they want, and you have the legal right to remove yourself. They do it because they can, and you should leave because you can.

Comedy and its Utility

And yet, Tina Fey regretted her *SNL* response to Charlottesville. In a later interview with David Letterman, Fey said the events unfolded like "a fast-moving train... I felt like a gymnast who did a very solid routine and broke her ankle on the landing. Because I think it's in the last two, three sentences of the piece, I think, that I chumped it. And I screwed up, and the implication was that I was telling people to give up and not be active and not fight. That was not my intention, obviously... If I had a time machine, I would end the piece by saying, 'Fight them in every way except the way they want'."[20]

This, of course, brings us to the last of our responses for why we permit *SNL* to perform offensive sketches: because they *should*. There is something valuable in what *SNL* is doing in offensive jokes. Two arguments can be made here, both of which pack a serious punch, though for different reasons. The first argument for not only permitting but also encouraging offensive *SNL* material is a philosophical one: we permit free – even offensive – speech because it contributes to human knowledge, leading to a greater understanding of the world in which we live. This is a progressive and teleological view of humanity: we're aiming at something, and constantly striving to get better at it. We're not wandering in total darkness or getting worse. Rather, things are getting better. And free speech contributes to that goal.

Again, Mill's *On Liberty* is instructive: humans are fallible creatures, and we rarely arrive at the whole truth, at least not at first. Without knowing the whole truth, ideas are subject to public debate *through* speech. For Mill, freedom in speech, communication, and thought is vital for a society that desires to push its conclusions to their logical ends and evaluate alternative points of view. It displays courage to welcome a diversity of viewpoints, says Mill. If we do not have freedom of speech, "the price paid for this sort of intellectual pacification is the sacrifice of the entire moral courage of the human mind."[21] Only freedom in thought and communication allows us to test views in public, subjecting them to public scrutiny and the informed opinions of peers. For Mill, humans are also limited beings who need the corrective thinking of other free people. Mill puts it this way:

> That mankind are not infallible; that their truths, for the most part, are only half-truths; that unity of opinion, unless resulting from the fullest and freest comparison of opposite opinions, is not desirable, and diversity not an evil, but a good, until mankind are much more capable than at present of recognizing all sides of the truth, are principles applicable to men's modes of action, not less than to their opinions.[22]

Only by permitting nearly all speech are we able to root out incorrect views and pursue better ones. This isn't based on any abstract "rights" language. Rather, it's practical: a robust appreciation for the value of liberty will produce the greatest long-term good for the most people, according to Mill. Progress is at stake, the forward motion of humanity as a species. Freedom of speech has utilitarian value.[23]

If, as individuals and societies, we're constantly learning, constantly progressing, then it is entirely possible that the things we find offensive today – albeit for good reasons (e.g., they are thought to violate the rights of others) – may not be so offensive decades from now. It is possible, Mill thought, that a few voices in the wilderness might be calling humanity toward a new, better stage in our development, but the majority may not be ready for it. That is to say, Mill worried about situations in which the majority was of one mind and a small minority was of another. Borrowing language from Tocqueville, he worried about the "tyranny of the majority," the unfortunate "feeling in each person's mind that everybody should be required to act as he, and those with whom he sympathizes, would like them to act."[24] Mill argues instead for "absolute freedom of opinion and sentiment on all subjects, practical or speculative, scientific, moral or theological."[25]

The correction for bad speech is not less speech, for Mill. Rather, it is *more* speech, *more* debate. This is what Thomas Jefferson had in mind when he founded the University of Virginia, ironically the gathering place of hateful and bigoted white nationalists: "This institution will be based on the illimitable freedom of the human mind. For here we are not afraid to follow truth wherever it may lead, nor to tolerate any error so long as reason is left free to combat it."[26]

More than just an epistemological argument for freedom of speech, however, there are strong aesthetic reasons for permitting (and encouraging!) offensive speech on *SNL*. Here we return to the criticism of censorship mentioned above: we can tell that something different from hate speech is happening on *SNL*.[27] We may not be sure *how* they're different in their offensive jokes, but we can sense that they are. The "moral" argument for permitting *SNL* and other entertainers says that comedians have an important role in today's America: that of social critic. Intellectually, we should be unafraid to turn over any stone in search of the truth, but aesthetically, we should permit art that calls our norms and times into question. Artists who cause outrage seek truth by offering a purposefully distorted mirror, exaggerating those parts of ourselves we wish were different. They do so to point toward a different way to live in the world, one in which the subjects of jokes don't do things that can be joked about. Alec Baldwin's Donald Trump, racy and obnoxious as he is, demonstrates for viewers the character of the person he is lampooning. All of this is to say that art, especially comedic art, can do things that other forms of communication cannot. And this is a valuable social good. Not only *can* the *SNL* staff say the things they say, even when offensive, but also and more importantly, they *should*.

After reflecting on her *SNL* commentary on Charlottesville, Tina Fey said she would urge viewers to "fight," just not using the same methods as the haters. This is the moral argument for offensive material on *SNL*.

It allows us to fight oppression, bigotry, intolerance, hate, and all things hostile to human flourishing using every available tool in our toolbox short of physical harm. *SNL* has a unique and vital role in society, and I hope they continue to fight for social goods using comedy, yes, but also sarcasm, irony, and even offense. At the very least, jokes that cause outrage get people thinking and talking.

Robust Social Critique

In a way, *SNL* acts as a teacher. Parker Palmer says in *The Courage to Teach*, good instructors "shed light in dark places." What might *SNL* be teaching us? Perhaps chiefly, *SNL* reminds us of the necessity of free speech. But the show also teaches us to not to take ourselves too seriously. *SNL* has a prophetic role in today's culture, speaking speak truth to power through humor. And finally, *SNL* teaches us by inspiring us. By presenting awkward or insensitive or offensive material – like dating in a concentration camp – *SNL* performers remind us just how horrific some situations are, and hopefully it ignites the viewer's passion against the thing that is being mocked. Comedic timing is an art, not only the careful calculation within a performance of pauses and effective delivery of one-liners, but also timing in the sense of a specific joke within a cultural context that needs to hear it. Good comedians know which jokes will resonate at which times in history, and dark times call for robust social critique. This is only possible with free speech.

Notes

1. Ryan Gajewski, "'Saturday Night Live': 10 most controversial sketches ever." *Hollywood Reporter* (March 7, 2015). Retrieved from www.hollywoodreporter.com/live-feed/saturday-night-live-10-controversial-779939 on July 6, 2019.
2. Despite Kevin Nealon's meta-fictional PSA at the end, laced with ironic wit.
3. See, for example, Erwin Chemerinsky and Howard Gillman, Free Speech on Campus (New Haven, CT: Yale University Press, 2017), ch. 1: "The new censorship."
4. Dave Itzkoff, "Saturday Night Live: Alec Baldwin and Larry David contribute to an awkward episode" (Nov. 5, 2017). Retrieved from www.nytimes.com/2017/11/05/arts/television/larry-david-snl-monologue-holocaust-joke.html on July 6, 2019.

5. Avi Selk, "The debate over Larry David's holocaust joke on SNL: bad taste, or just bad comedy?" *The Washington Post* (Nov. 5, 2017). Retrieved from www.washingtonpost.com/news/arts-and-entertainment/wp/2017/11/05/was-larry-davids-holocaust-joke-on-snl-bad-taste-or-just-bad-comedy/?noredirect=on&utm_term=. b1e236093fc7 on July 6, 2019.

6. Jeremy Dauber, "Why Larry David's holocaust joke was so uncomfortable." *The Atlantic* (Nov. 7, 2017). Retrieved from www.theatlantic.com/entertainment/archive/2017/11/why-larry-davids-holocaust-joke-was-so-uncomfortable/545105/ on July 6, 2019.

7. Dauber, "Why Larry David's holocaust joke was so uncomfortable," online.

8. Richard Delgado, "A tort action for racial Insults, epithets, and name calling," in M. Matsuda (ed.), Words that Wound: Critical Race Theory, Assaultive Speech, and the First Amendment (Boulder, CO: Westview Press, 1993). Passages from *Words that Wound* are taken from Erwin Chemerinsky and Howard Gillman, Free Speech on Campus (New Haven, CT: Yale University Press, 2017), 84.

9. Mari Matsuda, "Public response to racist speech: considering the victim's story," *Words that Wound*.

10. Richard Delgado and Jean Stefancic, Critical Race Theory: An Introduction (New York: New York University Press, 2001), 135.

11. John Stuart Mill, The Collected Works of John Stuart Mill (33 vols., J.M. Robson, ed., Toronto and London: University of Toronto Press and Routledge, 1963–1991), esp. *On Liberty* (in CW, XVIII, 213–310). Or see the single volume edition, edited by Currin V. Shields (New York: Bobbs-Merrill Company, Inc., 1956).

12. Mill, *On Liberty*, 13.

13. Gary Younge, "The misremembering of 'I have a dream.'" *The Nation* (August 14, 2013). Retrieved from www.thenation.com/article/misremembering-i-have-dream/ on July 6, 2019.

14. Mill, *On Liberty*, 13 (emphasis mine).

15. Joel Feinberg, The Moral Limits of the Criminal Law (4 vols.; New York: Oxford University Press, 1984–1988), vol. 2, *Offense to Others* (1985). See also *Social Philosophy* (Englewood Cliffs, NJ: Prentice Hall, 1973) and *Rights, Justice, and the Bounds of Liberty* (Princeton, NJ: Princeton University Press, 1980).

16. Feinberg is of great help to readers sorting out what they believe the state is or is not permitted to interfere with in a person's life, because he poses a number of situations for the reader to evaluate which situations call for non-interference and which call for some sort of legal response. See, e.g., "A ride on the bus," in *Offense to Others*, 10–13.

17. Feinberg, *Harm to Others*, 45.

18. Feinberg, *Offense to Others*, 219.

19. *Saturday Night Live*, "Weekend update: summer edition," Season 42, Episode 24 (August 24, 2017).

20. Katie Kilkenny, "Tina Fey tells David Letterman she wishes she could change 'SNL' Charlottesville sketch." *The Hollywood Reporter* (May 4, 2018). Retrieved from www.hollywoodreporter.com/live-feed/tina-fey-tells-david-letterman-she-wishes-she-could-change-snl-charlottesville-sketch-1108095 on July 6, 2019.

21. Mill, *On Liberty*, 40.

22. Mill, *On Liberty*, 68.

23. Mill, *On Liberty*, 14: "It is proper to state that I forego any advantage which could be derived to my argument from the idea of abstract right, as a thing independent of utility."

24. John Stuart Mill, On Liberty (Peterborough, ON: Broadview, 1999), 48.

25. Mill, *On Liberty*, 16.

26. Letter from Thomas Jefferson to William Roscoe (December 27, 1820). A.E. Bergh, ed., *The Writings of Thomas Jefferson* (Washington, DC: The Thomas Jefferson Memorial Association, 1907) vol. 15: 302. Summary retrieved from www.loc.gov/exhibits/jefferson/75.html on July 6, 2019.

27. For a thorough discussion of racially charged language on SNL, see J. Jeremy Wisnewski's "Word associations, black Jeopardy, and Mr. Robinson's neighborhood: *SNL* tackles race," which is chapter 7 in this volume.

SNL, Satire, and Socrates:
Smart-Assery or Seriousness?

Joshua J. Reynolds

Picture yourself in an audience witnessing a live comedy performance. You and other crowd members laugh hysterically as various sketches unfold on stage. Celebrity actors lampoon an assortment of social trends and political figures. Sarcasm flows thick, as do impressions, physical comedy, and of course sexual innuendo. Ridiculous costumes, excessive gesturing, and exaggerated speech emphasize familiar features of targeted personalities. Silly dance routines proceed from punch lines while a musical ensemble heightens the festiveness. Overkill abounds, but you keep laughing.

A last detail: even though you're enjoying live comedy, more than pure entertainment is taking place. Indeed, careful observers will notice that the amusing scripts and ridiculous drama package serious reflections on society, religion, politics, and human nature.

Now, where and when were you? New York, circa 1992? Was it Saturday night? Perhaps. Such silliness does describe *Saturday Night Live*. But what about the seriousness? Just how philosophical is *SNL*'s brand of comedy? Is it satire? Picture a spectrum. The spectrum represents artistic forms of social/political criticism according to depth. On one end, there's philosophy; on the other, smart-assery. Somewhere in the middle lies satire. This chapter argues that *SNL* tends, with some exceptions, away from the philosophical and satirical areas of the spectrum and more towards the smart-assical, silly side.

Saturday Night Live and Philosophy: Deep Thoughts Through the Decades, First Edition. Edited by Jason Southworth and Ruth Tallman.
© 2020 John Wiley & Sons Ltd. Published 2020 by John Wiley & Sons Ltd.

I'm Chevy Chase and You're Not

Let's begin with some hairsplitting:

ME: Oh, most infallible of oracles, Great Google, tell me ... What is satire?

GOOGLE: Thank you, seeker, for your query. Yours is a difficult question, though the answer will be short. According to my algorithms, satire is *The Colbert Report*.

ME: No, I'm afraid you misunderstand. You seem to be saying what lots of folks today think is really super awesome satire, not...

GOOGLE: Silence! The Google has spoken!

ME: I didn't mean to offend, oh Engine Most Divine. But please shed LCD light on another question of mine.

GOOGLE: You may proceed once the page has loaded.

ME: Google, please *define* satire for me.

GOOGLE: Satire is "the use of humor, irony, exaggeration, or ridicule to expose and criticize people's stupidity or vices, particularly in the context of contemporary politics and other topical issues."[1]

ME: Thank you, Godly Google. You've been of service. As a final request, what does the wise and weighty Wikipedia have to add?

GOOGLE: Just that satire uses ridicule "with the intent of shaming individuals, corporations, government, or society itself into improvement."[2]

Now then, with all that arduous research out of the way, let's consider an example and then collect some observations.

On the surface, it may seem tough to find much meaning in *SNL*'s Mr. Bill clips from the 1980s. But here, *SNL* does fit the definition of satire. These sketches feature a clay figurine who offers safety tips to children, but who always ends up getting mangled, crushed, suffocated, electrocuted, dismembered, drowned, or otherwise abused in the process. Humor? Check. Irony? Oh yeah. Exaggeration? Big time. But, at the same time, "Mr. Bill" also criticizes violence in children's cartoons (think *Looney Tunes*, *Tom and Jerry*, etc.). It thus indirectly forces the viewer to reconsider the content of such programs instead of taking it for granted. Often, extreme exaggeration and overkill are needed to get people to see familiar things for what they are.

So then, judging by the definitions and example above, it's safe to say that anything exhibiting the following features is satire, whereas anything without them (for instance, a cardigan or a carburetor) is not:

- Satire involves *humor*. So here, *SNL* qualifies. Think, for instance, of all the random characters who make the crowd burst out in laughter: Phil Hartman's Unfrozen Caveman lawyer; Chris Farley's Matt Foley; Martin Short's Ed Grimley, a neurotic bi-polar man with greasy pointed hair who constantly entertains (to himself, out loud) contradictory possibilities, all the while smiling and posing awkwardly, hands on hips, or prancing around while practicing the triangle. I must say: the humor might make you mental.

- Satire relies on *irony*. What's irony? At the most basic level, we call it ironic when one thing is said, expected, or intended but something else is meant or occurs. So, think here of the *SNL* sketch "The Librarian" (2016), which parodies a nerdy kid's hot teacher fantasy. Of course, that repetitive 1980s song "Oh Yeah" begins to play as the librarian starts to strip away her clothing. Naturally, the boy gets excited in anticipation. The song's lyrics, however, turn to "Oh no" when the woman suddenly starts to strip away even more, like her hair and teeth, eventually becoming a lizard monster that licks the kid's face, giving him way more than he bargained for.
- Satire employs *exaggeration* rather than an objective account of how things are. That said, satire doesn't involve pure make-believe either. It offers a blown-up, skewed, or bastardized version of reality. For instance, take the "More Cowbell" sketch (2000), which clearly overstates the extent to which the cowbell actually features in Blue Öyster Cult's song "Don't Fear the Reaper."
- Satire is *critical*. It aims to condemn perceived vice, folly, ignorance, corruption, and hypocrisy. In so doing, it involves the attempt to shame the naughty target and induce contempt towards it/them. No one who has watched *SNL* depict the American president, especially when conservative, would doubt that those sketches fail at all in the criticism department.
- Satire aims at *improvement*; thus, it proceeds through moral judgment about how things should be. Specifically, a satirist presumes to know that the target personality, state of affairs, or belief is unethical, unsafe, unintelligent, or uncivilized. So, satire's got a constructive message.

Note: such improvement must be possible. So, simply mocking physical features, mannerisms, race, class, health, speech, sexuality, and handicap doesn't qualify as satire. That style of humor is superficial, deconstructive, and aims at making fun. Satire, on the other hand, has depth and targets changeable things, such as policies, ideologies, conventions, power structures, and moral codes. It's on this last point, as we'll see, that *SNL* typically comes up short. Although there are exceptions, we rarely find a deep, constructive message behind all the mockery and silliness.

We Are Two Wild and Crazy Guys!

Setting aside how accurately the scenario sketched at the outset depicts typical *SNL* performances, it should be noted that it does paint a fair picture of staged satire in Athens, Greece, circa 2,400 years ago. Greek satirists thrived on the use of impressions, offensive language, sexual and scatological references, and stereotypes. The vulgarity and offensiveness, however, went deeper than getting cheap laughs from dirty minds. It also served as a foil for highlighting the dirt on society and delivering a critical message.

One of the earliest such comedians was Aristophanes (ca. 449–ca. 386 BCE). Politically, Aristophanes resisted many of the changes that were rocking Athens in his day. He opposed the rise of so-called sophists, who taught aspiring politicians rhetorical tricks for a fee. He also criticized new forms of philosophy. These appealed to natural causes rather than divine will, and they embraced *relativism*: the idea that opposites like right/wrong and good/bad are not absolute but change according to who is perceiving them, from what perspective, in what situation, and as a member of which culture.

In short, Aristophanes was a conservative man with a message who carefully pondered matters of politics, reality, and morality. That said, not unlike conservative-leaning *SNL* alums Dennis Miller and Norm Macdonald, this man had a knack for making people laugh in ways that could be as cheap and raunchy as they were clever and thought-provoking. So, Aristophanes was by no means conservative in the sense of prudish, reserved, or respectful.

Moreover, just like *SNL* sketches, Aristophanes' plays often subjected contemporary figures, celebrities, and politicians to intense ridicule. A handful of scenes from his play *Clouds* should suffice to set the stage for further comparison.

Clouds was produced in Athens in the 420s BCE during a time of radical intellectual change. As mentioned, Aristophanes was critical of the forms of education, science, and philosophy trending at the time. So, he set out in this play to vilify the slick-talking sophists and godless natural philosophers. Socrates (469–399 BCE), a contemporary thinker already famous for his wisdom, served as Aristophanes' scapegoat.

The play opens with Strepsiades (a sort of lovable loser, whom perhaps Chris Farley or Will Ferrell would have played well) having a restless morning. The rooster crows, yet his son sleeps. He complains: "[That boy] never wakes up before sunrise ... [but] just farts merrily away wrapped up in five or six blankets."[3] Strepsiades is worried about debts that have accrued due to his son's gambling addiction.

Suddenly, Strepsiades has an idea. He wakes the boy and tries to convince him to enter a school he's heard about. It's called The Thinkery, where "if you pay them well, they can teach you how to win a case whether you're in the right or not."[4] Strepsiades continues: "They say they have two Arguments in there – Right and Wrong... and one of them, Wrong, can always win its case even when justice is against it."[5]

At the school, a student answers the door and complains that Strepsiades has interrupted Socrates' research. The student then goes on to describe one of the Master's discoveries: how gnats produce their hum:

> [You see], the intestinal passage of the gnat is very narrow, and consequently the wind is forced to go straight through to the rear end. And then the arsehole, being an orifice forming the exit from this narrow passage, makes a noise owing to the force of this wind.[6]

Now, on the surface, this seems like just another fart joke. But a degree of depth is involved. The idea is that a sophisticated explanation of a mundane matter brings philosophy down to earth, equating it, essentially, with triviality or trash.

Perhaps we see this idea in the *SNL* sketch "The Playboy Philosophy" from 1977, starring Hugh Hefner as Hef, Garrett Morris as Plato, and John Belushi as Socrates. The scene is ancient Athens, where philosophers gather "to learn at the feet of the one they called Hef," who, it turns out, was the "wisest and most swinging of the Greeks." After Socrates and Plato identify the nature of the good life, Hef wants to know how man is different from the beasts. Comically, he then suggests that man is different not because of his courage, which lions also possess, but rather because the lion doesn't "decorate his cave with leather bedspread and shag carpeting," while the fox cannot "choose the aftershave lotion that is right for him." The others just nod wisely in approval, which further detracts from the authority of real philosophers.

Historically, the Athenians believed that comedy could influence public opinion and policy. A similar assumption lies behind Will Ferrell's portrayal of George W. Bush as a childish moron and Tina Fey's harsh caricature of Sarah Palin. In Aristophanes' case, however, the distorted representation of Socrates did more than influence opinion. It brought harm, as the Athenians voted to execute Socrates in 399 BCE on charges of impiety and corrupting the youth.

Details of Socrates' life are vague. The only direct evidence comes from those who knew him, especially his student Plato. In *The Apology*, Plato's Socrates recalls how a friend once consulted an oracle, asking who the wisest man in Greece was.[7] The oracle replied that Socrates was wisest. This shocked the philosopher, so he set out to disprove it by questioning all presumed authorities. Years of conversations, however, turned up nothing. So, Socrates concluded that he was wisest only because he didn't think he knew what he in fact didn't know.

Although he was a serious philosopher, Socrates' critical tendencies liken him to a satirist.[8] For one thing, he's witty and indirectly emphasizes flaws in people's opinions to get them to think.[9] His habit of exaggerating his own ignorance is also relevant. Despite claiming he knows nothing, Socrates never loses a debate. In addition, he comes off as sarcastic, as when he pretends to compliment the intelligence of arrogant characters who have trouble with logic.[10]

Given these traits, one of Socrates' opponents accuses him of being ironic.[11] "To be ironic" here is a rough translation of a Greek verb that means to pretend or feign ignorance and refers to the acts of those who misrepresent their abilities and agenda to win an argument.[12] This is key. Self-deprecation, feigning ignorance, and adopting other personas are tools that satirists use to criticize their targets and deliver their messages. A comedic mask offers the critic a safe and insidious way to disarm the opponent, rouse resentment, and get others to think.

I'm Gumby Dammit!

This catchphrase is funny. But why? Gumby was a sweet kids' claymation character in the 1950s and 1960s. But in 1982, Eddie Murphy began to portray Gumby (complete with floppy green foam costume and face paint) as a short-tempered actor who would cuss others out behind the scenes, constantly reminding them: "I'm Gumby, dammit!"

So why does that make us laugh? Well, for one thing, it's unexpected. Let's think of laughter as an emotional reaction to odd twists of fate, as a non-rational way of dealing with what seems to be an irrational break from routine. We laugh at the unexpected, the strange, the absurd, the random. Laughter itself mimics such aberrations. Far from melodious and soothing, laughter lacks structure and thus stands out against usual speech and behavior.

Now, armed with my armchair theory of laughter, it's fair to say that Murphy's Gumby is funny because he is so opposite to the Gumby we grew up loving. His portrayal creates an unexpected awkwardness to which we respond with awkward noises and random motions.

Consider Murphy's parody of *Mr. Rogers' Neighborhood*. Mr. Rogers was calm, methodical, and articulate. He kept an orderly home, sang songs, and educated kids. Murphy, too, adopts this kind, pedagogical persona. But he adds the twist that Mr. Robinson happens to be a hoodlum whose lessons include how to shoplift and evade capture. Like Fred, Eddie sings, smiles at the camera, and adheres to rituals. Mr. Robinson is funniest, however, when he unexpectedly breaks from routine and begins to yell threateningly at whoever comes poking around the door of his gritty ghetto apartment.

Most *SNL* sketches consist of such parodies. The idea is to provide a convincing portrayal of some familiar scenario, personality, or pop culture phenomenon. Any mannerisms, physical appearances, or sceneries are imitated closely. To this superficial realism, however, is added some absurd, unexpected twist that skews the original, bastardizing and rendering it opposite to itself. Laughter ensues.

One of the all-time classic *SNL* sketches is "Star Trek: The Last Voyage" (1976). John Belushi nails the voice and gestures of Shatner's Kirk. Also realistic are the bridge backdrop, ship sounds, and camera work. So, there's superficial realism. But the twist comes when an object appears on the viewscreen. Following computer analysis, Chevy Chase's Spock concludes that the object is a "1968 Chrysler Imperial with a tinted windshield and retractable headlights." He then adds that the car's license plate was registered to "a twentieth-century company called NBC."

After a brief chase, the occupants of the 300-year-old vehicle board the Enterprise. As it turns out, the aliens are NBC executives who've come to cancel *Star Trek* due to its low Nielsen ratings. Upon hearing the news, Kirk and crew remain in persona, desperately refusing to drop the act even as workers dismantle the set and remove Spock's plastic ears. The sketch ends with Kirk slumped in his chair, alone on what had been the bridge. The final entry in the Captain's Log states that the crew had tried to explore "strange new worlds" and "boldly go," and "except for one TV network" they had found intelligence "everywhere in the galaxy."

In Murphy's "Gumby" and "Mr. Robinson's Neighborhood" there was no discernible point other than to provide funny parody with a twist of the absurd. For this reason, they hardly qualify as satire. What's the message? Who's being criticized? What change is urged? The *Star Trek* parody, however, contains something more since it moves towards a critical point. That point, ostensibly, is that NBC, the network which originally aired *Star Trek*, is run by dimwits because it canceled such a great show. In addition, the sketch provided *SNL* a way of criticizing its own network (also NBC) by allowing the writers and actors to adopt a different persona, thus creating a safe distance between critic and target.

Jane, You Ignorant Slut

Now, calling a TV network's intelligence into question isn't the most philosophical of messages. But it's a message nonetheless. Most *SNL* sketches, however, tend to be aimed solely at getting laughs. For instance, viewers don't have to work for giggles in the Harry Potter sketch from 2004. Here, the character Hermione (played by Lindsay Lohan) returns to Hogwarts after summer vacation and is depicted with appreciable cleavage bursting from her school uniform. Harry and Ron notice the change but don't want to mention it to Hermione, who remains oblivious and strictly interested in practicing spells. The whole sketch consists of shots of Lohan's boobs and the boys tripping over their words as they try to make casual conversation. Simplistic innuendos abound. Other male characters enter. More of same.

Again, there's no real point here. The potential for humor, rather, resides in familiar pop culture icons acting in persona except for an unusual twist. The same model applies to "Hobbit Office" (2014), which mimics *The Office* as closely as possible, right down to camera work, lighting, backdrop, mockumentary style, and characterization. The twist, however, consists in the fact that the actors play characters from Tolkien's *The Lord of the Rings*. Everything else is business as usual, including the deadpan humor.

Or consider a sketch from 2017 that parodies the filming of an Olive Garden commercial. The actor who plays the director remains professional in tone, even as he begins to give the supposed commercial actors more and more ridiculous directions. Here's an example:

> Now, Blue Shirt. Someone just said something funny. Big laugh [*white guy in blue shirt laughs*]. And even funnier [*Blue Shirt guy nods*]. You're about to pee yourself [*Blue Shirt nods harder*]. I'm peeing, I'm peeing, I'm peeing, ahhh [*Blue Shirt strains expression*]. Fantastic. Great, great, great. Okay, now, Yellow Top, you're looking at the menu and you really want that Chicken Ciao Bella [*African American woman in yellow top views menu with interest*]. Oh, you want it really bad [*Yellow Top woman shakes the menu in excitement*]. You're looking at that pasta going, "Oh, Lordy! I must be in heaven!" [*Yellow Top's jaw drops*].

This sketch, like many others, turns on racial stereotypes; and yet, the audience finds it amusing. But why? What is so funny about a director who unabashedly directs a black woman to recite her lines in a stereotyped African American voice? Sure, it's risqué. It's shocking. But what's the point? Could it just be that audiences, even today, find stereotypes funny?

To repeat: none of these sketches quite qualifies as satire. Sure, audiences find them humorous. They may involve a modicum of irony and plenty of exaggeration. But what they lack is an urge towards social/political criticism and change. They are ultimately just as silly as *SNL*'s 1989 sketch "Toonces the Driving Cat" (in which a couple's cat takes them on a drive but ends up plunging the car off a cliff, only to drive away again) or 2005's "Monkeys Throwing Poop at Celebrities," which is pretty much just crap as far as messages go.

Not Gonna Do It

Judging from the examples above, constructive social criticism is rare for *SNL* (Mr. Bill is an exception). It's not that the show can't do it, because it can. It would just rather engage in parody, impressions, stereotypes, and plain ol' smart-assery. That's its brand of comedy. That's what gets the laughs. So why, then, does *SNL* have a reputation for being a satire, or, as one commentator puts it, "the Empire State Building of satire, the one that you find first on the crowded skyline"?[13]

As in the case of Aristophanes, most of *SNL*'s satirical qualities revolve around political debates, issues, and, most famously, figures. Specifically, it has always specialized in parodies of the American president. Chevy

Chase's Gerald Ford was clumsy and absent minded. Will Ferrell depicted G.W. Bush as a clueless but dangerous child-man with a speech impediment. And Alec Baldwin, though doing a decent job on Trump's voice and mannerisms, portrays the current president as an overt racist. Bill Clinton and Barack Obama got off easy: the former depicted with an obsession with food and women; the latter portrayed as so cool that it was funny.

Here we see neither pointless parody nor smart-assery, but satirical propaganda. As usual, superficial realism is maintained. But instead of an absurd twist, some flaw (whether fictional or based loosely on reality) is ascribed to the target to evoke contempt and detract support. A clear example is "The Undecided Voter" (2012), which ridicules people who didn't know as of September 2012 which candidate they would support. The campaign ad thus depicts such voters as clueless idiots who don't even know basic things like "When is the election?", "What are the names of the two people running?", and "Can a woman have a baby just from French kissing?"

Another example of *SNL*'s political satire is "Racists for Trump" (2015), a mock campaign ad that depicts what it brands as "real Americans" praising Trump for being a winner, a jobs creator, a skilled negotiator, a Washington outsider, authentic, and a good business man. Sounds reasonable, right? Apparently not. The problem is that these "real Americans" are all later shown as casually embracing bigoted symbols and behaviors: a Nazi armband; a KKK outfit; book burning; painting "White power" on a farm house; torching a cross in a field. The ad concludes that it has been a message from "Racists for Donald Trump."

Politicians aren't the only targets of *SNL*'s political satire. An episode from March 2018 included a spoof of an exterminator commercial offering an alternative to roach spray. Charles Barkley plays Ned, the exterminator, who insists that "the only thing that can stop a bad roach is a good roach with a gun." The sketch then proceeds to show animated roaches armed with tiny AR-15 rifles shooting up a house, killing (unarmed!) roaches. Ned also assures customers not to worry about giving roaches guns because he arms only "god-fearing" roaches. Incidentally, Ned adds, "and none of my roaches are gay."

The point isn't hard to miss. The writers are mocking the familiar claim of gun rights advocates that good people, trained and armed with guns, could stop a mass shooter. At the same time, the sketch takes a broad swipe at stereotypical conservatives by tossing in gratuitous homophobia humor. The message is clear, but it's hardly profound: "Guns are bad. Arming good people means more violence. Gun owners are religious and don't like gay people."

And Now, Deep Thoughts...

So, what constitutes depth? What is seriousness? Aristophanes himself relied on shallow, skewed versions of the truth. Perhaps it's impossible to be funny otherwise, at least before a live crowd. Now, recall the spectrum pictured at the start of this chapter, according to which satire lies somewhere between philosophy and seriousness on the one side, and smart-assery, parody, and mockery on the other.

Philosophy attempts to discover and convey hidden truths about the world (usually to determine how we ought to live). Like Socrates, philosophy is critical and peers behind appearances, looking to motivations and causes, transcending assumptions and conventions. Philosophy is difficult and relatively unpopular. Often inducing doubt, it is a thought process that involves dialogue, formulating questions, and proposing answers in the form of timeless truths.

Smart-assery, on the other hand, attempts to entertain by appealing to appearances and superficialities. Aristophanes' comedy is certainly critical and reaches some depth; but his humor also depends on projecting an easy image of the target. Audience responses involve little thought, consisting instead of knee-jerk reactions to merely plausible representations of reality. Symbolism abounds, as staged comedy is a communal ritual that trades on the popular and contemporary. Most comedy, in fact, is aimed at the times in which the material is produced and usually comes off as dated when viewed even ten years later.

SNL, on this reading, tends heavily towards the smart-assery end of the scale. But this is not to say that the show doesn't ever make timelessly profound observations. It's just that what you're more likely to find is the superficial and symbolic, the knee-jerk and plausible. Take, for instance, *SNL*'s stock-in-trade. In the late 1980s and early 1990s, it seemed impossible to avoid people who would go around expressing themselves via *SNL* catchphrases: "That's the ticket," "Buh bye," "the ...-Meister!" "We're here to pump [*clap*] you up," "Makin' cop-ieees," and "Party on!" Like today's internet memes, this prepackaged slogan mentality involves some serious profundity... not! Mind you, this isn't a criticism. *SNL* isn't trying to be profound. It simply does what it does best: silliness and exaggerated mockery of contemporary culture.

But is there nothing more to say about *SNL* and philosophy? Is there not a deeper point to the bastardizations, the stereotypes, the catchphrases and caricatures? Let's think of it this way. Exaggerated mockery can serve to magnify the world's absurdities. So maybe all the wild 'n crazy scenarios and absurd twists aren't pointless. Perhaps the message is: "Life's absurd. Screw seriousness." The world is a mess of insane situations, insane people, and little, if any, sane meaning. It only makes sense, therefore, that a comedy reflective of this world would itself be insane, even inane. Seen in this light, *SNL* is as philosophical as it gets. It's an absurd form of art mocking an absurd world, part of which are absurd forms of mockery of that world. How's that for a deep thought, Mr. Handey?

Notes

1. For this definition, see also https://en.oxforddictionaries.com/definition/satire.
2. Wikipedia. "Satire." Retrieved from https://en.wikipedia.org/wiki/Satire on March 13, 2018.
3. Alan H. Sommerstein, *Aristophanes: Lysistrata and Other Plays*. Revised Edition. (New York: Penguin Books, 2002), 75.
4. Ibid., 78.
5. Ibid., 79.
6. Ibid., 80.
7. *Apology*, 21a–23b.
8. See R. Bracht Branham, "Satire," in Richard Eldridge (ed.), *The Oxford Handbook of Philosophy and Literature* (Oxford: Oxford University Press, 2009), 139–161. For Socrates, "to practice philosophy is to satirize in public anyone with a reputation for wisdom... to show that reputation to be baseless via question and answer... Socrates invented a form of satire just as offensive [as comedy]... he was devoted to unmasking all those considered wise for the amusement and edification of fellow citizens" (143–144).
9. Socrates also insists that he is a sort of god-sent gadfly who never ceases to rouse the citizens and constantly persuade them to cultivate virtue and think for themselves (*Apology* 30e). See also *Theaetetus* 150c–d, where Socrates compares his own ignorance to the sterility of a midwife who determines whether other people are "pregnant" with viable ideas and, if so, helps them "give birth" to those ideas.
10. For instance, *Euthyphro* 5b.
11. *Republic* 337a.
12. Aristotle says that self-deprecators, like Socrates, downplay their abilities and so seem more civilized than arrogant people who presume knowledge (*Nicomachean Ethics* 1127b21–26).
13. Todd Purdum, "S.N.L.: the skyscraper of satire." *Vanity Fair*, April 2011. Retrieved from www.vanityfair.com/news/2011/04/todd-purdum-saturday-night-live-201104 on March 13, 2018.

Part II
SOME POLITICAL SKETCHES

5

Saturday Night Live and the Political Bubble

William Irwin

During the Weekend Update for December 9, 2017, Michael Che said, "Sometimes I'll tell a joke that offends a marginalized group and I'll get a lot of mail about it, mostly from super liberal white women. Which made me think maybe I should try to see things from their perspective by trying to walk a mile in their shoes the best way I knew how, by going undercover as a white woman named Gretchen."

The resulting video clip is hilarious. As promised, Che goes undercover as a liberal white woman, but his skin is still black[1] – and despite his wig, crochet hat, and several scarves, he is still obviously a man. It was enlightening for Che to learn what it is like to have your parents send money while you read Huffington Post articles and eat brunch with your friends. But did the *SNL* audience learn anything? Did they see how satire misrepresents to make a point?

Caricature: What's So Funny about That?

Seeing your own view mocked and caricatured is very unlikely to get you to change your mind or do things differently. Instead, the typical emotional response is to become defensive. The "I'm not like that" response to Michael Che's depiction of liberal white women grasps an important truth: satire misrepresents to make its point. You are not like that, but neither are all the conservatives (and their views) that you enjoy seeing lampooned. Comedy elicits an emotional response. Although laughter is often pleasant and a kind of relief, it can have a dark side. We may be laughing at someone and indulging in *schadenfreude*. We laugh

Saturday Night Live and Philosophy: Deep Thoughts Through the Decades, First Edition. Edited by Jason Southworth and Ruth Tallman. © 2020 John Wiley & Sons Ltd. Published 2020 by John Wiley & Sons Ltd.

at a mean-spirited portrayal of Donald Trump and implicitly say to ourselves, "They really nailed him. That's what he's really like." But when we find ourselves lampooned, we may become upset, angry, or defensive, remarking "That's not fair. That's not what I'm like." We need to walk a mile in the other side's shoes to see how it feels. More important than how it feels, is what it misrepresents. Misrepresentation is fair game in comedy, but when we forget or ignore the comedic misrepresentation, we do ourselves and our opponents a disservice.

Consider the way that Aristophanes caricatured Socrates in *The Clouds*, depicting him as an impractical person with otherworldly concerns, who was out of touch with reality. In the play, Socrates is the head of a school called The Thinkery where, among other things, he has devised a unit of measurement for the leap of a flea and discovered the exact cause of the buzzing noise made by a gnat – its ass resembles a trumpet. Aristophanes' portrait was hilarious, and it was valuable for exposing the pretensions of philosophers in general and perhaps Socrates in particular. Alas, it was also an unfair representation that contributed to the popular prejudice against Socrates that, in turn, led to his execution. According to one ancient source, Socrates was in the theater for a performance of *The Clouds* where he heard some foreigners asking who Socrates was. In response, Socrates stood up in mid-performance to show them.[2] As this example illustrates, parody only works as parody when you know the subject being parodied – otherwise it's misinformation. No philosopher thinks that Socrates was served well by being satirized the way he was, so we should be careful not to assume fairness and accuracy when we see a politician satirized.

There is much that is true and correct to be said about the value of using humor to critique politics. Several chapters in this book do an excellent job of discussing the subject. But the potential problem with using humor this way is that it distorts in order to highlight a truth. This is the essence of caricature, a technique that *SNL* uses to great success in the political realm, perhaps most notably in the cases of Sarah Palin and Donald Trump.

Caricature does not follow the principle of charity, whereby one interprets and understands one's opponent in the best possible terms. However, an ideal political debate format would follow the principle of charity. The candidate would have to state the position of his opponent in terms that she accepts and approves before going on to offer criticism or delineate his own view. In turn, the other candidate would do likewise for her opponent. Of course, there would be nothing funny about that, but it would be informative to watch such a debate.

When instead one learns the views of one's opponents through caricature and other forms of humor, as on *SNL*, one may be able to abstract away the implicit criticism and distortion to be well informed, but one will not be ideally informed or properly sympathetic.

The Ideological Turing Test

Throughout its history and certainly in recent years, *SNL* has exhibited a liberal bias. I use the word "liberal" loosely here to mean what it does in contemporary American politics, roughly the orientation of the Democratic party. This liberal bias is not surprising inasmuch as *SNL* has always aimed to be edgy and to reach a young, hip demographic. In fact, there is nothing wrong with *SNL* exhibiting a political bias. The problem comes when people watching *SNL* simply have their prior beliefs and opinions confirmed. *SNL* has no obligation to avoid political bias, but it provides a valuable service when it reaches beyond its core audience, as arguably it has when effectively lampooning Sarah Palin and Donald Trump. Most of the time, though, *SNL* does not challenge its core audience. It's understandable why: challenging your core audience is biting the hand that feeds you. If your core audience stops watching, then you stop getting paid. *SNL* does not have a duty to challenge its audience, but audience members do have a duty to challenge themselves by getting outside their bubbles.

Consider the Ideological Turing Test.[3] The original Turing Test involves a scenario designed to test whether a computer could communicate so effectively that its human dialogue partner would have no better than a 50% chance of guessing whether it was a computer or a person. The Ideological Turing Test calls for you to present your political opponent's view so effectively that a neutral observer would not be able to guess with better than 50% accuracy whether the view was your own or not. To effectively pass the Ideological Turing Test, you need to present the opposing side both accurately and sympathetically. To be sympathetic requires getting the tone right, which involves genuine understanding. There is no obligation for comedians to pass the Ideological Turing Test, but it is possible.

It has become a truism that many of us exist in political bubbles, echo chambers in which our views are reinforced by friends and newsfeeds. Everyone thinks political bubbles are bad, but no one thinks they are in one. In a fake ad that aired November 19, 2016, shortly after the election of Donald Trump, *SNL* depicted liberals who wanted to remain in their bubble, a near replica of Brooklyn but one where liberals could be sheltered from the effects of the 2016 election. The Bubble is advertised as "a planned community of like-minded free-thinkers, and no one else. If you're an open-minded person come here, and close yourself in." You'll still be able to enjoy things "everyone loves," such as hybrid cars, used book stores, and raw milk.

"The Bubble" passes the Ideological Turing Test. If the fake ad were shown to liberals and conservatives who did not recognize the *SNL* cast members, they would not be able to guess that it was made by liberals. In fact, I wouldn't be surprised if more than half thought it was made by conservatives. Bravo *SNL*! This is not easy to do, and *SNL* does not do it very often.

In *On Liberty* the philosopher John Stuart Mill (1806–1873) not only championed the value of minority opinion but advocated that we learn the opposing side as well as or better than our own. Mill makes sense, because you really don't know your side of an issue if you don't fully understand the other side. We're naturally inclined to learn our side well, but we need to be pushed and reminded to learn the other side. Mill added that to do so we should seek to learn the other side *from* the other side.[4] The difficulty in doing this is not a matter of access, at least not these days. The conservative or liberal point of view (or any other point of view) is as close as the click of a remote or a mouse. The difficulty is the tone. Well-motivated liberals may attempt to watch Fox News or read Breitbart, but they will likely find the tone tough to take. The same goes for conservatives who tune into MSNBC or peruse the *Huffington Post*. But learning the other side from partisans of one's own view is often no better than getting a caricature – and in the case of watching *SNL*, it is exactly that.

SNL does not need to stop presenting caricatures, but we need to be more careful consumers of news and opinion, including *SNL*. The source matters and the tone matters. Comedy is good for laughs and for speaking truth to power, but it can sour discourse and keep us trapped in our bubble. In light of that, let's consider the possibility of neutral political satire and the possibility of a conservative alternative to *SNL*.

Diversity in Comedy?

One way of dealing with caricature consumption is to ingest politically neutral satire. There is plenty to satirize about politicians apart from their partisan views. Politicians in general are corrupt, ineffective, hypocritical, and self-serving. *The Simpsons* has, at times, aimed at this kind of neutral political satire and succeeded in creating fictional politicians whose party affiliations are ambiguous.[5] But this is not always possible, and it is perhaps easier in a fictional cartoon world than in a sketch comedy. With the freedom of a fictional world, *The Simpsons* can develop scenarios in which to ensconce satire. *SNL*, by contrast, takes the real world as its jumping off point into satire. The real world, of course, includes real politicians with partisan views and party affiliations.

South Park could be perceived as an equal opportunity offender with its characterization of the American electoral process as resulting in the choice between a Douche and a Turd, but in some ways that is giving the show too much credit for neutrality. In truth, *South Park* is not so much neutral as libertarian in its politics, which suits me perfectly. So, while the show is right to satirize both the left and the right, *South Park* does not do so from a neutral point of view but rather from a libertarian point of view.

To its credit, *SNL* does not present the left as without foibles. The hilarious portrayal of sighing Al Gore and his "lockbox" in the 2000 election highlighted the sanctimonious vacuity of the Democratic candidate, and in an election decided by a few votes in Florida, may have cost Gore enough votes to lose. Larry David's portrayal of Bernie Sanders in 2016 was clearly done from a place of love and affection, and yet it was effective in highlighting the candidate's crankiness and economic illiteracy. Of course, Larry David and the writers took it only so far; it seemed more like they were roasting Sanders for his personal eccentricities than satirizing his socialism. Kate McKinnon's portrayal of Hilary Clinton in the 2016 election was often biting, but it was done with affection. Contrast McKinnon's portrayal of Clinton with Tina Fey's portrayal of Sarah Palin in 2008 – no affection there.

Barack Obama got a pass for the most part during his eight years in office. There were sketches with Fred Armisen and Jay Pharoah portraying him, but Obama was a tough target. The president had his faults, but they were not easy to parody, or at least *SNL* did not want to go there. *SNL* never saw fit to satirize Obama's sanctimony and sense that he always knew what was best. Worse, the show could potentially have had an effect on policy if it were willing to critique and satirize Obama's militarism from the left, but it passed on that opportunity. Portraying Obama, Fred Armisen admitted that he got the Nobel Peace Prize just because he was not George Bush. But an easy regular target for *SNL* would have been the Peace Prize winner's continuing wars in Iraq and Afghanistan and employing drone strikes.

Likewise, *SNL* has taken it easy on liberals who suffer something akin to PTSD in Trump's America. The Bubble video was a good start, but there was no follow-up. To be sure, it is not *SNL*'s responsibility to be fair and balanced in its satire, but it might serve its audience better if it were. Then again, the argument could be made that, in light of Trump's egregious behavior, giving equal time to satirizing the liberal response would be a distortion and a disservice.

Much has been made of diversity on the *SNL* cast, and rightly so. In its earliest days, *SNL* was a boys' club in which brutes like John Belushi did not give women like Gilda Radner their due. Things changed and improved with time, reaching a peak when Tina Fey and Amy Poehler co-hosted Weekend Update. Garrett Morris was a minor player in the original cast, but over time black stars rose, with Eddie Murphy, followed by Chris Rock, Tracy Morgan, Tim Meadows, Jay Pharoah, Keenan Thompson, and Michael Che.

Maya Rudolph departed in 2007, and there was no new black female cast member hired to replace her. In an attempt to draw attention to the situation in 2013, guest host Kerry Washington played the roles of multiple black women in a single sketch. Finally, Sasheer Zamata was hired in 2014. For the sake of diversity in viewpoints, not to mention the ability to portray black female characters, the cast needed black women.

But if diversity of viewpoints is important, why not add conservative cast members? Has that possibility been seriously entertained? Probably not. Then again, if it could boost ratings, perhaps it would be considered. Before her racist Twitter implosion, Roseanne Barr had a tremendous hit with the reboot of her eponymous sitcom and her character's support for President Trump. If nothing else, this shows there is an audience for comedy with a favorable portrayal of a conservative. Of course, Roseanne's reboot was balanced by characters expressing dissenting, liberal views, lending dramatic tension.

Would there be an audience for a show that skewered both liberals and conservatives? *South Park* has answered that question in the affirmative. In his early days on *The Daily Show*, Jon Stewart made at least an attempt to criticize and satirize liberals, but as his audience grew larger and more liberal, Stewart's critiques of liberals became fewer and less biting.[6] From the standpoint of ratings and audience size, Stewart made the right move. Similarly, if *SNL* attempted to integrate conservative cast members and writers, the result might have more integrity but find fewer viewers.

It also might produce an unsatisfying weak tea. When liberal strongholds give a token slot to a conservative, they sometimes satisfy no one. Consider the place of David Brooks at the *New York Times*. Most conservatives do not care what Brooks has to say, but liberals are routinely enraged by him. Beyond that, liberals who read his column congratulate themselves on exposing themselves to conservative viewpoints, and yet Brooks is not regarded as much of a conservative by most conservatives. So the liberal self-congratulation and self-satisfaction is unearned. Something similar might happen if *SNL* integrated a token conservative or two.

But what about the past? Haven't there been conservatives on *SNL* in the past? It's hard to know for certain, and we don't always really know the political views of actors and writers. Dennis Miller comes to mind as a possible conservative cast member, especially given his association with Bill O'Reilly in recent years. Miller, though, was a liberal during his time on *SNL*. His political views shifted to the right in the 1990s after he had left the show. Joe Piscopo has supported Donald Trump and voiced displeasure with Trump's portrayal on *SNL*, but Piscopo remains a Democrat. Victoria Jackson is a conservative Christian and a Tea Party supporter, but she seems to have developed and voiced her political views after her departure from *SNL*. The *SNL* writer Jim Downey has been mislabeled as a Republican by his critics, but he is in fact a Democrat.[7]

We might be led to conclude that the reason there are no conservatives on *SNL* is that conservatives aren't smart and funny – they don't have a sense of humor. Besides, reality has a liberal bias. I mean, can you name any great conservative comedians? When liberals respond this way they prematurely close off the question with a self-satisfied ejaculation. A couple of things need to be considered. First, the entertainment industry is not hospitable to conservatives, so many conservatives may just stay in the closet. Others who come out of the closet before they have become successful may find their careers cut short. Second, writers and cast members are typically unknowns before they come to *SNL*, so conservatives may be out there. If *SNL* put out the word that they were looking for conservatives, there would probably be no shortage of applications and audition tapes.

Ultimately, *SNL* may just be too old and established as an institution to become politically integrated at this late date. A politically balanced show might have to start from the grassroots by people who really want to be part of such a project.

Live from Omaha?

If conservative comedians and writers really exist, what about the free market that conservatives are so fond of? Why doesn't some conservative comedy troupe take up the challenge? Conservative columnist Mike LaChance has suggested the idea for a conservative *SNL* set in red state America – it could be "live from Omaha" instead of "live from New York."[8] LaChance is not a comedy writer, and so predictably some of his ideas for sketches were pretty lame and earned him abuse on the internet. But a couple of his ideas were not bad:

> "A sketch featuring Sarah Palin playing Tina Fey upset about Hillary losing."
>
> "The Social Justice Warriors: A group of college undergrads who are trying to advance radical social change but can't get anywhere because they're constantly at war with each other over pronouns."

There is no doubt that seasoned comedy writers and actors could come up with more and better ideas and sketches.

Even so, I'm not sure that a conservative *SNL* would be a good idea. Conservatives don't need to have their views reinforced by a new *SNL*-type show any more than liberals need to have their views reinforced by the real *SNL*, or any more than libertarians, like me, need our views reinforced by *South Park* – I hardly ever watch it. Watching shows that reinforce our beliefs through satire is the problem. The solution involves conservatives watching *SNL* to get a feel for how their views and icons look to the left. If someone made a conservative *SNL* alternative, it would likewise benefit liberals and libertarians to watch it to get a feel for how their views and icons look to the right.

But perhaps the best thing would be a new show founded by people from all political persuasions who want to work together. Isn't that what democracy is all about?[9]

Notes

1. Contrast this with Eddie Murphy's whiteface performance in the video "White like me," which aired December 15, 1984 on *Saturday Night Live*.
2. Aelian, *Historical Miscellany* (Cambridge: Harvard University Press, 1997), 85.

3. Bryan Caplan, "The ideological Turing test." Retrieved from http://econlog.econlib.org/archives/2011/06/the_ideological.html on July 6, 2019.

4. John Stuart Mill, On Liberty (New York: Penguin, 1974), 99.

5. John Hugar, "How *The Simpsons* mastered the art of neutral political satire." Retrieved from https://tv.avclub.com/how-the-simpsons-mastered-the-art-of-neutral-political-1798246386 on July 6, 2019.

6. As Jason Holt pointed out to me, on Trevor Noah's *Daily Show* there have been some halfhearted attempts to target the left, as if the writing team recognizes the importance of doing so. Alas, the criticism of the left from Noah and company does not work as well or come across as authentic.

7. Other *SNL* alums who have been mislabeled as Republicans or conservatives include John Lovitz who calls himself a Kennedy Democrat; Rob Schneider who was a registered Democrat during his years on *SNL*; Adam Sandler who considers himself an independent; and Norm Macdonald who describes himself as apolitical.

8. Mike LaChance, "If conservatives want to win the culture war, we need our own 'Saturday Night Live'." Retrieved from https://townhall.com/columnists/mikelachance/2018/06/07/if-conservatives-want-to-win-the-culture-war-we-need-our-own-saturday-night-live-n2487982 on July 6, 2019

9. Thanks to Jim Ambury, Jason Holt, Joshua Reynolds, Sharon Schwarze, Jason Southworth, Ruth Tallman, and Mark White for very helpful feedback and ideas.

Saturday Night Live and the Production of Political Truth

Foucault Explains the Danger of Late Night Comedy

Kimberly S. Engels

Saturday Night Live has become a staple of each political season. Viewers delight as their favorite cast members or guest celebrities impersonate major political candidates. Sometimes the candidates themselves get in on the act, appearing as guest stars on the show. In recent years, though, late night comedy has taken on a role that goes beyond entertainment and comedic relief. Many viewers interpret the comedy as reflecting a level of truth about the candidates and as revealing shortcomings in the coverage of traditional news programs. This was especially true in 2016. To make sense of this phenomenon, let's look to the philosopher Michel Foucault (1926–1984).

Foucault famously argued that truth and knowledge are neither static nor objective. In his view, what can be considered true and what can be considered knowledge emerge in a historical context amidst a set of contingent power relations. Bodies of knowledge do not reflect inherent or timeless truths about the world, rather they emerge in relation to existing knowledge fields, institutions, and authorities. What is considered true in a specific historical and geographic context is produced by frameworks of rules governing what can be spoken about and in what ways. These frameworks include "authorities of delimination," the individuals and institutions in a given historical context who are trusted to define the boundaries of what is true and false regarding a particular subject.

Saturday Night Live and Philosophy: Deep Thoughts Through the Decades, First Edition. Edited by Jason Southworth and Ruth Tallman.
© 2020 John Wiley & Sons Ltd. Published 2020 by John Wiley & Sons Ltd.

In this chapter, we'll see how late night comedy programs such as *Saturday Night Live* have joined traditional TV news programs as authorities of delimination for defining the boundaries of political truth in our historical epoch. In the spirit of Foucault's work, I will not argue whether or not *Saturday Night Live* ought to serve as an authority of delimination, but instead uncover its effects. In short, we'll see that *SNL*'s authority is not necessarily bad, but it is potentially dangerous.

Foucault: Knowledge, Truth, and Power

In *The Archaeology of Knowledge,* Foucault argues that the way we order and arrange information is governed by justificatory frameworks (or rules) that operate below our reflective awareness. The rules, called "discursive practices," determine what can be thought of and spoken about at a certain time.[1] We don't have thoughts or ideas *before* we are able to speak about them. Rather, our thoughts and ideas develop through the language that we use and the concepts that are available to us.

The rules dictate who is trusted as an authority to speak about certain subjects based on what institutions these people are part of. Foucault calls these "authorities of delimination." For example, in our contemporary epoch, therapists and psychiatrists are authorities trusted to speak the truth about mental health and illness. If these professionals have degrees from prestigious universities and are associated with therapy centers, mental health clinics, or psychiatry wards at major hospitals, they are more trusted by the public to speak the truth about mental illness. Additionally, the ability to study individuals and their behavior in institutional settings led to the development of psychology as a body of knowledge.

Foucault shows that different historical epochs and different geographical locations have different frameworks of verification for something to be considered true. These frameworks of verification include people who are trusted to speak the truth, and the institutions that they speak from which legitimate them. In the next section, we'll explore how TV serves as the primary shaper of the truth about American political candidates and events, and how late night comedy is included alongside traditional news programs as an authority of delimination for political truth.

Late Night Comedy as a Contemporary Authority of Delimination

In our contemporary epoch, news programs and the well-known journalists who appear on them, are trusted authorities of delimination. In other words, whether or not a particular event is legitimated as important has to do with it being featured on the news. TV continues to be the most widely used news platform; 57% of U.S. adults often get TV-based news, either from local TV (46%), cable (31%), network (30%) or some combination of the three.[2] While this number varies slightly for younger demographics who increasingly turn to online sources for their news, TV still remains the most common source of news delivery. What individuals understand to be important in their society, as well as how they interpret events or form attitudes about other places in the country are formed by what they see on news programs.

All news programs make choices about what to cover and in what ways. In terms of politics, these choices and portrayals then shape the narrative of an election season. For example, in 2015, five Republican candidates – Donald Trump, Jeb Bush, Ted Cruz, Marco Rubio, and Ben Carson – each got more news coverage than Senator Bernie Sanders during the 2015 season leading up to the primary, and Hillary Clinton received three times as much press as the Vermont senator.[3] These choices by major media sources about which candidates to focus on influenced viewers' perceptions of who were the leading contenders for the presidency. Some commenters have partially blamed the election of Donald Trump on the attention he was given by the mainstream media. Trump's campaign, while not being taken very seriously early on, was given unfiltered airtime on major news networks. According to the data from mediaQuant, Trump received $4.96 billion in free media in the year leading up to the presidential election. He received $5.6 billion throughout the entirety of his campaign, more than Hillary Clinton, Bernie Sanders, Ted Cruz, and Marco Rubio combined.[4] Clearly, major TV news networks play a role not just in revealing or communicating the truth, but in actually *creating it*. The portrayals of the TV media shape the beliefs of viewers and consequently the way that people think, act, relate to others, and form conceptions of truth about the world. Ultimately, this influences people's perceptions of the candidates and who they vote for.

Alongside traditional news programs, as well as cable news, late night comedy is now seen as a legitimate news source, especially by younger people. According to a 2004 report from the Pew Research Center, young people get campaign information from traditional news sources (newspapers and national news) less than any other age group. The results indicated that 21% of young people (ages 18 to 29) reported learning something about the presidential campaign regularly from comedy shows like *The Daily Show* or *Saturday Night Live*.[5] When it comes to important events such as presidential elections, late night comedy programs are seen as trustworthy, informative, and able to influence public opinion.[6]

SNL is different from other comedy programs such as the *The Daily Show* because of its focus on parody. Parody "recasts something that is already settled."[7] Parodying a debate takes the events that transpired and comically emphasizes or exaggerates specific aspects of them that viewers might not have picked up on the first time. Viewers then reconceptualize the events as they happened with these new points of emphasis. During the 2008 election season, after an *SNL* sketch spoofed the fact that Hillary Clinton was asked tougher questions than Barack Obama, reporters became noticeably tougher on Obama.[8] The truth that the press had been going easier on Obama than Clinton was partially produced through *SNL*'s parodies. From this we can see that *SNL* has influence as an authority of delimination regarding political events and has the power to influence how other media sources cover the news.

As another example of *SNL's* ability to produce truth, consider the depiction of vice presidential candidate Sarah Palin, who was unknown to the public until her surprise announcement as John McCain's running mate. In her third televised interview with Katie Couric, Palin failed to answer basic questions about Senator McCain's policies and was unable to name a newspaper that she read. Right after the interview, journalists focused on the McCain campaign as a whole and generally ignored Palin's answers. Two days later, though, *SNL* aired a sketch with Tina Fey impersonating Palin in which Fey used many of Palin's lines from the interview verbatim.[9] Following the sketch, journalists' focus shifted to Palin herself. A study by Angela Abel and Michael Barthel showed that before the sketch, 34% of news articles, editorials, and broadcasts placed blame on Palin herself for her failures in the Couric interview rather than the McCain campaign. After the *SNL* sketch, 80% of articles and broadcasts placed blame on Palin herself. Clearly, *SNL* sketches have the ability not only to influence public opinion, but to shift the focus of journalists and the media and call into question the narratives presented by other news programs.[10] Part of the reason *SNL* can shape viewpoints is that it affects other media outlets. When other news sources fail to notice something, *SNL* may highlight it. After the *SNL* sketch, viewers may interpret other news coverage as biased, leading some to trust comedy sources more than traditional news programs.

SNL and the 2016 Election

The portrayal of the 2016 candidates by TV sources, including what candidates were given airtime and whether that airtime was positive or negative, undoubtedly had an influence on who won both the primary races and the final contest. *SNL* featured many sketches focused on the election, which also contributed to the production of the truth. Three of the stars of the forty-first and forty-second seasons of *SNL* were Kate McKinnon impersonating Hillary Clinton, Larry David as Bernie Sanders, and Alec Baldwin playing Donald Trump. Larry David made his first appearance as Bernie Sanders during the Cold Open, spoofing the first Democratic debate. As David enters the stage he says, "We're doomed. We need a revolution. Millions of people on the streets. And we got to do something and we got to do it now." He continues: "I don't have a Super PAC, I don't even have a backpack. I carry my stuff around loose in my arms like a professor, you know between classes. I own one pair of underwear. That's it!?"[11] The sketch portrayed both Sanders' enthusiasm and also his strong conviction that our political system needs to be shaken up. Yet it also portrayed him as disheveled and a bit crazy. At the end of the sketch, David says, "I'm Bernie Sanders, and come next November, I'm going to be Hillary Clinton's Vice President!" signifying that Sanders had no chance of winning the Democratic nomination. These points of emphasis by *SNL* were also reflective of how Sanders was portrayed by the mainstream media, who either failed to cover his campaign at all or framed him as a "fringe candidate."

Future sketches featuring David as Sanders had a similar tone. Sanders was portrayed as a hopeless idealist who could never be elected, despite being a passionate politician with a good heart. In a sketch spoofing the town hall with Rachel Maddow, when Sanders was directed to choose an envelope containing a question, he requested the "one on the far left. So far left it could never be elected."[12] Sanders was also portrayed as having homogenous supporters, in one clip stating, "My message is resonating with a very diverse group of white

people. And I've got supporters of all ages – 18-year-olds, 19-year-olds...
eh, that's it,"[13] suggesting Sanders was only popular among very young
people and white people.

Throughout the season, the portrayal of Hillary Clinton was quite
different. Clinton was portrayed as obsessively seeking the White
House, but also as an obvious shoe-in for the nomination (and later
the presidency), as well as qualified, grounded, and realistic – everything Sanders was not. Sketches also highlighted the fact that Hillary
Clinton's candidacy was judged more harshly because she was a
woman, and she was often required to prove herself in a way that
male candidates were not. In her opening remarks for Democratic
Debate Cold Open, McKinnon, impersonating Clinton, greeted the
audience saying: "I think you're really going to like the Hillary Clinton
my team and I have created for this debate. She's warm, but strong;
flawed, yet perfect; relaxed, but racing full-speed toward the White
House like the T-1000 from Terminator."[14]

In another sketch, Clinton sings solemnly in the background while
a group of young voters confess they were leaning toward supporting
Bernie Sanders. "Hillary has every single thing I want in a president,
but at the same time, she's no Bernie," one man says as the group discusses politics in a restaurant. The voters tout Clinton's experience
and say she's the "most qualified candidate in history," but say they're
still drawn to her rival's "vibe."[15] The message of the sketch was that
Hillary Clinton was obviously a much better candidate than Bernie
Sanders, but sexist double standards prevented voters from seeing
that. It also may have caused some viewers to question how other
media sources were portraying the candidates and wonder whether
other news sources were guilty of the sexist double standard that *SNL*
was emphasizing. After Clinton had secured the nomination, she was
portrayed as self-evidently the best candidate and the obvious even-
tual winner. In the Cold Open sketch spoofing the first debate, after
Trump rambles incoherently, Clinton is asked, "What do you think
about that Secretary?" to which McKinnon responds, "I think I am
going to be president."[16] In the sketch spoofing the second debate, she
says, "Just last Friday, he handed me this election."[17]

Donald Trump was depicted as inconsistent, prejudiced, easily
agitated, provocative, lacking in actual policy proposals, and not a
serious candidate. Two minutes into Alec Baldwin's first appearance in "Donald Trump vs. Hillary Clinton: Cold Open," he
announces, "I won the debate, I stayed calm" suggesting Trump did
not have the poise to be president. Hillary Clinton also yields her

two minutes of speaking time to Trump, suggesting that every time Trump speaks he makes the situation worse for himself and better for Clinton. Later in the debate she says, "Can America vote right now?" Then she starts tearing up, "Sorry Lester, just, this is going so well...It's going how I always dreamed," implying that Trump was handing Clinton the election.[18] In "Donald Trump vs. Hillary Clinton Third Debate: Cold Open," it was again emphasized that Trump had no chance of winning. The moderator stated, "Mr. Trump, it has become clear that you are probably going to lose" and then makes him repeat "I, Donald Trump, promise to accept the results of this election."[19]

In summary, Senator Sanders was presented as enthusiastic, well-meaning, and a good person, but naive, unprepared, disheveled, inexperienced, and unelectable. His appeal was limited to white liberals and young people, because they too were naive and idealistic – they liked the sounds of his plans but didn't know how difficult it would be to implement them. Hillary Clinton was portrayed as tough, experienced, judged by a double standard, struggling to make herself appealing to ordinary people, and despite this, a shoe-in for the Democratic nomination and later the presidency. Donald Trump was portrayed as incompetent, sporadic, unpredictable, bizarre, constantly sabotaging his own campaign, and the obvious loser of the presidency. Ultimately, these representations, alongside the portrayals by other news sources, produced truth and knowledge about the candidates and the election.

Saturday Night Live as an Authority of Delimination for Political Truth

When reflecting back on his works, Foucault once commented, "My point is not that everything is bad, but that everything is dangerous, which is not exactly the same as bad. If everything is dangerous, then we always have something to do."[20] Foucault never said that a particular framework for producing truth was bad, but that it had the potential to be dangerous. Thus, it is not necessarily bad for TV news programs as well as *SNL* to function as authorities of delimination for the emergence of political truth, but it could be dangerous.

As an authority of delimination for political truth, *SNL* emphasized the sexist double standard to which Clinton was held. Viewers of debates or interviews may have missed subtleties that were then exaggerated in the sketches. This brought the sexist double standard into the spotlight, emphasizing that Clinton was judged more harshly than the male candidates. If she wore wild hair like Sanders she would not be taken seriously; if she spoke as incoherently as Donald Trump, she would never win an election. Framing this in a comedic light allowed viewers to laugh and learn from it simultaneously. It also helped them evaluate how Clinton was being portrayed by traditional news networks and whether this portrayal was fair. There is a very real benefit in using comedy, and parody in particular, to emphasize important dimensions that may go unexamined by traditional news sources.

At the same time, danger was apparent. One way in which it was dangerous for *SNL* to be considered an authority of delimination is that *SNL*'s writers are fairly removed from a sizeable portion of the U.S. electorate. As elites, their knowledge of working-class people and the political climate in some of the rural states was badly misread. Despite the repeated portrayal in the sketches that Hillary Clinton had the presidency in the bag, she lost the election. Sketches made it seem crazy that anyone could be fooled by Trump's ridiculous rhetoric and obvious incompetence. Trump wasn't convincing to any of the *SNL* writing staff, and they lacked knowledge of the lifestyles, experience, and worldviews of working-class people. *SNL* is far from the only media source that falsely assumed Clinton would win, but *SNL*'s reputation for focusing on things that other news sources conveniently omit or fail to see makes the mistake more glaring.

In the same vein, viewers were encouraged to see Senator Sanders as a fringe candidate, with ideas outside the mainstream. *SNL* suggested that the enthusiasm for his candidacy was due to unrealistic voters, not to the popularity of his proposals. However, Senator Sanders' proposals were very popular in states like Wisconsin and Michigan that ended up going to Trump in the general election, again showing a disconnect between the portrayals offered by *SNL* writers and the worldviews of working-class people. While portrayals of Sanders as a fringe candidate were common in traditional news programs as well, *SNL* sketches acted as confirmation, suggesting that the mainstream media was getting this one right. It was also emphasized repeatedly that Sanders would lose the general election, even after polls showed him beating Donald Trump by as many as 15 points in a head to head match up, with a polling average lead of ten points.[21] *SNL* helped create the truth of Sanders' unelectability, which became a self-fulfilling prophecy. These inconsistencies call into question whether *SNL* should take greater care with how situations and people are portrayed.

Foucault argued that the concept of madness changed over time. In the nineteenth century, madness became medicalized and hospitals and doctors became trusted authorities to speak the truth about who was mad and who was not. Research has shown that, in a similar way, comedy program writers are now trusted to speak the truth about political events and candidates. But the specific rules or processes used to determine what is most important to emphasize about events and people are unclear. Doctors had established methods for diagnosing madness based on what behavior was observed in each subject. The same structured care is not taken when setting the boundaries of political truth through sketch comedy. The fact that it was repeated in multiple sketches that Trump would not win reflected a refusal to even entertain the possibility. So, there is danger in trusting late night comedy writers with political prediction.

Another danger is that *SNL* sketches focus on the personality traits and quirks of the candidates, rather than the actual policies that candidates support. Thus, sketches did not reflect the actual policy proposals of Hillary Clinton and Bernie Sanders: these differences in policy accounted for why some voters preferred Sanders over Clinton and vice versa. Focus was kept to the "qualified" versus "unqualified" dimension of the race, while ignoring that "qualifications" are not the only thing that matter, nor are they what is most important to many voters. Substantive policy differences between Sanders and Clinton and then Clinton and Trump were never emphasized or explored on *SNL*. Ignoring this dimension of the primary and the general election may have affected the outcome of both contests.

"We Always Have Something To Do"

In years to come, *Saturday Night Live* sketches will continue to shape what viewers find important to focus on regarding candidates and political events. In short, *SNL* will continue to play a role in the production of political truth and knowledge. While this has definite benefits, it also has potential dangers. Going forward, it could be useful to acknowledge those dangers and perhaps try to remedy them – as Foucault says, danger means "we always have something to do."[22]

Notes

1. Michel Foucault, *The Archaeology of Knowledge and the Discourse on Language* (New York: Pantheon Books, 1972), 117.
2. Pew Research Center, "Pathways to news" July 7, 2016, Retrieved from www.journalism.org/2016/07/07/pathways-to-news/ on November 24, 2018.
3. Thomas Patterson, "Pre-primary news coverage of the 2016 race: Trump's rise, Sanders' emergence, Clinton's struggle," *Shorenstein Center on Media, Politics, and Public Policy*, June 13, 2016. Retrieved from https://shorensteincenter.org/pre-primary-news-coverage-2016-trump-clinton-sanders/#_ftnref22 on November 24, 2018.
4. Emily Stewart, "Donald Trump rode $5 billion in free media to the White House," *The Street,* Nov 17, 2016. Retrieved from www.thestreet.com/story/13896916/1/donald-trump-rode-5-billion-in-free-media-to-the-white-house.html on November 24, 2018.
5. Pew Research Center, "Where Americans go for news," June 8, 2004. Retrieved from www.people-press.org/2004/06/08/i-where-americans-go-for-news/ on June 19, 2018.
6. P. Moy, M.A. Xenos, V.K. Hess, "Priming effects of late night comedy," *International Journal of Public Opinion Research* 18 (2006), 198–221. J.S. Morris and J.C. Baumgartner, "The Daily Show and attitudes towards news media," in J.C. Baumgartner and J.S. Morris (eds.), Laughing Matters (New York: Routledge, 2008).
7. Angela Abel and Michael Barthel, "Appropriation of mainstream news: how Saturday Night Live Changed the Political Discussion," *Critical Studies in Media Communication* 30.1 (2013), 5.
8. Ibid.
9. Seth Meyers (Head Writer), *Saturday Night Live,* "Sarah Palin and Hillary Clinton," Season 34, Episode 1, September 13, 2008.
10. Abel and Barthel, "Appropriation of mainstream news," 8.
11. Rob Klein and Bryan Tucker (Head Writers), *Saturday Night Live,* Season 41, Episode 3, October 17, 2015.
12. Rob Klein and Bryan Tucker (Head Writers), "MSNBC forum: Cold Open," *Saturday Night Live*, Season 41, Episode 4, November 7, 2015.
13. Rob Klein and Bryan Tucker (Head Writers), "Carson endorsement: Cold Open," *Saturday Night Live*, Season 41, Episode 15, March 12, 2016.
14. Rob Klein and Bryan Tucker (Head Writers), "Democratic debate: Cold Open," *Saturday Night Live*, Season 41, Episode 3, October 17, 2015.
15. Rob Klein and Bryan Tucker (Head Writers), "I can't make you love me," *Saturday Night Live*, Season 41, Episode 13, February 13, 2016.
16. Chris Kelly, Sarah Schneider, Bryan Tucker, and Kent Sublette (Head Writers), "Donald Trump vs. Hillary Clinton debate: Cold Open," *Saturday Night Live,* Season 42, Episode 1, October 1, 2016.

17. Chris Kelly, Sarah Schneider, Bryan Tucker, and Kent Sublette (Head Writers), "Donald Trump vs. Hillary Clinton town hall: cold open," *Saturday Night Live*, Season 42, Episode 3, October 15, 2016.
18. Chris Kelly, Sarah Schneider, Bryan Tucker, and Kent Sublette (Head Writers), "Donald Trump vs. Hillary Clinton debate: cold open," *Saturday Night Live,* Season 42, Episode 1, October 1, 2016.
19. Chris Kelly, Sarah Schneider, Bryan Tucker, and Kent Sublette (Head Writers), "Donald Trump vs. Hillary Clinton third debate: cold open," *Saturday Night Live*, Season 42, Episode 4, October 23, 2016.
20. Michel Foucault "On the genealogy of ethics: an overview of work in progress: afterword," in Hubert L. Dreyfus and Paul Rabinow (eds.), *Michel Foucault: Beyond Structuralism and Hermeneutics*, 2nd ed. (Chicago: University of Chicago Press 1983), 343.
21. Realclear Politics, "General Eeection: Trump vs. Sanders." Retrieved from www.realclearpolitics.com/epolls/2016/president/us/general_election_trump_vs_sanders-5565.html on June 19, 2018.
22. Michel Foucault "On the genealogy of ethics: an overview of work in progress: afterword," in Hubert L. Dreyfus and Paul Rabinow, Michel Foucault (eds.), *Beyond Structuralism and Hermeneutics*, 2nd ed. (Chicago: University of Chicago Press 1983), 343.

Word Associations, Black Jeopardy, and Mr. Robinson's Neighborhood
SNL Tackles Race

J. Jeremy Wisnewski

Comedy reveals our assumptions by exploiting them in exaggerated form – and boy do we have a lot of assumptions, particularly about race and racial identity. For over forty years now, the evolving cast of *SNL* has used comedy to navigate our attitudes about what it means to belong to a racial group, and particularly what it means to be African-American. Revealing what we take for granted about race has an essential political and ethical function. In this respect, *SNL*'s comedy and philosophy have something fundamental in common: both re-tune our attention by challenging our assumptions about the world and each other.[1]

Word Associations: *SNL* and the N-word

SNL has been using comedy both to reveal and to challenge our notions of race since its first season, when Chevy Chase and Richard Pryor appeared in "Word Association."[2] The sketch is deservedly famous.[3] Under the auspices of a job interview, an interviewer (Chase) presents a series of words to a job candidate (Mr. Wilson, played by Richard Pryor). The candidate is instructed to say the first term that comes to mind after being presented with a word. After a few harmless examples, we see what the interview is really about: a demonstration of racial superiority.

Saturday Night Live and Philosophy: Deep Thoughts Through the Decades, First Edition. Edited by Jason Southworth and Ruth Tallman.
© 2020 John Wiley & Sons Ltd. Published 2020 by John Wiley & Sons Ltd.

INTERVIEWER (CHEVY CHASE):	Negro
JOB CANDIDATE/MR. WILSON (RICHARD PRYOR):	White
INTERVIEWER:	Tar baby.
MR. WILSON [SURPRISED]:	What'd you say?
INTERVIEWER:	Tar baby.
MR. WILSON:	Ofay.
INTERVIEWER:	Colored.
MR. WILSON [ANGRY]:	Redneck.
INTERVIEWER:	Jungle bunny.
MR. WILSON [ANGRIER]:	Peckerwood.
INTERVIEWER:	Burr head.
MR. WILSON:	Cracker!
INTERVIEWER:	Spear chucker.
MR. WILSON:	White trash.
INTERVIEWER:	Jungle bunny.
MR. WILSON:	Honky.
INTERVIEWER:	Spade!
MR. WILSON:	Honky-honky!
INTERVIEWER:	Nigger!
MR. WILSON:	Dead honky!
INTERVIEWER [SCARED]:	You seem qualified for this job … how about a starting salary of $5,000?
MR. WILSON:	Your Mama!
INTERVIEWER:	uh…how about $7,500?
MR. WILSON:	Your Grandmama!

Notice that the slurs aren't passively accepted by Mr. Wilson (Pryor) – he asserts himself by counter-slurring his interviewer. The racial slurs paint a picture of black persons as primitive, animalistic, irrational. Mr. Wilson won't have it. His responses *resist* the social identity being foisted on him. He asserts his autonomy and his personhood, by not passively accepting what his potential employer is saying. Mr. Wilson is *not* simply a hireling, not simply a black man, and not someone who can be brushed aside by stereotypes. He demands to be recognized as a full-fledged human being, even to the point of intimidation (and winds up being the highest paid janitor ever for his efforts!).

We see this same dynamic – the assertion of one's humanity through struggle – in Frederick Douglas's (1818–1895) famous account of his fight with Covey the slaveowner.

After resisting [Covey], I felt as I had never felt before. It was resurrection from the dark and pestiferous tomb of slavery, to the heaven of comparative freedom. I was no longer a servile coward trembling under the frown of a brother worm of the dust, but, my long-cowed spirit was roused to an attitude of manly independence. I had reached the point at which I was *not afraid to die*. This spirit made me a freeman in *fact*, while I remained a slave in *form*.[4]

Compare the dynamics of identity in "Word Association" (don't you dare scoff!). Based on certain concepts of race, the interviewer attempts to humiliate Mr. Wilson. Mr. Wilson refuses to be defined by others, refuses to be merely an object at the whim of an employer. African-American philosopher Lewis Gordon suggests that Douglas's struggle with Covey is emblematic of the experience of black persons in the United States and Europe more generally, who must struggle against the historical ways in which black identity has been constructed. In this respect, Gordon argues, black experience *cannot* be understood as simply a modified version of white experience. Indeed, the struggle to be seen as more than a stereotype, as more than "not white," lurks at the core of black identity.

Racism, properly understood, is a denial of the human being either on the basis of race or color. This denial, properly executed, requires denying the presence of other human beings in such relations. It makes such beings a form of presence that is an absence, paradoxically, an absence of human presence.[5]

When the interviewer refers to Mr. Wilson with slurs, he addresses a human being and *simultaneously* designates him as *subhuman*.[6] This contradiction marks our historical understanding of race: to be understood as black is to be understood as less worthy than a full-fledged human. As the Jamaican-American philosopher Charles W. Mills argues, non-white races have been *invented* as a means to ensure the existence of a class of "superior" persons. At the heart of our commitment to the idea of race, historically, has been the idea that some races are *better* (more civilized, more intelligent, more capable of governing) than others. Mills argues that this form of thinking pervades Western thought from the seventeenth century onward, forming what he calls "the racial contract": a commitment to sorting people into different races as a means of placing one sort above another.

Mr. Robinson's Neighborhood: The Genius of Eddie Murphy

Stereotypes and biases reinforce this racial contract. Such biases are not innocent falsehoods; they structure the way people experience and *are experienced* by those around them. In "Mr. Robinson's Neighborhood," which appeared multiple times from Season 6 to Season 10, Eddie Murphy plays the ghetto version of Fred Rogers, from the PBS show *Mr. Rogers' Neighborhood*. Robinson introduces words of the day like "bitch" and "rehabilitation"; he offers advice on how to steal from little old ladies, or escape capture, or get top-dollar through conning children. The sketches usually end with Mr. Robinson leaving his apartment by fire escape, typically to avoid violence or arrest. The "neighborhood" we're exposed to is one of pure fancy: a comedic rendering of all the stereotypes and biases that are carried by our notion of "black."

In a famous bit on Weekend Update celebrating Abraham Lincoln's birthday, Eddie Murphy announces that the Emancipation Proclamation was never signed, so "Tomorrow, if you happen to be out and see a black person that you like, by all means, take him home with you."[7] The absurdity of the idea is also the point. In Murphy's comedic work, slavery could be re-instituted on a technicality. Our attitudes have not improved enough to create *actual* equality; indeed, our attitudes imprison us in the idea that non-white persons *are* inferior. As Murphy riffs on the re-instatement of slavery, he tells Weekend Update viewers "Enjoy your Negro!"[8]

But Murphy's work doesn't end at displaying our ridiculous assumptions. He also brilliantly demonstrates how these assumptions impact us in concrete ways in our everyday lives. In "White Like Me," Murphy goes undercover in white America, using make-up and a wig to pass as white.[9] He discovers a world of privilege unavailable to anyone but the white (presumably male) majority. He goes to a bank to get a loan and is in the process of being turned down by an African-American loan officer when a white loan officer intervenes. "That was close," he says to a be-whited Murphy, and then lets him have all the money he wants, telling him not to worry about when he pays it back, or even if he pays it back.

Though white privilege is perhaps not quite as egregious as "White Like Me" suggests, the exaggeration allows us to laugh *while also* recognizing the underlying point: whiteness is a social category that affords people opportunities. The point here is *not* that people consciously *decide* to discriminate against persons of color (though of course this also happens). The point is rather that we operate with certain assumptions – those implicitly attached to our ideas of race – that inform the way we interact with people *despite our best efforts to avoid prejudice*. Implicit bias is just that – implicit. This hierarchical ranking of the white over the black, as we've seen, is what Mills calls the "racial contract": we construct an idea of race *so that* we can hold one group ("white") higher than another ("black"). "White Like Me" allows us to see this racial contract function explicitly. If Mr. Robinson or Buckwheat had been applying for a loan rather than white Eddie Murphy, reactions *would have been different*, and this difference is part of the way we have socially constructed "blackness" in the United States. It's for this reason that at the height of his fame on *SNL*, Eddie Murphy still couldn't hail a cab in New York City. No matter how talented and beloved, he was still just a stereotype to every cabbie that saw him on the street.[10]

SNL's Double Consciousness

In "The Day Beyoncé Turned Black," the white world realizes that Beyoncé isn't "one of them" when she releases a song embracing her African heritage.[11] "This isn't for us!" a white woman yells, "But usually everything is!" As the awareness of Beyoncé's racial identity spreads through the lily-white world, chaos ensues. One woman tells her black friend the news as people scream in the background. "But I'm black," the friend says. The woman's face registers her disbelief. "But you're my girl!" she replies, unaware that her friend can be *both* black and "her girl." Here we see what W.E.B. DuBois (1868–1963) called "double consciousness," a condition he claimed characterized black experience. One is both a cherished friend and an alien presence.

> It is a peculiar sensation, this double-consciousness, this sense of always looking at one's self through the eyes of others, of measuring one's soul by the tape of a world that looks on in amused contempt and pity. One ever feels his two-ness – an American, a Negro; two souls, two thoughts, two unreconciled strivings; two warring ideals in one dark body, whose dogged strength alone keeps it from being torn asunder.[12]

"The Day Beyoncé Turned Black" shows us the racial other, what the *significance* of being black means to the white world – and by implication, what it means for everyone living in the white world. In the context of the west, to be black means to be *African* and *then* to be American, Canadian, European, and so on. Being black *means* being foreign, different, an outsider to white culture – despite the fact that one isn't an outsider at all. In double consciousness, one is perpetually a stranger at home.

We tend to understand race as an *essential* element of a person, something *inescapable* and *unavoidable*. While Eddie Murphy can "pass" as a white man, he's *really* black – or so this line of thinking goes. While I can stop being a fan of the cowbell, I can't stop being a member of the race to which I belong. The Ghanaian-American philosopher K. Anthony Appiah calls the view that race is essential to who one is *racialism*, and contrasts it with racism. Racialism involves the belief that:

> "We could divide human beings into a small number of groups, called "races," in such a way that the members of these groups shared certain fundamental, heritable, physical, moral, intellectual, and cultural characteristics with one another that they did not share with members of any other race."[13]

As Appiah goes on to argue, no such groups exist. Indeed, grouping races "for biological purposes, your classification will contain almost as much human genetic variation as there is in the whole species."[14] The most we can classify as a "race" is a group of (partially) reproductively isolated people. As Appiah points out, though, this means that "no large social group in America is a race."[15] Indeed, the Amish (a partially isolated reproductive population) might have a better claim to being a race *in this sense* than any of our current categories of race.

Appiah's view is not uncommon. There's actually a great deal of agreement now among biologists that races are not biologically "real." The problem is that we seem to be stuck thinking that they *are* real. The comedy of *SNL* often highlights the *involuntary* aspects of our identity – the way thinking that race is biologically real leads to oppression and discrimination.

> Once the racial label is applied to people, ideas about what it refers to, ideas that may be much less consensual than the application of the label, come to have their social effects. But they have not only social effects but psychological ones as well; and they shape the ways people conceive of themselves and their projects.[16]

Behind our thinking about race, then, is a kind of *racialism* – the view that race is essential to who one is and what one does.

Consider "Leslie Jones Wants to Play Trump."[17] As the title suggests, the sketch revolves around the African-American comedian deciding she wants a shot at impersonating Trump. No one will tell her she can't play Trump because she's black (though someone does reference the casting of *Hamilton*). Some suggest that playing Trump *as a woman* is gutsy, though the misdirection of the remark is all-too-obvious: women have *routinely* played men on *SNL* (like Melissa McCarthy playing Sean Spicer, or Amy Poehler playing Michael Jackson). Leslie is undaunted by the skepticism of her peers: she gets into costume as Donald Trump and makes her pitch to Lorne Michaels. Needless to say, it doesn't end well.

Why is it *more* outrageous to have Trump played by a black woman than it is to have Sean Spicer played by a white woman? The answer, in a word, is racialism: we think of race as something that *must be intrinsic* to the person, something without which they would no longer be themselves.[18] The central problem with our racialism is that it leads us to impose an identity on people – to make their race, negative connotations and all, a core of who they are.

Here we see a potential dark side of comedy that traffics in racial stereotypes. For whatever the delights of exaggerating stereotypes, there's always a danger that comedy will only serve to reinforce what it aims to critique. In revealing racial assumptions, *SNL* may well inadvertently perpetuate them. It was this very worry that motivated Dave Chappelle to end his award-winning *The Chappelle Show*: perhaps people were laughing at the *wrong thing* – not at the absurdity of our racial stereotypes, but at the belittling of black persons.

Black Jeopardy and a Trumped-Up *SNL*

As we've seen, *SNL*'s comedy reminds us of our racial assumptions and the real-world consequences of our biases. After examining differences in the experience of whites and non-whites, it's natural to ask whether or not there can be any common ground between oppressor and historically oppressed. If, as French writer Albert Memmi has argued,[19] the oppressed group is *necessarily* regarded as inferior, real communication isn't possible. True communication requires equality among participants, and this is ruled out between oppressor and oppressed. This logic led Frantz Fanon (1925–1961) to the conclusion that violence was required to change such relations[20] – a primal assertion of one's worth through struggle (much like Fredrick Douglas' struggle with Covey was an assertion of Douglas's worth).

A more hopeful response is presented in "Black Jeopardy" when Tom Hanks plays a white, Trump-supporting contestant named Doug.[21] The usual questions on the show traffic in standard stereotypes of black culture, arguably performing a comedic function similar to Eddie Murphy's early work on the show. Things get interesting when Doug (who is wearing a "Make America Great Again" hat) chimes in to answer a question.

CONTESTANT:	Let's go with "They Out Here Saying" for $200.
HOST (KENAN THOMPSON):	Okay, they out here saying the new iPhone wants your thumb print for your protection. [*bell dings*] Oh, okay, then, Doug.
DOUG:	What is, I don't think so. That's how they get you.
HOST [*AMAZED*]:	Yes, that's it! That's it!

To everyone's surprise, Doug gets the answer correct – and he doesn't stop there.

CONTESTANT:	Let's go to "They Out Here Saying" for $800.
HOST:	All right, the answer, they out here saying that every vote counts. [*bell rings*] Oh, Doug again.
DOUG:	What is, come on, they already decided who wins even before it happens.
HOST [*WIDE-EYED AND AMAZED*]:	Yes! Yes! The illuminati figured that out months ago. That's another one for Doug.

Even as Doug finds common ground with the contestants (and host) of "Black Jeopardy," they all have to work to overcome lingering prejudice. When the African-American host (Kenan Thompson) approaches Doug to shake his hand, Doug assumes he's about to be attacked. He quickly realizes his mistake, and the two shake hands, amazed they both enjoy Tyler Perry movies. "Black Jeopardy" emphasizes the uniqueness of black culture while playing with the stereotypes surrounding it. In so doing, it raises an important question: How can we address problems of racial inequality when we live in a climate that aims to accentuate differences, to polarize attitudes? "Black Jeopardy" seems to provide an answer: we can look to those basic features of our experience that we happen to share, given our common humanity, despite the different histories that define white and black experience.

Lest we start singing Kumbaya together too soon, the sketch quickly presents a core limitation to looking for shared everyday experiences. The final category is "Lives that Matter." The contestants turn to Doug shaking their heads. "Well, it was fun while it lasted," the host says, laughing. For whatever the similarities revealed throughout the course of the show, for whatever bridges may have been built, the question on Final Jeopardy comes down to the litmus test of our racial and cultural differences. The sketch implicitly asks us this very question: for all that both unites us and divides us, how seriously do we take the issue of racial violence? Doug says "I have a lot to say about this," but the host cuts him off, saying "I'm sure you do!" The sketch ends by reminding us that the problem of racial violence needs to be addressed, no matter what we do or do not have in common. Historically, we've largely ignored the issue – but any commitment to racial equality must involve a recognition of the precarity in which African-Americans live, and the responsibility we *all* have for it.

Where in the Hell is Chris Rock?

Why hasn't Chris Rock been more prominent in these pages? Why no mention of Damon Wayans getting fired, or of the under-utilized genius of Juilliard-trained Garret Morris? What's at stake is representation: do my examples *really* capture the diversity of *SNL*'s comedy dealing with race? The same issue has been raised about the show itself: do the voices of *SNL* adequately represent the diversity we find in the world? When Chris Rock was hired in 1990, it had been a few years since *SNL* had a "black guy."[22] Rock ultimately left the show because it didn't afford him enough opportunity to explore race issues. He didn't think this was due to explicit prejudice. It came down to numbers: there were a lot of people with material, but he was the only one writing about race.

One of the perennial issues facing *SNL* has been the composition of its cast. A frequent criticism of the show has been that it privileges white males over persons of color and women: does the cast adequately represent its diverse audience? Is the show participating in large-scale patterns of racism and sexism by privileging a white, male perspective?

The wisdom of "Black Jeopardy" will once again aid us, if only to see how complicated the issue is. Consider black contestants who are *not* African-American. The African-Canadian rapper Drake, for example, appears as Toronto-native Jared.

HOST (DARNEL HAYES):   You're Canadian?
JARED: Yo! There's thousands of us! I'm sure you've met one of us before.
HOST [SMILING]:   No, never met one.

The sketch continues.

JARED: C'mon, Darnell! Black people live all over the world. You can't just
          put us all in one category.
HOST: Maybe so, Jared. I'm gonna let you tell that to our American police.[23]

Jared goes on to complain that the host is pre-judging him. "Why do
I have to be your definition of black?" he asks. "You're making me so
angry inside, dawg!" Drake, as Jared, represents a place where blackness and African-American culture don't overlap. This is possible
because there's no *single* thing called "black identity," or even "African-
American identity," for that matter.

When Chadwick Boseman appears as T'Challa (also known as the
Black Panther), ruler of African utopia Wakanda, the show again
challenges the assumption that "being black" is a unified identity.[24]
Introducing T'Challa leads the host to speculate that "This might be
the blackest Black Jeopardy yet," presumably because there is something "blacker" about being directly from Africa (a strange idea!). The
assumption soon unravels. When a clue asks why you might put your
cable bill in your grandmother's name, T'Challa replies: "To honor
her, as the foundation of the family." "That's really nice," the host
replies, "it's wrong but really nice." He then goes on to the correct
answer ("I don't need all that on my credit!"). The same dynamic
repeats, revealing the decidedly *different* assumptions and expectations of *non-African-American* black persons. In this way, even our
understanding of racial identity is tied to more culturally-specific
factors.

"Black Jeopardy" reminds us that *many* things affect our identities,
not just the putative race to which we belong. This web-like composition of social identity was termed "intersectionality" by activist and
critical race theorist Kimberle Crenshaw.[25] Our economic class, our
level of education, our gender and sex – these and more intersect to
provide us with a sense of who we are. Even adding a dozen African-
Americans to the cast of *SNL* might only increase *apparent* diversity.
If all members are the same sex, or in the same economic class, or the
same religion, or the same sexual orientation, the diversity in question
is only skin-deep.

The point here is not to diminish the significance of race, but to
recognize how race intersects with other aspects of who one is. It's
likely that any attempt at *perfect* representation is doomed to fail.
Identities are multifarious, changing over time. Any reflection of such

changes is bound to lag behind. Obviously, this doesn't mean it's pointless to try to be more diverse. It means that criticism comes with the territory, and in many cases the criticism will probably have some merit. Rather than ignore it, we must simply try to do better.

For over four decades, *SNL* has used comedy to present us to ourselves: the prejudices, assumptions, and privileges that populate our racial world. I daresay *SNL* has helped people be open to the problems of race by allowing them (and us) to laugh at ourselves. And although *SNL* has never been immune to criticism for insensitivity or lack of diversity in its cast, it has routinely attempted to address – often through comedy – the criticisms it faces. One could hardly ask for more from comedy.

Notes

1. Indeed, the Austrian philosopher Ludwig Wittgenstein once remarked that all philosophy could be done with jokes, presumably because jokes rely on revealing our assumptions for what they are.
2. Season 1, Episode 7.
3. The sketch itself reflects not only the underlying racial tensions present in race relations; it also directly criticizes NBC's own hiring practices. When hosting *SNL*, Pryor brought a writer with him who was subjected to an interview process that inspired the skit. Not only was *SNL* drawing attention to the ways in which we belittle persons for their racial identities, it was also highlighting, albeit obliquely, the way that NBC itself engaged in racial discrimination.
4. *Narrative of the Life of Frederick Douglas, an American Slave,* (New Haven, CT: Yale University Press, 2001), 151–152.
5. *Existentia Africana* (New York: Routledge, 2000), 67.
6. When Mr. Wilson uses slurs, these slurs often designate whites as oppressors rather than sub-humans – "white trash" being a notable exception. Nevertheless, one can't separate anti-black slurs from the history of slavery, an institution that leaves its mark on everything. I would suggest that anti-white slurs developed in *reaction* to practices of white supremacists, while anti-black slurs often developed as a means of trying to *justify* behavior like murder and enslavement.
7. Season 6, Episode 9.
8. Michael Che's brilliant "Twelve Days Not A Slave" makes essentially the same point: twelve days after the abolition of slavery, a freed slave (Jay Pharoah) is surprised that people aren't yet over their prejudices (Season 39, Episode 4).
9. Season 10, Episode 9.

10. Murphy's performance as the singer Tyron Green adds an additional level of complexity to race issues. His reggae band performs a song called "Kill the White People" at the VFW. The white audience watches as a dread-headed Eddie Murphy sings "Kill the white people, Oh we're gonna make them hurt, Kill all the white people, but buy my record first." Race relations have created a divide that warrants anger (Kill the white people!), but material success in white culture seems to require appeasing white people (but buy my record first).

11. Season 41, Episode 23.

12. *Souls of Black Folks* (New York: Norton Publishing, 1999), 38.

13. *Color Conscious* (Princeton, NJ: Princeton University Press, 1996), 69.

14 Ibid.

15. Ibid., 73.

16. Ibid., 78.

17. Season 42, Episode 14.

18. On the other hand, Amy Poehler played Michael Jackson. Fred Armison played President Obama. Is Leslie Jones "too black" to play Trump? Is Trump so intrinsically "white" that we need Alec Baldwin?

19. In *The Colonizer and the Colonized* (Boston, MA: Beacon Press, 1967), Memmi explores this logic in some detail. Although he is explicitly discussing colonial situations, his analysis applies equally to any relation between oppressor and oppressed.

20. In *The Wretched of the Earth* (New York: Grove Press, 1963), Fanon argues that only violent insurrection will lead to the end of the European occupation of African territory.

21. Season 43, Episode 17.

22. See Tom Shales and James Andrew Miller, *Live from New York! A Complete, Uncensored History of Saturday Night Live* (New York: Back Bay Books, 2015), where Rock also discusses his reasons for leaving the show.

23. Season 40, Episode 21.

24. Season 43, Episode 19.

25. Retrieved from https://philpapers.org/archive/CREDTI.pdf on July 6, 2019.

John Belushi, Chris Farley, and Stuart Smalley

Drugs and Recovery on *Saturday Night Live*

William Irwin and J.R. Lombardo

It's no secret that drugs and alcohol have been fuel for some *Saturday Night Live* cast members. Sadly, though, John Belushi and Chris Farley both lost their lives to overdoses at the young age of 33. Their fates call for philosophical reflection. We would like to understand why some people find drugs and alcohol to be a creative muse. And we would also like to consider what lessons can be learned from the ways Belushi and Farley lived and died. Although Stuart Smalley pokes fun at the Pollyanna tone of recovery gurus, Al Franken himself has been a great advocate for the kind of twelve-step programs that Chris Farley succeeded with for a time. If Farley could speak to us from the grave, what would he say to young comedians?

Lend Me Your Ears and I'll Sing You a Song

What makes John Belushi decide to combine an impression of a samurai warrior with a deli owner? What makes Chris Farley hike up his pants, raise his voice, and warn kids about living in a van down by the river? Where do artists get their ideas from? It's a perennial philosophical question, even if philosophy can't deliver a definitive answer.

In search of the wisest person in Athens, Socrates (470–399 BCE) went to the poets. To his disappointment he found that they did not even seem to know the meaning of their own work. Socrates concluded that it was a kind of divine inspiration; the poets were just

Saturday Night Live and Philosophy: Deep Thoughts Through the Decades, First Edition. Edited by Jason Southworth and Ruth Tallman.

vehicles through whom the muse speaks. Not everyone would agree, but through the ages it has been common for even artists themselves to suggest that they don't know quite where their ideas come from, and that a spirit or muse must be at work.

One problem with counting on the muse for creativity is that she does not always show up. Authors suffer from writer's block and artists of all types endure creative dry spells. Sometimes the muse needs some help or a substitute. Indeed, it's not a big step to go from thinking that a divine spirit speaks through you to thinking that wine and spirits of the alcoholic variety can help produce artistic and creative works. Why this is so becomes clear when we consider the limited nature of creativity.

As the cliché has it, there is nothing new under the sun. Creativity is usually not so much a matter of producing something totally new and original as it is a matter of coming up with a new combination or arrangement. *Star Wars* took the movie Western and set it in outer space; the Beatles borrowed from the blues; and Shakespeare stole the plots of his plays from *Holinshed's Chronicles*. Of course, these examples over-simplify, but the point remains: creativity is frequently a matter of assembling old parts into new wholes. As the philosopher David Hume (1711–1776) said, "All this creative power of the mind amounts to no more than the faculty of compounding, transposing, augmenting, or diminishing the materials afforded to us by the senses and experience. When we think of a golden mountain, we only join two consistent ideas, *gold* and *mountain*, with which we were formerly acquainted."[1]

One of the artistically beneficial effects of alcohol and drugs is that they lower inhibitions and encourage unlikely associations as well as the willingness to voice them. Often such associations and connections will seem more creative and funnier to the person while drunk or high, but some of them will be genuinely creative or funny and worth preserving. Both Belushi and Farley were trained in improvisational theater – and without a script, it all comes down to the creative impulses of the actor. Self-censorship is the enemy. Of course, drugs and alcohol can hurt timing – a real hazard for actors and comedians – but they can also be an aid in removing the barrier of self-censorship. We don't know where inspiration and ideas ultimately come from. What we do know, though, is that writers and performers need to generate lots of bad ideas along with the good ones.

A writer's motto, sometimes mistakenly attributed to Hemingway, instructs, "Write drunk and edit sober." In other words, you need to allow yourself the uninhibited freedom to create. Alcohol can be your muse, but she does not dictate golden prose. You need to look at your work later with sober eyes, throw much of it away, and make corrections and adjustments to what remains. Friedrich Nietzsche (1844–1900) said, "Artists have an interest in the existence of a belief in the sudden occurrence of ideas, in so-called inspirations; as though the idea of a work of art ... flashed down from heaven like a ray of divine grace. In reality, the imagination of a good artist or thinker is productive continually of good, mediocre, and bad things, but his *power of judgement*, sharpened and practised to the highest degree, rejects, selects, knots together ... All great artists have been great workers, inexhaustible not only in invention but also in rejecting, sifting, transforming, ordering."[2]

Some writers favor drugs for their visions: Samuel Taylor Coleridge reportedly wrote the poem "Kubla Kahn" under the influence of opium, and Alan Ginsberg claimed to have written some of his best poetry under the influence of peyote. Many writers and artists prefer to rely on unaided imagination but require something to keep their mood and energy up. Caffeine, usually in the form of coffee and energy drinks, is the benign drug of choice among most writers today. As a stimulant, caffeine provides the energy and sense of well-being that pushes the writer forward. Amphetamines and cocaine have been used for similar purposes. Cocaine was particularly popular among writers in the early days of *Saturday Night Live*, who felt the tremendous pressure to meet a weekly deadline. Scripts needed to be written by the end of Wednesday to allow time for blocking and rehearsing. Pressure and procrastination routinely led writers to rely on cocaine to stay up all night and finish the job.

The idea of alcohol as "spirits" and inspiration finds its companion in the idea of alcohol as demon – demon alcohol or demon rum. It's as if the drunk person is possessed by an evil spirit. Alcohol, which first serves to provide inspiration, then ceases to serve and becomes the demonic master. Chris Farley, who was a very serious Catholic, seems to have thought of it that way. Drugs in particular, he saw as evil, and so he saw himself as losing a battle of good and evil. Certainly, some artists can use drugs and alcohol and reap the benefits at little or no cost. Belushi and Farley were not so fortunate. Drugs and alcohol took more than they gave, ultimately taking the comedians' lives.

The audience might want to assume that Belushi and Farley could turn it on and off for the camera, but actually their craziest behavior took place off camera. There is an ugliness to substance use disorder that we miss when we consider only how Belushi and Farley appeared on screen. They both had friends who enjoyed their company and cared about them. But as their substance use disorders progressed over the years and as their behavior became intolerable over the course of a given night, those friends did not want to be near them. As Farley's friend Ted Dondanville said, "The first hour of drinking with Chris was fun. The second hour was the best hour of your life. The rest of the night was pure hell."[3] When an average person alienates his friends, he may experience a moment of clarity. But for celebrities like Belsuhi and Farley there were always plenty of false friends and hangers-on to keep them company and validate them even at their worst.

I Get High with a Little Help from my Friends

John Belushi was defined by contrasts. He was a cuddly teddy bear with menacing intentions; an actor of sloppy appearance delivering a precision performance; a grown man who behaved like a spoiled baby when he didn't get his way; a party animal married to his high school sweetheart. And it was a combination of contrasting drugs (sedative/opiate and stimulant) that took his life.

Belushi approached his work and his life with great intensity. Watching John, you knew he was up to no good, but that somehow it would all be okay. On stage or on screen, all eyes were on him. John was a performer, but he was not much of a writer. He didn't even like to learn lines that he or others had written, preferring to improvise. Much of John's comedy was physical, and facial – a raised eyebrow, brilliantly communicating thoughts without words.

Belushi was not always the bloated out of shape mess that we knew and loved. His portrayal of Joe Cocker was perfect not just because he resembled the rocker, but because his athleticism allowed him to move and twitch and writhe in ways that were both hilarious and accurate in their imitation. As a star linebacker in high school John weighed 170 pounds, but he was more than 50 pounds heavier when he was imitating Cocker, doing cartwheels as a Blues Brother, and winning the decathlon in the mock Wheaties commercial ("Little Chocolate Donuts").

In the early days, the culture and writing of SNL were fueled by drugs, particularly cocaine and marijuana. So John's drug use was not at all unique, and it justified his belief that people in the entertainment business needed to do drugs to cope with pressure and stress. He simply took it further than others. Cocaine gave him a positive feeling about himself and made everything feel important and intense. Belushi believed that he used drugs (not the other way around). His goal was to harness the power of cocaine with the least amount of destruction. But the only kind of destruction he seems to have considered was physical. In reality, substance use disorder is pervasive and insidious. It destroys not just one's physical health and appearance, but one's mental health and stability. Relationships suffer; productivity declines; peace of mind, integrity, and morality erode.

Many of the original *SNL* cast and writers believed that cocaine was non-addictive and that it was a logical drug to use to sustain the long hours of intense preparation necessary for a weekly live show. Al Franken said, "John was partly a casualty of the ignorance of that period. There have been times through American history when drug use surges and becomes 'new' again, and coke became kind of new again in the middle to late seventies. People had forgotten or didn't realize what it could do."[4] Belushi was arrogant in his belief that he could handle the excess of drugs, and the culture wasn't correcting him.

In hindsight, we can see that John's career and his life were in trouble when he got too big for *SNL*. Cursed by the success of *Animal House*, he was led to think he could do anything. John lived like Bluto from *Animal House* even though he wanted to get away from that role on screen. *The Blues Brothers* movie paled by comparison, and his other movie performances – in *Continental Divide*, *Neighbors*, and *1941* – were weak and forgettable. Instead of being humbled by lack of success, John blamed others, and up to the time of his death he fought with studios, producers, and directors, insisting that he knew best. Undoubtedly, John's cocaine use disorder fed his ego and clouded his vision of reality, but the drugs cannot take the blame for all of John's faults.

Belushi glorified the creative process driven by drugs and alcohol and the death it could bring. In this regard his two icons were the comedian Lenny Bruce, who died of a heroin overdose, and the poet Dylan Thomas who, according to legend, drank himself to death in the White Horse Tavern – a bar that Belushi frequented. As with death itself, heroin both attracted and repelled John. Fascinated by the unknown and tempted by the darkness, John began using heroin in conjunction with cocaine – both drugs were in his system on the night he died. A man of contrasts, he apparently craved the high of the coke and the dulling effect of the heroin (often referred to as a "speedball"). This is the cocktail that killed him.

John never went to twelve-step meetings, and never went to rehab. In fact, that option never seems to have been suggested to him by his wife or friends or business associates. They all wanted him to stop doing cocaine or at least stop doing so much of it, but no one close to him seems to have seriously suggested that he should get sober. Perhaps this was just a sign of the times. It's inconceivable today that a celebrity like Belushi, with a clear substance use disorder, would not spend some time in rehab. Of course, rehab and twelve-step programs are not magic cures. If a person does not have a genuine desire to get sober and a willingness to do what it takes, their substance abuse will continue. John showed no signs of having that desire or willingness. Nonetheless, rehab, or multiple stays in rehab, might have planted seeds in his mind and might have slowed him down enough to keep him alive long enough to develop the desire to get sober and the willingness to do what it takes. We'll never know. Instead, at one period John employed a kind of bodyguard named Smokey to keep him away from cocaine. Predictably, Smokey was not fully successful – people with substance use disorders can be cunning in their efforts to get what they want.

How Do I Feel by the End of the Day?

John Belushi was Chris Farley's muse. Farley grew up idolizing Belushi, memorizing movie lines and *SNL* sketches. Like Belushi, Farley was surprisingly athletic and played football in high school. Indeed, Farley's athletic career continued at Marquette University where he played rugby. It wasn't all power though; there was plenty of finesse. The sketch that made Farley famous on *SNL*, the Chippendale's dance competition with Patrick Swayze, showcased his ability to move. Chris Farley was not built like Patrick Swayze, "... and that's ... okay," as Stuart Smalley would say. Aside from their size and penchant for physical comedy, Farley and Belushi did not share much in common as performers. Farley was inspired by Belushi but he didn't imitate him, at least not on stage.

Truly, it would not have worked for Farley to imitate his idol because they were two such different people. In comic form, one can picture Belushi as the devil on one shoulder and Farley as the angel on the other shoulder, both whispering in your ear. *SNL* writer Tom

Schiller described Farley as "a kind of secret, angelic being who tore too quickly through life, leaving a wake of laughter behind him. As corny as that sounds, it's the truth."[5] No one would be tempted to describe Belushi that way. Belushi could be a teddy bear or a little boy, but not an angel. Belushi was driven by a huge ego, whereas Farley just really enjoyed making people laugh. Belushi was selfish as an actor and as a person, whereas Farley was generous both professionally and personally – he loved being part of a team whether it was rugby or comedy.

Unfortunately, Farley was like Belushi in one undeniable way: he had a huge appetite for drugs, alcohol, and food. Chris was never much of a student, but he loved the camaraderie and the debauchery of the rugby team at Marquette University. His college years were filled with drunken exploits rivaling those of Bluto and the boys in Delta House. According to a friend, "*Wired* was the only book that Chris Farley read in college. The only one."[6] That's probably one more book than Bluto read, but Farley would have been better off not reading it. After all, the book wasn't even assigned for class. No, *Wired* was Bob Woodward's warts-and-all biography of John Belushi. A friend of Farley reports that, "When Chris read *Wired*, he just took completely the wrong thing away from it. You could tell what he saw in Belushi and what you and I saw in Belushi were two different things. Chris wasn't blindly imitating Belushi, but reading that book validated all the addictions and impulses that Chris already had inside him."[7] So the stage was set, but not before Chris honed his craft and inflamed his substance use in Chicago, performing with Second City as Belushi had before him.

One would have hoped that what happened to John would never happen again. In fact, Lorne Michaels and others were keen not to let it happen again. The culture of *SNL* was very different by the time Chris got there. Drug use was not pervasive among the cast and writers – indeed it was frowned upon. *SNL* writer Tom Davis reports that, "*Saturday Night Live* had really changed. The smell of marijuana no longer hit you when you stepped off the elevator; that sort of thing just wasn't tolerated anymore."[8] This was not lost on Farley. Concerning his drug and alcohol abuse at *SNL*, Farley said, "It wasn't hip anymore. I stuck out like a sore thumb, taking my clothes off at parties and making a fool of myself."[9] David Spade, Farley's close friend and fellow cast member, was not into drinking or drugs. And other young cast members like Chris Rock, Adam Sandler, and Mike Myers were Boy Scouts compared to Belushi and the original cast.

Everything that culturally or environmentally was to blame for Belushi's sad fate was counteracted when it came to Farley, and yet Farley met the same fate at the same age: a lethal mix of cocaine and heroin at 33. Tom Davis reports that, "I said to him once, 'Chris, you don't want to die like Belushi, do you?' And he said, 'Oh, yeah, that'd be really cool.' And I actually started crying. I wept for him."[10]

Farley concealed a lot of pain beneath his jovial exterior. Food, drugs, and alcohol could not take it away. According to Brian Dennehy (co-star of *Tommy Boy*), Farley had a sense that "the world can never take away the pain that I feel, pain that I know that I have, but that I don't fully understand."[11] On screen, Farley felt trapped in the image of the fatty who falls down. As *SNL* writer Steven Koren said, "He wanted to give people laughter so much that it was okay if it hurt him a little bit. It was a conscious decision, I think."[12] Off screen, Farley felt trapped in the role of the foolish drunk even when he no longer wanted to play it and people no longer wanted him to.

As Stuart Smalley likes to say, "Denial ain't just a river in Egypt." Chris was in denial, and so was his family. As Chris's older brother Tom said, "Nobody was willing to face the truth. Nobody confronted Chris about his problem, because doing so would have meant acknowledging that Dad had a problem – that we all had a problem."[13] Eventually this attitude changed for several of the Farleys who confronted Chris and got sober themselves. But the patriarch of the family kept drinking until after his son's funeral, at which time he gave up drinking and gave up on life, dying about a year later at age 63. Chris loved his father, spoke on the phone with him regularly, and sought his advice. For Chris, admitting that there was something wrong with himself would be pointing a finger at his beloved father. At the time of his death, the elder Farley weighed 600 pounds. Chris's brother Kevin reports that one time, "Chris said to me that he should stay heavy for Dad."[14]

Despite his own denial and the initial denial among some of his family, Chris did get sober for a time. No, Stuart Smalley did not save him. Stuart Smalley "is a caring nurturer, a member of several 12-step programs, but not a licensed therapist." He's also not a real person. Al Franken, who portrayed Smalley, was not only a real person, but a real member of Al-Anon, the support group for families and friends of alcoholics. Indeed, Franken was an advocate for 12-step recovery, and Farley would talk with him about it after his time in rehab.[15]

Thanks to his time in rehab and in twelve-step recovery, Farley, unlike Belushi, understood the importance of abstinence. Belushi repeatedly fell prey to the idea that he could use just a little cocaine or use it only in certain situations. Farley realized that once he started with drugs and alcohol there was no controlling his use or reining it in. Because of the characters he played on *SNL* and in *Animal House*, Belushi had a drunken, wild man persona. People expected him to misbehave, and he complied. Farley, by contrast, was a drunken wild man off camera. It wasn't a necessary part of his comedic persona, and so he was able to succeed quite well during his three years of continuous sobriety (and during other sober periods), including a good chunk of time on *SNL* and for the filming of *Tommy Boy*. By all accounts, he was happiest and funniest during that three-year period.

During a St. Patrick's Day episode, Stuart Smalley tried to help Chris Farley in the role of Mike Flannagan, the drunken camera-man who is in denial about his problem. Predictably, things did not work out. We can see why when we consider Stuart's mode of oper-ation. He routinely takes refuge in stock phrases and clichés from twelve-step recovery meetings. On his show, he's unable to see the truth about his guests, like Michael Jordan – no he doesn't suffer from insecurity about whether he's good enough. And comically, Stuart is unable or unwilling to see or admit the truth about him-self. He prefers to bullshit himself with his standard affirmation, "I'm good enough, I'm smart enough, and doggone it, people like me." Well, that's not exactly true, but Stuart would like it to be true, and he thinks that if he repeats it often enough he will believe it. The facile one-liners and ready-made solutions that he dispenses fail to reckon with reality, which is much more complex. Is anyone really going to be helped by his instructions to "Trace it, face it, and erase it"? What would Stuart Smalley have to offer John Belushi or Chris Farley? Belushi was much too cynical – just think of him as Bluto smashing the folk singer's guitar in *Animal House*. Farley by contrast would probably have liked Smalley. During his three years of continuous sobriety, Farley dug deep and did the hard work of recovery. It wasn't all pink clouds and Stuart Smalley sayings for him, but with his innocence and naivete it's not hard to imagine Farley finding trite sayings to be profound.

Farley illustrates the fragility of sobriety. He had been happy and successful during a three-year period of continuous sobriety, but he blew that sobriety by drinking before the premiere of his movie *Black Sheep*. Farley had not let up on his program of recovery; he just made the choice to drink again. Like many people in recovery, he returned to his twelve-step program after his relapse, but unfortunately he was not able to maintain lasting sobriety despite numerous stints in rehab. He would put together some sober time and then drink again. As his friend Ted Dondanville put it, "The first relapse, that was the big one. The rest were just dominoes."[16]

During his time as a cast member on *SNL*, Farley's performance on screen did not suffer from impairment. But when he returned as a guest host, his substance use disorder was so out of control that Lorne Michaels considered the unprecedented move of replacing him with a different guest host. Doing so might have sent Farley the wake-up call that he needed, but Lorne Michaels reasoned that Farley's performance might be a more effective wake-up call. His performance was indeed poor, including a disastrous opening sketch and monologue, both of which were cut from the syndicated version of the show. Alas, Farley did not heed the wake-up call.

And in the End

In his memorable interview of Paul McCartney on *SNL*'s "The Chris Farley Show," Chris asks the Beatle if it is true that, as the song says, in the end, the love you take is equal to the love you make. Sir Paul responds that yes, in his experience, the more you give, the more you get. Chris is totally psyched to hear it. It's hard to imagine John Belushi or any character played by John Belushi being similarly moved by such news. Farley really was all about putting love out into the world in the form of laughter, and he was glad to hear from Paul that he could count on getting some love back. As Farley's friend Pat Finn said, "If he made somebody's day better, if he could ease the pain and sadness in the world just a bit, that was why he felt he was there."[17]

We honor the memory of Chris Farley and John Belushi best by recognizing their problem. Drugs and alcohol can fuel creativity, but they demand a high price from some people. A sober Chris Farley was a funny Chris Farley, and perhaps the same could have been true of John Belushi. We'll never know. Comedians and artists will always look for inspiration, and some will succeed in dancing with drugs and alcohol. So, what would Chris Farley advise a young comedian? We don't know, of course, but we'd like to think he'd say something like this: Don't imitate my life. Even if drugs don't kill you, over the long run they will not make you stronger ... or funnier. Look elsewhere for the muse.[18]

Notes

1. David Hume, "Of the origin of ideas," in *An Enquiry Concerning Human Understanding*, Peter Millican (ed.), (Oxford: Oxford University Press, 2008), 13.
2. Friedrich Nietzsche, *Human All Too Human*. Tr. R.J. Hollingdale (Cambridge: Cambridge University Press, 1996), §155 p. 83.
3. Tom Farley, Jr. and Tanner Colby, *The Chris Farley Show: A Biography in Three Acts* (New York, Penguin Books, 2008), 83.
4. Judith Belushi Pisano and Tanner Colby, *Belushi: A Biography* (New York: Rugged Land, 2005), 177.
5. Farley and Colby,145.
6. Ibid., 48.
7. Ibid.
8. Ibid.,121.
9. Ibid., 7.
10. Ibid., 137.
11. Ibid., 270.
12. Ibid.,158.
13. Ibid., 35.
14. Ibid., 280.
15. Ibid., 135.
16. Ibid., 239.
17. Ibid., 40.
18. Irwin thanks Jim Ambury, Dave Baggett, Greg Bassham, Richard Davis, and Mark White for helpful conversations and feedback on earlier drafts. Lombardo thanks all the fine people with whom he has had the privilege to work and with whom he has shared the journey of recovery.

Part III

SOME SKETCHES FEATURING YOUR FAVORITE RECURRING CHARACTERS

Dana Carvey vs. Darrell Hammond

What Does it Mean to be "Spot On," and Does it Matter?

Tadd Ruetenik

Fans sometimes describe a great impression as "spot on." However, though, a great comedic impression is never a "spot on" realistic depiction of the subject. The true skill of an impressionist is in making a new and creative experience out of the subject, and making it so new that it stretches recognizability to the limits. In short, the best impressionists from *SNL* have *not* been spot on.

A New Experience of Bush and Brokaw

The best example of an *SNL* impressionist who goes beyond "spot on" to offer a creative impression is Dana Carvey. Just consider his impression of George H.W. Bush. Carvey performed Bush in cold opens and other sketches, developing a character that was not, in the ordinary sense of the term, spot on. If one compares the voice, the word choice, and the gestures – particularly the hand gestures – one finds that they are barely noticeable in the actual Bush. And, there's no evidence of the catchphrase "wouldn't be prudent" coming from the lips-readable face of Bush – look it up! The only time Bush himself uses the phrase is when he is referring back to Carvey's impression of him. At the groundbreaking of his presidential museum in Texas, Bush joked about how his son, recently elected as governor, might upstage him. "Well let me tell you this doesn't help with my identity crisis," he said to reporters, who probably were cringing in anticipation of an awkward attempt at self-deprecating, Reaganesque humor. "First I was known as (first dog) Millie's owner, then it was Barbara's husband, now it's the father of the governor-elect of Texas." The *Deseret News* offers this description: "Shifting into the clipped speaking pattern Carvey uses in his impersonation, Bush continued: 'Now I have to share Dana, too? Not gonna do it. Wouldn't be prudent.'"[1] The former president thus tries a spot on impression of Carvey doing his creative impression of the president. This is vexing, as it negates the point of an impression. Carvey displacing Bush is funny, but Bush being a part of it is not funny. Though we might hope for a small sense of satisfaction seeing Bush display the virtue of humility, upon closer inspection we discover that he is engaging in political calculation rather than displaying humility.

Bush's intention matters, and so does the intention of any impressionist. *Hostile impressions* are intended to degrade their target. Such impressions involve the artistic version of what philosophers call the straw person fallacy, constructing a weak version of an argument in order to knock it down more easily. Although logically fallacious, the straw person is artistically valuable, not to mention funny. *Friendly impressions* are intended to be either neutral with regard to the subject, or to in some way even upgrade the subject. Imitation is the sincerest form of flattery, as the saying goes. The more spot on the imitation is, the more flattering it is. Likewise, someone might quote a venerated person directly rather than paraphrase them. After all, if the figure is so important, the speaker finds it inappropriate to add their own interpretation to the presentation.

The difference between a hostile impression and a friendly impression is, somewhat unfortunately, difficult to determine in many cases. Intentions are notoriously difficult to ascertain. This is why I would say that an impression is best when it exploits as much as possible the connection between hostility and friendliness. Many of our relationships seem to be ambiguous in this regard. We love our friends, and yet we compete with them in various ways. We enjoy getting in a good dig, one that is made good precisely by both degrading the person and displaying one's affection for them. Yet it is problematic – both aesthetically and politically – if politicians try to make friends with our impressions of them. You cannot have revolution if you are palling around with the bourgeoisie!

We might disagree about whether the intent at the heart of Carvey's impression of Bush is friendly or hostile. But we can all agree that the impression is hostile to the ideal of spot on representation. Indeed, at times, Carvey's impression of Bush became an impression of itself, with the comedian taking his own gestures as the subject of new exaggerations. Carvey was so selective in his representation that it became an experience in itself, a Carvey-Bush that is admirable for its artistry more than its fidelity. The impression becomes so little about Bush himself, that one is disappointed to hear Bush joke along with it.

As another example of an extremely selective impression, we can consider a 1996 sketch called "Tom Brokaw Pre-Tapes." The premise is philosophically interesting, involving the idea of newscasters recording descriptions of possible events ahead of time so that they are ready for immediate broadcast, presumably before other news outlets are able to do it.

Beginning with "Gerald Ford dead today at age of 83," Carvey's Brokaw must do a dramatic rehearsal of varying scenarios in which Ford dies, including being "chopped into little bits by the propeller of a commuter plane." The jarring absurdity of considering all possible worlds in which Ford dies is held together by one common element, namely the one feature of Brokaw that Carvey decided was representative, the subtle slurring of his voice on particular words.

But the star here is Carvey himself. Whenever his version of Brokaw says "Gerald Ford," Carvey highlights the slackened r sound in the last name. Everything else is almost irrelevant. This is evident when the scenario of the United States being invaded by Zimbabwe comes up, and Brokaw gives the news using clicks and pops stereotypical of African language. The sketch seemed designed as much as anything else to showcase Carvey's impressionist talent, because Brokaw is forced to speak a click-language (forgive us for laughing at the stereotype) with a Brokaw accent coming through on the "Geh-rald Fooohrd." The brilliance comes from the fact that, at this point, the impression was as far from spot on as possible. As contemporary philosopher Steven Fesmire puts it, "when a single experience becomes sufficiently demarcated from other experiences to be called an experience (as when we say "Now that was an experience!") a coherent story may be told …".[2] Carvey is creating a new experience of Brokaw, and for better or worse, every time that we experience the newscaster, we ourselves select out that sound as most significant. Again, listening to Brokaw has become *an* experience.

SNL's use of impressions begins in the first season. Then-president Gerald Ford (Fohhrd) was portrayed by Chevy Chase. But Chevy Chase, more of a comic genius than a trained actor, did nothing to

look or sound like Ford. The feature that was interesting about Ford
was his supposed clumsiness, and Chase was known as a good physical comedian, specializing in falls. The young Chase was far from a
spot on choice for Ford, but that didn't matter. The point was to
depict Ford's clumsiness with maximum creativity. In the sketches,
Chase would simply say a few words and then trip and stumble across
the stage.

Chase was not a brilliant impressionist in the way Carvey was. The
art was merely in the selection of Chase as the actor to "represent"
Ford. Similarly, Amy Poehler portrayed Michael Jackson in Season
29. The artistry here was again in the choice to emphasize one particular feature in the impression. Poehler was a talented writer and
actor, but not a gifted impressionist. This again was irrelevant, because
the point was in the very fact that all you needed to do to have an
impression of Jackson was use a petite white woman. The joke was
that Jackson had bleached and emasculated himself so much over the
years that he was, practically, a white woman. The fact that *SNL* also
had the services of black comedian Dean Edwards, who could do the
impression spot on, indicates either that *SNL* thought spot on was not
as important as artistry, or, perhaps at the same time, that *SNL* was a
little racist.

On this last point, the words of the philosopher John Dewey (1859–
1952) are relevant: "art tells something to those who enjoy it about
the nature of their own experience of the world."[3] An impression,
then, must not just represent the subject, but represent the subject in
a way that tells us something interesting about the subject – as well as
the people who enjoy the impression. This can be something as harmless as the weird voice of Brokaw that we didn't notice before, or the
clumsiness of the former college football player as president. Or it can
also be something more significant, such as the fact that *SNL* chose to
go with Poehler over Edwards, and thus, revealingly, promote the
white woman over the black man.

Darrell Hammond as a Tribute Band

To better understand the difference between creative representations
and spot on representations, we should consider for a moment the
subject of music, and specifically the phenomenon of tribute bands. A
tribute band is one that attempts, as accurately as possible, to represent a famous band to a concert audience. With tribute bands, there

really is no room for creativity, since they are judged entirely by their ability to be spot on. If a tribute band were to do a creative impression of the original band, with, for example, the guitarist performing a solo using his own improvisational style, the crowd would be disappointed. The people are paying for spot on representation in a live performance.

Some might argue that Darrell Hammond was one of *SNL*'s greatest impressionists, but I would argue that he was much like a tribute band. Yes, his range of characters is extraordinary, as are his creative choices regarding whom to impersonate. Hammond was available to offer a spot on impression of whomever the show might need for a given sketch. To that end, he was invaluably useful to the show, but as an artist, he was not as admirable as Carvey. For instance, one might see it as a vice, rather than a virtue, that his impression of Don Pardo is so spot on many people don't even realize Pardo has died.

This is why an understanding of the philosophy of pragmatism is important. The term "pragmatism," unfortunately, has become overused, and thus subject to common misunderstanding. Many people think of a pragmatist as one who compromises principles for the sake of some, usually cynical, view of reality. For example, if a politician doesn't do what she said she would do in the campaign because she has to adapt herself to the grubby world of politics, we might consider her a pragmatist.

The kind of pragmatism Dewey espoused is different. I would define Dewey's philosophical pragmatism as the belief that human experience is not simply a representation of reality, but is a work of art based in part on selective interest. *Empiricist* philosophers stress that knowledge comes from sense experience. Pragmatists accept this basic idea, but add to it a psychological factor, namely the fact that human beings do not merely take in the world passively, but instead pay attention to some things more than others. William James (1842–1910), who was known both as a philosopher and a psychologist, said that "accentuation and emphasis are present in every perception we have. We find it quite impossible to disperse our attention impartially over a number of impressions...But we do far more than emphasize things, and unite some, and keep others apart. We actually *ignore* most of the things before us."[4]

In James' understanding of consciousness, every conscious human being relates to the world as an impressionist. And this impressionism can build on itself. "Among the sensations we get from each separate thing, what happens?" he asks. "The mind selects again. It chooses certain of the sensations to represent the thing most truly, and considers the rest as its appearances, modified by the conditions of the moment."[5]

We cannot, in fact, provide a spot on representation of the world. James uses the example of a table as he continues to highlight what for him are *The Principles of Psychology*:

> Thus my table-top is named square, after but one of an infinite number of retinal sensations which it yields, the rest of them being sensations of two acute and two obtuse angles; but I call the latter *perspective* views, and the four right angles the *true* form of the table's essence, for aesthetic reasons of my own.[6]

To grasp James' point more clearly, consider the fact that most objects in our line of vision are not represented to us as they actually are. Take doors, for instance. Doors are rectangular, yet when we glance over to our door as we watch *SNL* from our well-worn seat on the couch, we might notice – if we cared to – that the door does not appear rectangular at all, but at best quadrilateral, with sides of varying length based on the angle at which we are looking.

James' point, then, is that our experience of the world is always perspectival, and as a result, we have to select a certain perspective to be more "real" than the others. Now, it should be noted that pragmatists do not believe that reality is determined merely by individual perspective. Rather, they believe that a combination and negotiation of individual perspectives is required. And we cannot just choose the fullness of our sense impressions as the real one. The fullness of our experience, James says, famously, is really just a blooming, buzzing confusion. We re-present the world through our selective interest. This is the sense in which our experience is pragmatic.

Experience is not a tribute to reality. It is a creative reworking of reality. Consider receiving a gift from someone who knows you well – someone who you might say really "gets you." When someone is skilled at selecting gifts for you, it is not because they are able to summon an exact copy of you into their mind. Rather, when this skilled gift-giver sees an item that reminds them of you in a particular way, they are able to say, "That is exactly what they would like!" Perhaps the skill of gift-giving lies in this ability to discover a person's essence in found or created objects. Consider the difference between receiving this kind of gift – one that shows the giver "really gets you," as opposed to receiving a gift that was dutifully selected from a wish list that you provided to the giver. While it is known that every item on the list is one you'd be happy to receive, there is little skill in simply following directions. There is certainly less beauty in a gift that was selected from a list (although, in this analogy, that gift would be spot on) than in one that was discovered creatively by selecting some feature in the object that the giver somehow knew would appeal to your essence.

All Human Experience is an Impression

Admittedly, if all experience is selective, then all impressionists are selective. Hammond is different from Carvey only in degree. What I think distinguishes Carvey from Hammond – and what makes Carvey's impression better, is the non-specialization of the skill. Hammond was known primarily as an impressionist, and his skills seem to have been enlisted to fill particular needs. If the sketch required a specific person, Hammond could provide that person. Carvey, on the other hand, had impressionism as merely one of many skills. His most general skill is that of creativity. His now-famous audition bit, which became the "Chopping Broccoli" sketch in which a singer tries to come up with a song on the spot, is a work of improvisational thinking. Such a sketch seems much more difficult to imagine with someone who was almost exclusively a technical impressionist like Hammond.

Regardless of which impressionists are your long time favorites, now that you've had the chance to think about the difference between a spot on impression and a creative one, take a moment to consider what kind of impression is being done the next time an *SNL* impressionist has impressed you with his or her work.

Notes

1. *Deseret News*. December 1, 1994. "Share Dana: Bush says 'wouldn't be prudent.'" Retrieved from www.deseretnews.com/article/390700/SHARE-DANA-BUSH-SAYS-WOULDNT-BE-PRUDENT.html on July 6, 2019.
2. Steven Fesmire, "The art of moral imagination," in Casey Haskins and David I. Seiple (eds.), *Dewey Reconfigured: Essays on Deweyan Pragmatism* (Albany: State University of New York Press, 1999), 133–150.
3. John Dewey, *Art as Experience* (New York: Perigree Books, 1934), 83.
4. William James, *Principles of Psychology* (New York: Dover Publications, 1890), 285.
5. Ibid.
6. Ibid.

SNL's Blasphemy and Rippin' up the Pope

"Well Isn't That Special?"

David Kyle Johnson

> Religion, at best – at BEST – is like a lift in your shoe. If you need it for a while, and it makes you walk straight and feel better – fine. But you don't need it forever, or you can become permanently disabled. [And] don't ask me to wear your shoes and let's not go down and nail lifts onto the natives' feet.
>
> George Carlin, 10/11/75 (Saturday Night Live, Episode 1)

Saturday Night Live was birthed into existence in conflict with religion. That conflict came to a head on October 3, 1992 when Sinéad O'Connor – after singing an acapella version of Bob Marley's "War" – held up a picture of Pope John Paul II, sang the word "evil," tore the picture to shreds, and shouted "Fight the real enemy!" The audience was silent; Lorne Michaels kept the applause sign unlit.[1]

The backlash was fierce. NBC received 4,400 calls (and only seven were complimentary). The *New York Daily News* called her action a "HOLY TERROR," and other headlines included "Unpardonable Sin!" and "Is Sinéad Nuts?" The National Ethnic Coalition of Organizers crushed more than 200 donated copies of her album under a steamroller in front of *Chrysalis Records*' Rockefeller Center office, and Catholic groups everywhere demanded an apology.[2] NBC agreed to never run the performance again.[3]

But it wasn't even close to over. The next week's host, Joe Pesci, brandished the photo taped back together and said that, had he been hosting, he would have given her "such a smack." The audience erupted in applause. About a week after that (October 16), O'Connor was fiercely booed at a Bob Dylan tribute concert at Madison Square

Saturday Night Live and Philosophy: Deep Thoughts Through the Decades, First Edition. Edited by Jason Southworth and Ruth Tallman.
© 2020 John Wiley & Sons Ltd. Published 2020 by John Wiley & Sons Ltd.

Garden. When Kris Kristofferson came out and told her "don't let the bastards get you down," she nixed her planned song and attempted to reprise her version of "War." She didn't quite finish and nearly puked on Kris as she walked off stage.[4] Her career effectively ended soon thereafter.

"Could It Beeeeee...Satan?"

Why was everyone so upset? Presumably because what O'Connor did was considered a sacrilegious act – an act that violates, injures, or otherwise mistreats a sacred person or object. Some merely called it blasphemous, but blasphemy is sacrilege done with words. Technically speaking, O'Connor also committed desecration: an act of sacrilege done to a sacred object – at least according to those who would consider a picture of the Pope to be sacred (which O'Connor, being a Catholic at the time, presumably did).

But if you think about it, *SNL* is sacrilegious all the time. "Djesus Uncrossed," "God is a Boob Man," "The St. Joseph's Christmas Mass Spectacular," "The Bird Bible," The Church Lady, "The Religetables," "The Three Wise Guys," Father Guido Sarducci, that time Jesus visited Tim Tebow in the locker room...and what about when Louis C.K. implied God was a serial killer? Why didn't these cause the same kind of controversy? Was it because they were comedy? Were they less severe? Were they not actually instances of sacrilege? Or did they perhaps convey a message or lesson that justified them, or otherwise made them immune? And if so, what was that message? (And what was O'Connor's message anyway?) Might we learn from it? And what might all this tell us about whether or when we should risk our own well-being – like O'Connor did – to stand up for what we think is right? To explore these questions, I'd like to look at a few of the most famous instances of when *SNL* took on religion.

DJesus Uncrossed

Some *SNL* religion sketches are relatively harmless. Take "St. Joseph's Christmas Mass Spectacular" for example, which makes fun of how boring church is – lame jokes, sweaty handshakes, crappy organists, and all.[5] While it does involve sacred objects/events, since no harm is intended, no foul of "sacrilege" was called. Christian Molly

Hemingway of *The Federalist* even liked the sketch, saying it worked because "it doesn't hate Christians."[6]

"Djesus Uncrossed" wasn't so lucky.[7] Staged as a trailer for a new Quentin Tarantino movie, "Djesus Uncrossed" depicts a historical revenge fantasy where Jesus (played by Christoph Waltz) returns from the dead to inflict violent payback on those who wronged him. He kills a legion of Roman soldiers with a sword, shoots Judas (played by "Samuel L. Jackson") in the chest with a shotgun, and apparently says the N-word a lot. In response, Sears pulled their advertising from NBC's online posting of the sketch and Jim Baker argued that it was the "most blasphemous skit in *SNL* history."[8] So why didn't it end Waltz's career?

Well for one, it was satire (an attempt to use exaggeration and humor to criticize) – and satire sometimes gets a pass when other things (like protest songs) do not. As Megan LeBoeuf puts it, "Satire... has the ability to protect its creator from culpability for criticism, because it is implied rather than overtly stated."[9]

What's more, the target of this satire's criticism was Quentin Tarantino, not Jesus. Tarantino's movies are notoriously and gratuitously violent – so much so (the trailer suggests) that even his historical fiction movie about Jesus would include maximal bloodshed. Indeed, the joke doesn't work unless one recognizes the irony of Jesus as a mass murderer (because he was actually non-violent). Because of this, one might argue that "Djesus Uncrossed" isn't actually sacrilegious; although his image is used, Jesus himself wasn't actually maligned. This is perhaps another reason Watlz survived unscathed.

The Religetables

A piece of satire that unquestionably had religion as its target was "The Religetables," a TV *Funhouse* parody of the Christian cartoon *Veggietales*.[10] *Veggietales* retells biblical and moral stories with humor using digital vegetables, like "Bob the Tomato" and "Larry the Cucumber." "The Religetables" does essentially the same thing, except it illustrates the darker side of religious history: a potato screaming after being circumcised with a potato peeler, a crusade where non-Christian avocados are turned into guacamole, a pear and asparagus gleefully hanging a carrot as a witch, and a bearded tomato diving into a crowd of fruits and veggies with an electronic vegetable chopper in hopes of receiving seventy-two virgin cherry tomatoes in the afterlife. The sketch is interrupted by a news report about Fr. Rafael

Walsh (a cucumber) resigning his post after admitting to molesting six gherkins and fondling an adolescent mushroom. The piece ends with a scene from the end times, where all the Religetables are being peeled, roasted, and chopped. "Armageddon's finally here/ Armageddon out of here."

Despite all this, there wasn't an uproar and (as far as I could find) no one of import called "The Religetables" sacrilegious. Perhaps that's because what's being parodied, *Veggietales*, is not a sacred object. But what makes the piece funny is the juxtaposition of a kid friendly cartoon and the absolute worst horrors of religion. It therefore calls to mind those horrors and could raise serious questions about the moral responsibility of members of those religions. Are you morally culpable when members of your belief group do horrible things in the name of your shared belief? I mean, obviously not to the same degree – but do you bear some amount of moral responsibility since, by believing and belonging, you are adding legitimacy to the group and belief in question?[11]

With that in mind, we might think of the piece as a criticism of *Veggietales*. *Veggietales* indoctrinates children into religion without being honest about its dangers. And perhaps that is why the parody was not criticized. Any objection to it would provide the opportunity for everyone to point out that religious institutions actually are guilty of the crimes the piece depicts.

Tebow and Jesus

A sketch that *was* criticized aired at the time outspoken Christian NFL quarterback Tim Tebow had just led the Denver Broncos to a series of unlikely (fourth-quarter comeback) playoff wins. Tebow, who had become famous for making a show of praying during crucial moments in games and pointing up to heaven and saying "Thank you" after touchdowns, expressly said that the wins were a result of God's intervention. After beating the Chicago Bears in overtime he said, "I believe in a big God and special things can happen. Sometimes you can feel God has a big plan."[12]

A week after that win, *SNL* broadcast a sketch of Jesus appearing to the Broncos in their locker room.[13] Jesus takes credit for their last six wins but is visibly irritated by Tebow's enthusiasm. He makes fun of Tebow for saying that the Bible is his playbook, chastises Tebow for "being in everyone's face" about the fact that he prays, and tells him to "take it down a notch." Pat Robertson (of *700 Club* fame) criticized the sketch as "anti-Christian bigotry...that is just disgusting," and pointed out that if Muhammad had been depicted like that in a Muslim country "you would have found bombs being thrown off."[14]

He's perhaps right about the latter; depicting Muhammad (in any way) is considered sacrilegious by many Muslims, and people have been killed for doing so.[15] But depictions of Jesus are not automatically considered sacrilegious by Christians, and the sketch is not criticizing Jesus. Fox News' Bob Beckel said the sketch was "despicable" for the way it "display[ed]" Jesus Christ.[16] In reality however, Jesus comes off as likable and nice. And it can't be sacrilegious to simply depict Jesus in a modern setting or involved in helping people with sports. After all, *Catholic Supply* has a whole line of "Jesus Sport Statues," and I don't see anyone complaining about those.[17]

The real problem seems to be that Tebow is being made fun of. This, Robertson thinks, is equivalent to making fun of all Christians. But that follows only if all Christians are like Tebow. This is decidedly not the case. At worst, the sketch is criticizing the approximately 25% of Americans who think that God intervenes in sporting events.[18]

Such criticism, however, seems justified. "You're Welcome," Jesus says in the sketch. "I, Jesus Christ, am indeed the reason you've won your past six football games." The idea is ludicrous. First, Tebow's prayers seem pointless. How could anyone convince God, a perfect being, to do something that he wasn't already going to do? If helping the Broncos win was the best thing, wouldn't God have done it regardless?

Second, if God is willing to interfere in football games, why didn't he stop this or that car crash, or make the guns at Sandy Hook misfire? Why didn't he give Hitler a heart attack? To be concerned with sports, but not human suffering, is morally reprehensible.[19] Of course, to answer this, one might insist that "God works in mysterious ways." But that implies God's reasoning about what is good and bad is beyond us. So we can know that the Bronco's beating the Bears is a good thing, but for all we know the Holocaust wasn't evil? That's absurd!

Indeed, Philosopher Friedrich Nietzsche (1844–1900) argued that using God to explain mundane and chance occurrences cheapens God. It makes him a "domestic servant... a mere name for the stupidest sort of chance."[20] So the viewpoint being mocked in the sketch, it seems, deserves a hearty laugh.[21] Perhaps that's the reason it didn't inspire more objections.

God's a Boob Man

Something that did inspire objections was another fake trailer – this time for a movie called *God is a Boob Man*.[22] It tells the story of a small-town Christian baker named Beth who is asked to make a cake for a same sex wedding. When she refuses, the gay couple and their "Jewish lawyer" from the ACLU take her to court to get her to say three little words: "God is gay." She instead stands up in court and yells "God is a boob man," and everyone erupts in applause.

The sketch is a parody of *God's Not Dead 2*, a Christian movie about a public high school teacher forced to court because she quoted Jesus while answering a student's question about the similarities of the teachings of Ghandi, Martin Luther King Jr., and Jesus. In the film, the atheist ACLU lawyer says that he is going to use the trial to prove that God doesn't exist.

Actor Pat Boone, who starred in the film, objected to the *SNL* parody, equating it to an attack on God (sacrilege) and suggesting that the writers had earned themselves a place in hell. "They don't have to apologize to Christians [but] when you come against God...you are bringing upon yourself eternal condemnation... For those who dissent and disagree and reject God there is a place already prepared – for the devil, his angels and those who side with him."[23]

Given the title, perhaps the charge of sacrilege sticks.[24] But what's really being made fun of is *God's not Dead 2*, not God himself. Boone realizes this but suggests that the criticism is unfair. "The movie that we made has nothing whatsoever to do with homosexuality [and] there's not a reference to anyone Jewish. [There's] nothing whatsoever in the parody that relates to the film itself....it's made-up ... and criticizing us for something we didn't do."[25] The movie's producers, Michael Scott and Rice Broocks echoed Boone's sentiments, suggesting that – although they recognize humor and parody – *God's a Boob Man* goes too far because it distorts and twists their movie's message.

But the fact that their films have "nothing whatsoever to do with homosexuality," and the sketch does, is completely irrelevant. Although it's their film's plot that is being parodied, what's being *satirized* is the producer's assumptions and approach. Satire, recall, is the attempt to criticize something by exaggerating it. In this case, what's being satirized is the "God's Not Dead" movies' propensity to commit the strawman fallacy – to present someone else (or their position) in an uncharitable or weaker way so as to make it easier to attack. Both the films and the sketch cartoonishly vilify non-believers (whether they be gay, philosophers, or lawyers) by making them loveless curmudgeons with no morals who only do things for personal gain. This is completely unfair because, in reality, there is no difference between the moral behavior of the average believer and non-believer (whether they be an agnostic, an atheist, or a "none").[26]

Boone almost got the joke when he suggested that gay people should be offended by how they were portrayed in the *SNL* sketch. "[Gay people are] portrayed as more bigoted than the Christians. For them to be portrayed as demanding that God be declared gay is so over the top. I don't think any responsible member of the homosexual community would want to identify with that."

Of course they wouldn't! But the sketch isn't actually suggesting that gay people are like it depicts. It's making fun of the fact that the "God's Not Dead" movies suggest that non-believers actually are as they depict. For example, *God's Not Dead* has a philosophy professor insist that all his students declare that God is dead so they can skip the philosophy of religion section in his class. Suggesting that a philosophy professor would do such a thing is just as ridiculous as suggesting that there could be a court case about God being gay (or about God's existence.)

In fact, in certain ways, the sketch is more realistic than the movies. A case of a baker refusing to make a wedding cake for a gay couple actually did go all the way to the Supreme Court. But a case about a teacher quoting scripture in a classroom to respond to a student's question never would. Of course, the ends of both movies list a number of court cases, suggesting that this kind of Christian persecution happens all the time. But they are all false fake news boogeymen – stories that grossly exaggerate (or outright lie) to feed the intended victimization narrative.[27] (What's more, the bakery owners ended up winning the real-world court case on which the sketch was based.[28])

Speaking of which...the *SNL* sketch also parrots a number of common false evangelical assumptions. "They say we're bigots, but Christians are the most oppressed group in this country," says Beth in the sketch. "Gays are the most powerful force in America." [29] *God's Not Dead 2* suggests the same kind of things. Pastor Dave (a juror) says, "If we sit by and do nothing, the pressure we are feeling today will mean persecution tomorrow. We're at war!" And when he says "God bless you" after another juror sneezes, the defense lawyer says "Careful, or *you* might end up on trial."

In reality, of course, Christians make up the majority of the American population, the vast majority of elected officials, and control the Supreme Court. Indeed, every president in American history has been a Christian.[30] As far as I could find, no one has ever been killed in America by a non-Christian for being Christian, and no one has ever died by suicide after being ridiculed for being Christian.[31] (Sadly, atheists and gay people cannot say the same thing.[32])

Why isn't there a Hollywood style Christian movie about the social issues that Jesus cared about? He spent *his* life with the ill, poor, and outcast. Indeed, why aren't governments that are controlled by Christians addressing things like poverty, health, and teen pregnancy? Are the pressing issues really philosophy professors promoting atheism, teachers that can't quote scripture in class, and gay wedding cakes? Obviously, not. The reason, it seems, that *God's a Boob Man* didn't provoke consternation and outrage that ended careers was because the criticism it provided of the *God's Not Dead* movies was spot on.[33]

Louis C.K.'s God Monologue

Something else that seemed to slip under the radar was Louis C.K.'s opening monologue on March 30, 2014. He made fun of the idea that there is a heaven and suggested that God thinks we are "greedy dicks" for expecting one. He then followed with:

> I think if there is a God, I don't know if it's the one in the Bible because that's a weird story – it's "he's ours father, and we're his children." That's it. "Our Father who art in heaven." Where's our mother? What happened to our mom? What did he do to our mom? Something happened. Somewhere in heaven there's a porch with a dead lady under it and I want the story. Somebody's got to check the trunk of God's car for bleach, and rope, and fibers.

Implying God is akin to a creepy killer is clearly sacrilegious. So why didn't it threaten to end Louis' career (long before his sexual misconduct coming to light did)?[34] To be sure, a few were offended.[35] But it did not provoke the backlash that O'Connor did. Why?

Perhaps because it was a joke. But "Dejesus Uncrossed" was a joke, and that didn't keep people from calling it the most blasphemous sketch in *SNL* history. So why wasn't Louis' monologue called the most blasphemous monologue in *SNL* history? I think it's because Louis also made fun of disbelievers.

I'm not religious. I don't know if there's a God, that's all I can say honestly is "I don't know." Some people think that they know that there
isn't. That's a weird thing to think you can know. "Yeah, there's no
God." Are you sure? "Yeah, no, there's no God." How do you know?
"'Cause I didn't see him." How do you – there's a vast universe! You
can see for about 100 yards when there is not a building in the way.
How could you possibly – did you look everywhere? Did you look in
the downstairs bathroom? ...I haven't seen "12 Years A Slave yet," that
doesn't' mean it doesn't exist.

Actress Rosario Dawson thought the monologue was hilarious because
it offended everyone, and there is something to be said for that.[36] Christians
were upset about "God's a Boob Guy" and the Tebow and Jesus sketch
because they thought they were being singled out. But if you pick on both
sides, it seems that neither has much to complain about. Indeed, it would
seem hypocritical to only complain about how *you* were slighted.

Another reason Christians might not have been as upset at Louis is
that, while he only told a joke about God, he was actually presenting
an argument against atheism. *Atheists think they know God doesn't
exist because they can't see him, but not seeing something is no reason
to think something doesn't exist.* But to the extent that Christians
thought he was presenting a good argument, they were mistaken.

First of all, no atheist says God doesn't exist because they can't see
him. After all, if God exists, he's a non-physical being; so you wouldn't
be able to see him anyway. Louis is guilty of the straw man fallacy
here; he's misrepresenting an argument to make it easier to attack.
More commonly, atheists say they don't believe God exists because
they see no evidence of God's existence. And not believing that something exists because you have not seen evidence of it is a justified position to take. Without evidence that Bigfoot exists, I am justified in
believing he doesn't – and for those who do, the burden is on them to
provide the evidence he does. The burden of proof is on the believer.

What's more, Louis is wrong that not seeing something is never
evidence that it is not there. If you look in your fridge and see no milk,
that's good evidence there's no milk in your fridge. It's only when you
should expect to not see something (even if it was there) that not seeing it isn't reason to doubt its existence. Not seeing any spiders in my
garage from my kitchen window is no reason to think they aren't
there because I wouldn't see them if they were. But there is good reason to think that if God existed we would see evidence of his existence. Yes, the universe is vast, but God is supposedly infinite. And
atheists maintain that there is no good evidence of God's existence.[37]

Indeed, since God is supposedly perfectly good too, the large amount of gratuitous evil we have in our world would seem to be direct evidence against God's existence. Of course, some evil is our fault; such evil is called moral evil and theists often explain such evil by invoking human free will. But the existence of diseases, hurricanes, and earthquakes aren't our fault. Indeed, the fact that the laws of nature that govern our universe necessitate such things implies that, if our universe was created and designed by someone, it wasn't an all-powerful all-loving God. This is called the problem of natural evil.[38]

Ironically, the best way to solve this problem may be to embrace the theology of George Carlin – a theology he expressed in the same first-episode monologue that opened this chapter: "[I]f God is like us, I think he may perhaps be subject to physical laws. ... It would explain a lot of things. ...People say, 'Well, if God is so benevolent, how can He let people *suffer*?' [shrugs shoulders] He can't help it lady! He's subject to physical laws!"[39] If God is limited by the physical laws, he can't be held responsible for what they necessitate. Indeed, he likely couldn't have even created a universe better than the one we have.[40]

The Church Lady

Like Carlin, *SNL* likes to make fun of televangelists. One of my favorite examples is another *TV Funhouse* called "Jesus Today" that uses real audio from televangelists to show how televangelists would react to...well, Jesus today (and how he would react to them).[41] One televangelist punches Jesus in the face as the televangelist tries to raise money; another puts a curtain over Jesus as he berates the Clintons and "homosexuals." Jesus kicks another as he tries to heal someone in a wheelchair, and then the man in the wheelchair runs away. The only thing that makes him happy is seeing the ending of *A Charlie Brown Christmas*, which makes him dance away like a *Peanuts* character.

But no one on *SNL* was better at pointing out the foibles of televangelists than Enid Strict...also known as "The Church Lady." Played by Dana Carvey, The Church Lady would often berate (actors playing) televangelists on her show. Most famously she interviewed the disgraced "greedy media sluts" Jim and Tammy Faye Baker, right in the middle of their sex scandal.[42] The Baker sketch is famous for making fun of Tammy's running mascara, but it also nicely revealed The Church Lady's shtick: she's morally superior to everyone.

People, these are trying times. Everyone's trying everything and getting caught. ...I want to reassure my viewers that I am not a televangelist, with a maga-buck-ministry or a theme park. I'm just The Church Lady. Billy, can I have my special shaft of light? [Light shines down] I would just like to say to all the Swaggereds, and Schullers, and Falwells, and Roberts – Dragon-Boesky and all those Wall Street inside traders – to President Reagan and all his Iran scammers: Well, when trouble erupts, power corrupts – and I'm sure you'll all agree, that I'm just a *liiiiiittle* bit superior to all of thee.

That's why the Bakers' excuses for their sins are so "special" and "conveeeenient." That is why she explains their sin as the work of ... "could it beeeeee...Satan?" (You can add your own echo.) That's why the dance she does at the end of every sketch is called "The Superior Dance." (No one could ever quite do it like Carvey.) She thinks she's superior.

And it's not just televangelists. Of course, Enid often zeros in on easy moral targets like O.J. Simpson and Madonna,[43] the Kardashian sisters and Snooki,[44] and Donald Trump and Marla Maples.[45] But she also criticizes those much less deserving of criticism: not only relatively harmless celebrities – like Danny Devito, Ann Landers, and Willie Nelson[46] – but unexpecting innocents, like Jenny Baker (the "College Bible Student of the Year and President of the Christian Youth Activity League," played by Victoria Jackson).[47] Enid accuses Jenny – without evidence – of seducing minister Bob.[48]

The Church Lady bit doesn't elicit criticism because the bit is accurate. Just like Dana Carvey, who based the character on church ladies who would keep track of his church attendance as a child, we all know someone like Enid Strict.[49] But she also serves as a cautionary tale.

We all have a tendency to think that we are morally superior to others. Just like our propensity to believe that we have higher than average intelligence is usually wrong (we can't all be above average),[50] our propensity to think we are morally superior is also usually wrong.[50] (And if you're thinking, "But I'm different," you're probably wrong.[51]) Our sense of moral superiority therefore makes us less likely to admit, and thus discover, when we are in the moral wrong.

But unlike our false sense of superior intelligence, our false sense of moral superiority does not come so much from over-evaluating ourselves, but from under-evaluating others – thinking that others are guilty, or ascribing less than admirable motives to others, without sufficient evidence.[52] This is certainly what The Church Lady does. As Jenny Baker put it: "That's not true. You're making all that stuff up. I'm sorry Church Lady but you're the most judgmental person I've ever met. You twist everything people say into some sort of sordid perverted thing...why don't you even believe that anybody can be a nice good person?"

But feelings of moral superiority can not only be inaccurate, they can be harmful. According to philosophers Brandon Warmke and Justin Tose, they can lead to moral grandstanding – the act of trying to communicate one's moral superiority to others.

> Grandstanders want others to regard them as being morally respectable ... and the contributions they make to public moral discourse are intended to satisfy that desire. [T]hey may be sincere...their claim might even be true, or supported by reasons or evidence. But whatever the incidental features of grandstanding, the grandstander's primary concern is projecting an image of herself as someone who is on the side of the angels... In a quest to impress peers, grandstanders trump up moral charges, pile on in cases of public shaming, announce that anyone who disagrees with them is *obviously* wrong, or exaggerate emotional displays.[53]

To be clear, they are not talking about "virtue signaling" – a concept and term decried by Warmke and Tose, which is used by online bullies and trolls to belittle people taking moral positions the bullies and trolls can't refute. But Warmke and Tose do argue that grandstanding can lead to something else called "ramping up," a kind of "moral arms race" where each combatant feels they must show more moral outrage than the last.

> "I think they should censured."
> "I think they should be fired."
> "Well, I think they should go to jail!"

This can not only lead to underserved exaggerated punishments for minor moral crimes, but has led to a political polarization, in both Congress and public discourse, that has made compromise impossible. "This is an especially bad outcome in democratic societies," say Warmke and Tose. It also makes "many people stop taking moral conversations seriously... grandstanding devalues the social currency of moral talk [and] render[s] it a less useful tool for accomplishing aims more important than the promotion of reputation." [54]

The Church Lady is obviously grandstanding, and she is not willing to listen to anyone else's opinion.

> Well we have been getting gobs of letters, and lots of mail, and I'd like to share one in particular with you. Chuck Oliver of Redwood City California writes to me, he says: "Dear Church Lady, I think sometimes you don't want to listen to anyone's opinion but your own." [Rips up letter.] Well Chucky, [singing] I can't hear you. Alrighty, I think we both feel better now.[55]

But none of this is reason to start going around accusing everyone of grandstanding. After all, such an accusation is in danger of being an instance of grandstanding itself. It's also not a reason to never stand up for what you think is right for fear of being a grandstander yourself. Instead, it's a call for self-reflection, to consider that we might be wrong, to begin listening to others' points of view, and (as Warmke and Tose put it) "to reassess why and how we speak to one another about moral and political issues. Are we doing good with our moral talk? Or are we trying to convince others that we are good?"

Fighting the Real Enemy

This brings us back to Sinéad O'Connor. Was she grandstanding? It seems unlikely. For one, it wouldn't seem consistent with her character. Although some might argue that her refusal to accept a Grammy in protest of the music industry's materialism was grandstanding, in reality O'Connor shunned her fame and cared little about what the industry or the public thought about her. More importantly, however, she knew in advance that what she was going to do on *SNL* would convince most people that she was bad (not good). That's why she kept it a secret from the *SNL* crew. "I knew exactly where I stood," she said about her protest on VH1's "Behind the Music, "and I knew it would take years for it to become apparent what I was doing, and I was prepared to ride that."[56] So, although she was taking a stand, I don't think she was grandstanding. But what stand was she taking? What message was she trying to convey? And did it justify what she did?

There was a lot of confusion about her message in the media the next day – but this was primarily because they concentrated only on what she did at the end of the song. They ignored the song itself. The version of "War" she sang wasn't exactly like Bob Marley's. Not only was it acapella, but Sinéad changed some of the lyrics. Based on a speech by Haile Selassie, both versions start by essentially suggesting that, until racism and class structures are destroyed, and equal basic human rights and "international morality" are guaranteed, we should wage war against the powers that maintain those structures. But O'Connor's version deviates in the fifth verse. In his fifth verse, Marley harkens to a concern close to his heart: he calls for the freedom of his African brothers in bondage.

> Until the ignoble and unhappy regimes / That hold our brothers in Angola / In Mozambique / South Africa / Sub-human bondage / Have been toppled / Utterly destroyed / Well, everywhere is war. / Me say war.

But O'Connor changed that verse to be about child abuse.

> Until the ignoble and unhappy regime / Which holds all of us through / Child-abuse, yeah, child-abuse, yeah / Sub-human bondage has been toppled / Utterly destroyed / Everywhere is war.

Why did she do this? Partly because, as she put it in an interview the day after her *SNL* appearance, "Child abuse is the root of all evil...If you saw a child in front of you being raped...[or] beaten up, what would you do? Well, you'd stop it straight away wouldn't you? Well, OK, even though we can't see it in front of us now, it's happening as we speak to millions of people."[57]

But this issue was especially important to O'Connor because she had been abused as a child. She described the abuse she suffered from her mother a month after her *SNL* appearance in *Time*: "Sexual and physical. Psychological. Spiritual. Emotional. Verbal. I went to school every day covered in bruises, boils, styes and face welts, you name it. Nobody ever said a bloody word or did a thing."[58] The picture of the Pope she tore up belonged to her mother.

But why a picture of the Pope? Well, for one, O'Connor blamed the poor social conditions that led to a history of child abuse in her family (and in Ireland in general) on the Catholic Church. As she tells it, the Church sanctioned the devastation of the Irish culture.[59] More importantly, however, as a child she had also been abused by Catholic priests and knew that others had as well. As she told *Time*, "[T]he priests have been beating the shit out of the children for years and sexually abusing them."

What's more, she also knew that the Vatican was trying to hide it. As she put it in an interview for the aforementioned VH1 "Behind the Music" episode, "There were children who were being sexually abused by priests in Ireland, or had been sexually abused by priests in Ireland, whom the Vatican knew of but who the Vatican were doing nothing to help the families or the survivors of, and in fact were silencing the families."

In other words, she was protesting the Catholic priest sex abuse scandal before most people had even heard about it, much less believed it! Given that her American audience didn't know about the scandal or exactly what her message was, we can somewhat understand the public's negative reaction to what she did. But now that we know beyond any reasonable doubt that she was right, it not only seems that her protest was justified, but it would seem that we also owe her an apology![60]

O'Connor's example brings up a final question: when should we stand up for what is right? When should we make our position or moral stance known? It cost Sinéad her career. Is it always worth it, or is the cost sometimes too high?

In a way, this was the question of Plato's *Republic*: is it better to be a virtuous person who is decried by the public as a villain (like O'Connor was), or to be celebrated by the public as a hero but actually be a villain. (As an example of the latter, consider Jonathan King, a millionaire producer who was applauded when he said that O'Connor should be spanked for what she did, but was later convicted of sexually assaulting teenage boys.) The *Republic* is essentially one long argument that it's better to be like O'Connor because being virtuous comes with its own internal reward that far outweighs the reward of public recognition.

O'Connor would seem to agree. As she said the day after her *SNL* protest, when asked whether she was willing to face the consequences for what she did, "What consequences? Look at the alternative."[61] But it's not clear that Plato was right. Indeed, O'Connor's tragic life might serve as a counterexample to Plato's thesis. I don't mean to minimize the vacuousness of seeking fame; those who have it often wish they could give it up. But public scorn can be especially cruel, and O'Connor's political and social activism didn't exactly make her life easy.

Of course, you will likely never have an opportunity to take the kind of public stand, and garner the kind of public ridicule, that O'Connor did. But we all face similar decisions. Do you stand up at work and object to a company policy? Do you confront your best friend and tell them that you think they're wrong? Do you vocally object to your parents or in-laws who support political causes and candidates you find morally reprehensible?

On the one hand, you're standing up for what you think is right. On the other hand, have you considered the possibility that you might be wrong? Have you honestly tried to see things from their point of view? Do you know that you are right? Are you certain? If so, they might be convinced and change their ways – but people usually aren't. You could end up losing your job or alienating your friends and family with essentially "nothing to show for it" (so to speak).

Consider the story of professor Tayari Jones whose parents, at age 5, had taught her that Gulf Oil was financially supporting South African apartheid. What was she to do when, on the way to a much-anticipated visit to the zoo, her friends' mother stopped to refuel her car at a Gulf gas station? She protested, explained why, and then exited (and refused to reenter) the car when her friend's mother was not persuaded – thus sacrificing both the trip and her friendship. Did she do the right thing? It certainly wasn't wrong, but would it have been morally acceptable to ignore this minor transgression for the sake of the trip and her friendship? Or could she have instead found some kind of compromise?

Perhaps. But (as an adult) Jones argues that, when dealing with moral issues, compromise is often not acceptable.

> The middle is a point equidistant from two poles. That's it. There is nothing inherently virtuous about being neither here nor there. ... Where was the middle? Rather than chattel slavery, perhaps we could agree on a nice program of indentured servitude?... What is halfway between moral and immoral? ... Is it more essential that we comprehend the motives of white nationalists, or is it more urgent that we prevent them from terrorizing communities of color and those who oppose racism? Should we agree to disagree about the murder and dismemberment of a journalist? Should we celebrate our tolerance and civility as we stanch the wounds of the world and the climate with a poultice of national unity?[62]

On the other hand, if we took a stand against every injustice, we might not be able to function in the world. Because practically no person or corporation is innocent, we could buy no gas, or food, or work for any company. What's more, as Warmke and Tose pointed out, compromise is necessary for the functioning of democracy. At the 2014 American Humanists Associations annual conference in Philadelphia, I heard Barney Frank explain that he once supported a bill that protected gay but not transgendered persons, even though it pained him to do so, because he knew specific congressmen (whose votes were necessary for the bill to pass) would drop their support if it included the latter.

I have to admit, I don't have any answers here. I struggle with these kinds of questions myself. And, although these are philosophical questions, there may be no philosophical answer. Just like the O'Connor, and the writers of *SNL*, when you are faced with whether to stand up for what you think is right in the face of almost certain backlash, it's just something you will have to decide for yourself. I wish you the best of luck.

Notes

1. Surprisingly, he did let the incident air, unedited, on the time delayed West Coast broadcast the night the incident occurred.
2. William M. Reilly, "Steamroller crushes Sinead O'Connor recordings." *United Press International*, October 21, 1992. Retrieved from www.upi.com/Archives/1992/10/21/Steamroller-crushes-Sinead-OConnor-recordings/5284719640000 on 6 July, 2019.
3. Reruns of the episode feature her performance from the dress rehearsal where she held up a picture of a child instead.
4. Niall O'Dowd, "Sinead O'Connor booed off stage at Bob Dylan concert over tearing up Pope's picture." *Irish Central*, August 22, 2018. Retrieved from www.irishcentral.com/culture/sinead-oconnor-bob-dylan-pope on 6, July, 2019.
5. December 13, 2014.
6. Mollie Hemingway, "Saturday Night Live's Christmas parody works because it doesn't hate Christians." *The Federalist*, December 17, 2014. Retrieved from http://thefederalist.com/2014/12/17/saturday-night-lives-christmas-parody-works-because-it-doesnt-hate-christians on July 6, 2019.
7. February 16, 2013.
8. *The Jim Baker Show News.* "'DJesus uncrossed': most blasphemous skit in 'SNL' History?" February 20, 2013. Retrieved from https://jimbakkershow.morningsidechurchinc.com/news/djesus-uncrossed-most-blasphemous-skit-in-snl-history/ on July 6, 2019. See also Alexis Loinaz, "Saturday Night Live's 'Djesus uncrossed': Sears pulls online ads running with controversial sketch." *Eonline*, March 7, 2013. Retrieved from www.eonline.com/de/news/395169/saturday-night-live-s-djesus-uncrossed-sears-pulls-online-ads-running-with-controversial-sketch on July 6, 2019.
9. Megan LeBoeuf, "The power of ridicule: an analysis of satire" (2007). Senior Honors Projects. Paper 63. Retrieved from https://digitalcommons.

uri.edu/cgi/viewcontent.cgi?article=1065&context=srhonorsprog on July 6, 2019.

10. November 6, 2002.

11. For more on this topic, see my article "Moral culpability and choosing to believe in God," in Bill Anderson (ed.), *Atheism and the Christian Faith* (Wilmington, DE: Vernon Press, 2018).

12. Mark Maske, "Onward Christian soldier." *The Sidney Morning Herald*, Decembr 17, 2011. Retrieved from www.smh.com.au/sport/onward-christian-soldier-20111216-1oyma.html on July 6, 2019.

13. December 12, 2011.

14. Nellie Andreeva, "Televangelist Pat Robertson slams 'SNL's Tim Tebow skit as 'anti-Christian bigotry,'" *Deadline*, December 20, 2011. Retrieved from https://deadline.com/2011/12/televangelist-pat-robertson-slams-snls-tim-tebow-skit-as-anti-christian-bigotry-207260 on July 6, 2019.

15. "Charlie Hebdo attack: three days of terror." *BBC News*, January 14, 2015. Retrieved from www.bbc.com/news/world-europe-30708237 on July 6, 2019.

16. Jon Bershad, "Fox News' Bob Beckel: SNL's Tim Tebow sketch was 'despicable,'" *Mediaite*, December 19, 2011. Retrieved from www.mediaite.com/tv/fox-news-bob-beckel-snls-tim-tebow-sketch-was-despicable on July 6, 2019.

17. You can see their collection at www.catholicsupply.com/christmas/sports.html.

18. Jaweed Kaleem, "Half of Americans say God plays a role in Super Bowl winner: survey." *Huffington Post*, January 16, 2014. Retrieved from www.huffingtonpost.com/2014/01/16/super-bowl-prayer_n_4605665.html on July 6 2019.

19. For more on this particular issue, see William Irwin, "Tim Tebow, the problem of evil and divinely bestowed touchdowns." *Psychology Today*, December 22, 2011. Retrieved from www.psychologytoday.com/us/blog/plato-pop/201112/tim-tebow-the-problem-evil-and-divinely-bestowed-touchdowns on July 6, 2019.

20. Friedrich Nietzsche, *The Antichrist*, § 52. A copy of the work is available for free here: https://ebooks.adelaide.edu.au/n/nietzsche/friedrich/antichrist/complete.html.

21. For a more on the general philosophical implications of God interfering with sports see David Kyle Johnson, "The super bowl, atheists, and divine intervention in sports." *Psychology Today*. February 1, 2014. Retrieved from https://www.psychologytoday.com/us/blog/plato-pop/201402/the-super-bowl-atheists-and-divine-intervention-in-sports on July 6, 2019.

22. April 16, 2016.

23. Bob Unruh, "'God is a boob man' ignites Christian anger." *World Net Daily*, April 19, 2016. Retrieved from www.wnd.com/2016/04/god-is-a-boob-man-ignites-christian-anger on July 6, 2019.

24. Although, since merely liking boobs isn't a sin, and Jesus was supposedly 100% human, and a straight male, and also (according to Christian theology) identical to God himself…doesn't it follow from Christian theology that God did like boobs? (A logical joke for you to ponder.)

25. Ibid.

26. See Dimitris Xygalatas, "Are religious people more moral?" *The Conversation*, Oct. 23, 2017. Retrieved from http://theconversation.com/are-religious-people-more-moral-84560 on July 6, 2019. See also Sigal Samuel, "Atheists are sometimes more religious than Christians." *The Atlantic*, May 31, 2018. Retrieved from www.theatlantic.com/international/archive/2018/05/american-atheists-religious-european-christians/560936 on July 6, 2019.

27. Hemant Mehta, "Let's debunk the 'Christian persecution' court cases that inspired the 'God's not dead' films." *The Friendly Atheist*, April 8, 2016. Retrieved from http://friendlyatheist.patheos.com/2016/04/08/lets-debunk-the-christian-persecution-court-cases-that-inspired-the-gods-not-dead-films on July 6, 2019.

28. Robert Barnes, "Supreme Court rules in favor of baker who would not make wedding cake for gay couple." *The Washington Post*, June 4, 2018. Retrieved from www.washingtonpost.com/politics/courts_law/supreme-court-rules-in-favor-of-baker-who-would-not-make-wedding-cake-for-gay-couple/2018/06/04/50c68cf8-6802-11e8-bea7-c8eb28bc52b1_story.html?utm_term=.6fe8cedf6ba8 on July 6, 2019.

29. These assumptions are shared by most Christians. See Emma Green, "White evangelicals believe they face more discrimination than Muslims," *The Atlantic*, March 10, 2017. Retrieved from www.theatlantic.com/politics/archive/2017/03/perceptions-discrimination-muslims-christians/519135 on July 6, 2019.

30. Pew Research Center, "Religious landscape study," 2018. Retrieved from www.pewforum.org/religious-landscape-study on July 6, 2019.

31. There have been church shootings, but they usually are not motivated by religion – and of those that are, they are motivated by some kind of religious disagreements (for example, the shooter felt rejected by the church). Examples of atheists or gay people shooting up a church because they reject the church's teaching do not exist. See Daniel Burke, "The truth about church shootings," CNN.com, November 10, 2017. Retrieved from www.cnn.com/2017/11/06/us/church-shootings-truth/index.html on July 6, 2019.

32. See Haeyoun Park and Iaryna Mykhyalyshyn, "L.G.B.T. people are more likely to be targets of hate crimes than any other group," *The New York Times*, June 16, 2016. Retrieved from www.nytimes.com/interactive/2016/06/16/us/hate-crimes-against-lgbt.html on July 6, 2019. See also Austin Cline, "University study on American attitudes towards atheists," ThoughtCo.com, March 8, 2017. Retrieved from www.thoughtco.com/study-american-attitudes-towards-atheists-248478 on

July 6, 2019. See also, Kimberly Winston, "Study: atheists distrusted as much as rapists." *USA Today*, December 10, 2011. Retrieved from http://usatoday30.usatoday.com/news/religion/story/2011-12-10/religion-atheism/51777612/1 on July 6, 2019. See also Michael Stone, "Arizona woman shoots and kills atheist for not believing in God." Patheos.com, December 28, 2015. Retrieved from www.patheos.com/blogs/progressiv esecularhumanist/2015/12/arizona-woman-shoots-and-kills-atheist-for-not-believing-in-god on July 6, 2019.

33.   For a more detailed review of *God's Not Dead*, see David Kyle Johnson, "God's not dead? Neither is philosophy." *Psychology Today*, March 25, 2014. Retrieved from www.psychologytoday.com/us/blog/logical-take/201403/god-s-not-dead-neither-is-philosophy on July 6, 2019.

34.   Melena Ryzik, Cara Buckley, Jodi Kantor, "Louis C.K. is accused by 5 women of sexual misconduct." *The New York Times*, November 9, 2017. Retrieved from www.nytimes.com/2017/11/09/arts/television/louis-ck-sexual-misconduct.html on July 6, 2019.

35.   Angela Deines, "Louis CK 'SNL' monologue mocks god, doubts existence of heaven (Video)." *Newsmax*, March 31, 2014. Retrieved from www.newsmax.com/thewire/louis-ck-snl-mocks-god/2014/03/31/id/562848/ on July 6, 2019.

36.   Ibid.

37.   For a brief rundown of why one atheist thinks the best arguments for God's existence fail, see Jerry Coyne, "The 'best arguments for God's existence' are actually terrible." *The New Republic*, January 16, 2014. Retrieved form https://newrepublic.com/article/116251/best-arguments-gods-existence-dont-challenge-atheists on July 6, 2019.

38.   For more on this argument see David Kyle Johnson "The failure of Plantinga's solution to the logical problem of natural Evil." *Philo* 15 (2013), 145–157.

39.   October 11, 1975.

40.   For more on this kind of solution to the problem of natural evil, see Nancy Murphy, Robert John Russell, and William R. Stoeger (eds.), *Physics and Cosmology: Scientific Perspectives of the Problem of Natural Evil* (Vatican City: Vatican Observatory Foundation, 2007).

41.   December 13, 1997.

42.   March 28, 1987.

43.   October 26, 1996.

44.   February 5, 2011.

45.   February 24, 1990.

46.   February 21, 1987.

47.   December 23, 1987.

48.   Enid does something similar to the seemingly same character in one of her earliest sketches set at a church potluck on December 6, 1986.

49.   "The Church Lady." *Saturday Night Live Wiki*. Retrieved from http://snl.wikia.com/wiki/The_Church_Lady on July 6, 2019.

50. Tania Lombrozo, "Do you suffer from illusions of moral superiority?" *National Public Radio*, January 23, 2017. Retrieved from www.npr.org/sections/13.7/2017/01/23/511164613/do-you-suffer-from-illusions-of-moral-superiority on July 6, 2019.

51. And if you are looking at this endnote to find evidence that you might still be an exception, you're even more probably wrong.

52. Ben M. Tappin and Ryan T McKay, "The Illusion of Moral Superiority." *Social Psychological and Personality Science* 8.6 (2017), 623–631 You can download this article for free at http://journals.sagepub.com/doi/pdf/10.1177/1948550616673878.

53. Justin Tosi and Brandon Warmke, "Moral grandstanding: there's a lot of it, all of it bad." *Aeon*, May 10, 2017. Retrieved from https://aeon.co/ideas/moral-grandstanding-theres-a-lot-of-it-about-all-of-it-bad on July 6, 2019.

54. Ibid.

55. 24 January 1987.

56. "Behind the music: Sinead O'Connor," *VH1*. Season 1, Episode 128. Originally aired October 22, 2000.]

57. *Viddyms Reggae Video Vault*, "Sinead Oconner on ripping picture of the Pope – day after SNL." Recorded October 4, 1992. You can view the interview on YouTube at https://www.youtube.com/watch?v=6P0NwE9Xa2k

58. Michael Agresta, "The Redemption of Sinead O'Conner." *The Atlantic*, October 3, 2012. Retrieved from www.theatlantic.com/entertainment/archive/2012/10/the-redemption-of-sinead-oconnor/263020 on July 6, 2019.

59. Her explanation of this is complex. For more, see the aforementioned *Viddyms Reggae Video Vault* interview.

60. Mark Judge, "Does the Catholic Church owe Sinead O'Connor an apology?" *The Stream,* August 23, 2018. Retrieved from https://stream.org/catholic-church-owe-sinead-oconnor-apology/ on July 6, 2019.

61. See the aforementioned *Viddyms Reggae Video Vault* interview.

62. Tayari Jones, "There's nothing virtuous about finding common ground." *Time Magazine*, October 25, 2018. Retrieved from http://time.com/5434381/tayari-jones-moral-middle-myth/?fbclid=IwAR1YVNqP9tqwIGc-yM20E0r1avqnty0zSUvLFmMGKHwOJIpe-wi9bjj3-kc on July 6, 2019.

11

"Wayne's World" and the Philosophy of Play

Jason Holt

Many of Mike Myers' characters, both on *SNL* and in movies, take things either too seriously or too lightly. In the Austin Powers trilogy, for instance, Powers' nemesis, Dr. Evil, has no sense of humor, especially about himself, while Powers is incorrigibly amused about everything. There has been some suggestion that Dr. Evil is partly modeled on Lorne Michaels, producer of *SNL* and many *SNL*-based movies, including *Wayne's World* (1992). In what follows I'll respect the pop-cultural significance of "Wayne's World" by taking it broadly to include not just the *SNL* sketches but also the movies and various special appearances.

During Myers' tenure on *SNL* we see precedents for the too-serious Dr. Evil and the too-playful Austin Powers in two of his best and most memorable recurring-sketch characters: slick-haired, bespectacled, black leotarded "Sprockets" host Dieter, and longhaired, ballcapped, black t-shirted "Wayne's World" host, the excellent Wayne Campbell. Dieter's whole persona seems predicated on taking everything *super* seriously and deriving from this a twisted, arty enjoyment. For Dieter, all the world's a stage, a gorgeously agonized one. All the world's a stage for Wayne too, but at the opposite end of the spectrum: it's light, amusing, silly. Although Linda Richman ("Coffee Talk") and Lothar ("Lothar of the Hill People"), and even Simon ("Simon") are perhaps more nuanced in these respects, the contrast between being too serious and being too playful is in many ways the key to locating Myers' characters on the comedic stage.

In their way, Wayne and Garth (Dana Carvey) symbolize the importance of play, leisure, and fun in our lives, and in this respect touch on

Saturday Night Live and Philosophy: Deep Thoughts Through the Decades, First Edition. Edited by Jason Southworth and Ruth Tallman.

certain important aspects of applied philosophy, specifically the philosophy of play (and relatedly, the philosophy of leisure). Activities that are playful or leisurely have intrinsic value, and are intrinsically motivated, which means that they're done for fun, or, "for their own sake." Something has intrinsic value when it is valuable in itself rather than because of what it can lead to. By contrast, something has instrumental value not because of what it is but because of its consequences. Instead of extrinsic or instrumental motivation – working for a paycheck or swallowing bitter medicine – we engage in play and leisure for the sake of those activities themselves, and for the enjoyment we derive from them. We *choose* to engage in such activities, and we do so *because* they're fun. Without overplaying the philosopher, we'll think of play or leisure in terms of *intrinsically motivated elective activities*. Whatever effort (... *not!*) Wayne and Garth may put into it, doing "Wayne's World" counts as play for them, as they choose (elective) to do it (activity) for its own sake (intrinsic). And for that matter, whether we think of ourselves as participants or mere observers, we like playing along with them.

"Party Time! Excellent!"

One of the great twentieth-century philosophers who champions the lazier, more leisurely side of life is Bertrand Russell (1872–1970). One well-known brief, the title piece in a collection of essays, bears the provocative title "In Praise of Idleness."[1] There's a kind of irony in Russell being such a devotee of idleness: his writing output is among the most prolific in the history of philosophy, with some seventy-five books published during his lifetime. Toward the beginning of his essay he relates an anecdote: "Everyone knows the story of the traveler in Naples who saw twelve beggars lying in the sun (it was before the days of Mussolini), and offered a lira to the laziest of them. Eleven of them jumped up to claim it, so he gave it to the twelfth. This traveler was on the right lines."[2] One can imagine Wayne being that twelfth, or a disbelieving onlooker ("Yeah, right"). Russell continues, "I hope that, after reading the following pages, the leaders of the YMCA will start a campaign to induce young men to do nothing. If so, I shall not have lived in vain."[3] In this light, we can see Russell nodding through his pipe smoke with some approval at Wayne and Garth on their blanket-covered basement furniture.

You might think that when he writes in praise of idleness Russell is being a little tongue-in-cheek, that he can't really mean it. After all, we tend to value the very *opposite* of play, *work*, to the point that we think it a virtue. We often praise people highly for their *work ethic* – even to the point of workaholism. Even if we think of ourselves as working for the weekend, of working hard so that we can play hard ("Party on, Wayne." "Party on, Garth."), to value work not just for its instrumental value but as something valuable in itself, as a *source* of value, is deeply engrained in our culture. Though we don't usually speak of having a "play ethic" or a "leisure ethic" – as Wayne and Garth clearly have – Russell is really being quite serious. He sees danger, physical, psychological, social, and cultural danger, in both overworking and over*valuing* work. Russell praises idleness as an antidote, as a corrective, to unhealthy involvement in and attitudes toward work. He, along with other philosophers, and alongside Wayne and Garth, is a champion, over a hard work ethic, of a harder play ethic.

One of the reasons that Russell and other philosophers value the playful, leisurely side of life over work is, somewhat paradoxically, not just for the good times themselves, but for the good things that result: the parties, the headbanging rock concerts, the cable access hijinks, the street hockey games, or Stan Mikita's coffee (an often-unrecognized play on Canada's coffee shop chain Tim Hortons – that's right, no apostrophe). For Russell, the ancient Greeks "employed part of their leisure in making a permanent contribution to civilisation... Leisure is essential to civilisation, and in former times leisure for the few was only rendered possible by the labours of the many. But their labours were valuable, not because work is good, but because leisure is good."[4] Other works make such a commitment clear in their very titles. Just consider what the following titles suggest: Johan Huizinga's (1872–1945) *Homo Ludens: A Study of the Play Element in Culture* ('*homo ludens*': *playing* man, a play on '*homo sapiens*': wise man), and Josef Pieper's (1904–1997) *Leisure, the Basis of Culture*.[5] There's no doubt where Wayne, Garth, and company fall between the extreme *ludens* and *sapiens* sides of the human spectrum.

But you may be thinking, Wayne's beginning to sound like the grasshopper in Aesop's fable, the one who just played all day with his hair tucked back behind his ears under his ball cap – but the moral of that story is that the grasshopper got it wrong. Surely the ideal is *balance* between work and play, between a work ethic and a play ethic, with too much of either meaning not enough of the other, with the result that one is either dull (all work and no play) or useless (all play and no work). There's a point to this, of course, but only because of practical contingencies. For some philosophers, notably Bernard Suits (1925–2007), an ideal life for human beings would involve predominantly playing games. The title of his book, *The Grasshopper: Games, Life and Utopia*, says it all. In the preface Suits is quite clear: "The Grasshopper of this book is indeed the same Grasshopper whom Aesop made everlastingly famous as the model of improvidence. But while Aesop was content to cast this remarkable creature as the hero of a cautionary tale, he appears here as an exemplification – and articulate expositor – of the life most worth living."[6] [*smiling and nodding goofily*] Excellent.

"Dream Weaver"

In their grasshopperly way ("No way." "Way."), Wayne and Garth illustrate nicely Huizinga's theory of play. First of all, play is "a free activity standing quite consciously outside 'ordinary' life as being 'not serious,' but at the same time absorbing the player intensely and utterly."[7] It's clear how "Wayne's World" itself is a kind of play in this sense. Wayne and Garth don't have to do the show, but they do, because they want to, and it's Friday night, party time, excellent, quite apart from their viewers' (if not their own) normal workweek drudgery. Even in the relative ease in which Wayne and Garth live, it's a special time for them too. Something even as mundane as driving can become play when, say, you crank "Bohemian Rhapsody" and head-bang along when the guitar kicks in.

Play also, for Huizinga, "is an activity connected with no material interest, and no profit can be gained by it."[8] That's why the proper home of "Wayne's World" is cable access Channel 10, Aurora, Illinois, not network TV, as the movie *Wayne's World* makes painfully if comically clear. (The cable access show is publicly funded, a not-for-profit TV broadcast, and when they sign with a network to produce "Wayne's World," they end up losing both creative control and their love of the show.[9]) Play also "proceeds within its own proper boundaries of time and space according to fixed rules and in an orderly manner."[10] This applies no less to pick up street hockey and, oddly, parties than it does to "Wayne's World" broadcasts. Last of all, play "promotes the formation of social groupings" – headbangers, guitar noodlers, hockey fans, and other relevant subcultures – "which tend to surround themselves with secrecy and to stress their difference from the common world by disguise or other means" – think of the in-jokes between Wayne and Garth at outsiders' expense, the "... *not!*" and "A – sphincter says what?" fish-ins, for example.[11] More on these later.

Among Wayne and Garth's favorite kinds of play, we must acknowledge wordplay high up on the list, notably in their penchant for alternate puns on "babe" when sufficiently inspired: Wayne: "She's a robo-babe. In Latin she would be called 'babia majora'." Garth: "If she were a president she'd be Babe-raham Lincoln."[12] Another important type of play, and perhaps even an element in all forms of play, is make-believe. Pretending to sport an erection ("Schwing!") is yet one more habitual response to feminine pulchritude. Just doing their "Wayne's World" schtick, Wayne and Garth are in effect *pretending* to host a real or significant talk show, sometimes even raising intelligent questions completely out of step with the show's party atmosphere. As young kids play house, Wayne and Garth play "talk show" – and not just any talk show. With their top 10 (or 5) lists, sometimes silly camerawork ("Extreme close-up!"), poking fun at guests, and the like, they're also, more or less derivatively, playing at being David Letterman.

One of the more prominent kinds of "Wayne's World" make-believe is found in various daydream sequences ("Diddle-iddle-oo, diddle-iddle-oo"). Whether romping with Madonna in a "Justify My Love" video-inspired black-and-white sequence, beating Wayne Gretzky in one-on-one – or, counting the goalies, two-on-two – hockey, or showing up in a *Melrose Place* episode, these unapologetically adolescent daydreams would be the stuff of pop-psychological Freudian wish-fulfillment, if they weren't interspersed with peculiar slaps of reality (Madonna: "Call me, Wayne... *not!*"). Making-believe in the form of a daydream, whether making out with Madonna or besting the Great One himself, is a harmless if often private diversion. Yet Wayne's fantasies are *shared* with Garth, and the audience as well, another playful conceit. But the ultimate play here is the invariable appearance of a recognizable prop from the daydream after they've diddle-iddle-oo, diddle-iddle-oo-ed out again ("It was all a dream – or *was* it?").

"Game On!"

When we think of the word 'play,' the related term that inevitably springs to mind is 'game.' It's games that we think of as *what* we play when we play. Yet so far, I've said virtually nothing about

"Wayne's World" games, and I don't mean just street hockey (though philosophers include sports as *athletic* games in the class of games generally). We can play without playing games – just frolicking on the beach, for instance, or in a wood-paneled basement with the cameras off – but games are the form that we usually prefer our play to take. As opposed to more aimless, less structured play, games, we think, have *objects*, things we're trying to do to win, as well as *rules*, which we're supposed to follow in pursuing those objectives.

The idea that games have defining characteristics like objects and rules goes against one of the best-known arguments by one of philosophy's top rock stars ("We're not worthy!"), Ludwig Wittgenstein (1889–1951), who claims that games can't be defined: "Consider for example the proceedings that we call 'games.' I mean board-games, card-games, ball-games, Olympic games, and so on. What is common to them all?... For if you look at them you will not see something that is common to *all*, but similarities, relationships, and a whole series of them at that."[13] The idea here is that the class of games isn't held together by some kind of underlying essence, as, say, H_2O is the underlying essence of water. In Wittgenstein's view, what holds together many of the classes philosophers care about – knowledge, justice, beauty – is a set of overlapping resemblances, which means it's a mistake to try, as philosophers have tried for millennia, to give theoretical definitions of those things they care about most. Given the very radical nature of this view, more traditional-minded philosophers have replied, more or less, "Yeah, right. And monkeys might fly out of my butt."

Bernard Suits (remember him?) doesn't say anything about monkeys and butts, but he does offer the following theoretical definition: "To play a game is to attempt to achieve a specific state of affairs" – Suits calls this the *prelusory* goal – "using only means permitted by the rules... where the rules prohibit use of more efficient in favour of less efficient means... and where the rules are accepted just because they make possible such activity...."[14] In more compressed form, Suits describes playing a game as "the voluntary attempt to overcome unnecessary obstacles."[15] Although Wittgenstein would deny that all games have such goals or rules, Suits' theory can help us appreciate something we wouldn't appreciate otherwise: we may be surprised just how much "Wayne's World" fun counts as game-play, even if we aren't at all used to thinking of, or describing, such activities as games.

Sports fit particularly well into Suits' theory of games. In ice hockey, the prelusory goal or object of the game is to put the puck in the net, or to do so more times than your opponent. It makes no difference whether you're playing for the Chicago Blackhawks (Wayne's team) in the NHL (5-on-5 plus goalies) or facing off against Wayne Gretzky in daydreamland (one-on-one – Great One – plus goalies); the prelusory goal stays the same. It's also the same whatever motivates you to play, whether fun for an amateur, salary for a professional, or in the daydream, not just beating the best but winning Janet, the other Wayne's wife, in the process. It's likewise, at least as Suits sees it, the rules that *define* the game, which means that when Wayne resorts to playing dirty and breaking the rules to beat Gretzky, he's no longer playing the game at all! Other philosophers (with a "Yeah, right!") think that it's entirely possible to break the rules of a game and still win.[16] But I digress.

More important than sports to "Wayne's World" fun is wordplay, many forms of which count as not just wordplay but word *games* as well. In their classic "A – sphincter says what?" game, the prelusory goal, or object, is to get an unsuspecting target to say "What?" But the rules allow only one way of eliciting this response. You can't *ask* the target to say it, or speak in another language or so low a volume that the target says it. No, you've got to get them to say "What?" in *response* to the clear(ish) question "A sphincter says what?" and unwittingly confirm that they are, and in effect call themselves, a sphincter. As a rule of skill, this is usually done by slurring the first two words together although clearly enunciating the rest. That's why when Garth too-clearly asks the question in *Wayne's World 2*, he loses the game, for his target (Christopher Walken) is wise to the ploy. In the "… *not!*" game, the object is to have the target respond pleased at an apparent compliment (in an apparently completed sentence), only to have the sentence continued and negated, which turns the compliment into an insult. In what I'll call the "babe-x" two-player rally game, the object is to come up with alternating puns on the word "babe" when appropriately inspired ("She's the queen of Babe-ylon"), though Wayne and Garth usually tire after only one or two exchanges. Another classic is the "That's what she said" game, which was popularized on "Wayne's World" and later *The Office* (and later still, in the TV series *Archer*, became "Phrasing"). "That's what she said" apparently first beeped onto the pop-culture radar in 1975, *SNL*'s inaugural season, on "Weekend Update" with Chevy Chase.[17]

"We're Not Worthy"

Leisure and play do have a dark side, however, even if it happens to be a bangin' black t-shirted dark side. Getting back to what Russell wrote about the ancient Greeks, part of the picture is that the leisure that allowed them to make such "a permanent contribution to civilisation" was based on the fact that they were *slave-owners* whose achievements "would have been impossible under a just economic system."[18] Although we might be a little more sympathetic to Wayne and Garth, who inhabit a nebulous teens-to-twenties zone, in the following on-air exchange between Wayne and his Mom (Ana Gasteyer), the parallels between ancient Athens and 1990s Aurora are clear:

WAYNE: Hey, Mom! I'm doing a show here, okay?

MOM: Sorry, Wayne. Just doing a load of whites. On with the show. Hi, Garth. Wayne, I honestly don't understand how you manage to get everything you eat on the front of your t-shirt.

WAYNE: Uh, Mom, this is fascinating for everyone, all right? Myself, I'm enthralled. Can you go please?

MOM: All right, I get it, I get it. I'm good enough to do your laundry, but not good enough to be on [*whining*] "Wayne's World," "Wayne's World."

WAYNE: Good call, Mom. I think you have a firm grasp of our relationship.[19]

Being *too* playful also tends to make one careless, insensitive to others. It's because of a glibness he can't really help that Wayne, early on in *Wayne's World*, almost blows it with rock goddess Cassandra (Tia Carrere). When Cassandra fends off an attacker with some slick martial arts, as impressed and smitten as he is, Wayne simply can't help observing "Everybody's Kung Fu fighting" (a reference to the Carl Douglas song), which he wincingly recognizes, even while finishing it, as an offensive comment, insensitive to Cassandra's/Carrere's ethnicity. Though his regret is instant, he can't take the comment back, an outcome that could have been avoided with a hint more forethought and a dash less play.

Last, there's a downside of what otherwise is a good thing. By playing together, people in play-groups sometimes become extremely close-knit: "[T]he feeling of being 'apart together' in an exceptional situation, of sharing something important... retains its magic beyond the duration of the individual game."[20] This increased social cohesion is a good thing, of course. Think of the fun Wayne and (with him as always) Garth have in Wayne's basement during the magic of each "Wayne's World" broadcast beginning Friday night at 10:30 pm.

But the downside of drawing play-groups together is what happens to outsiders or those within the play-group who don't conform: they tend to be excluded, denigrated, ridiculed, or as Wayne says "denied." Think of the hazing rituals of secret societies or sports teams. Here's how Huizinga describes group insiders' attitude: "This is for *us*, not for 'the others.' What the 'others' do 'outside' is no concern of ours... Inside the circle... the laws and customs of ordinary life no longer count. We are different and do things differently."[21] Such treatment does seem fitting for insincere TV execs and cynical businesspeople in the "Wayne's World" world, but Wayne and Garth behave no less badly toward those like their teachers or parents (except for Garth's Mom, saved by her babe status) who try to help them and whose work makes their play possible.

There's a decent chance that, as a later teenager or early twenty-something, I might have been welcomed into the magic circle of "Wayne's World," especially since my taste ran to hard rock and ripped jeans. There's absolutely no doubt, though, that as a professor in his late forties, I couldn't be a riper target for Wayne and Garth's relentless mockery – and as I bring this chapter (of all things) to a close, I can't say I'd blame them.

Notes

1. Bertrand Russell, "In Praise of Idleness," in *"In Praise of Idleness" and Other Essays* (New York: Routledge, 2004 [1935]), 1–15.
2. Russell, "In Praise of Idleness," 1.
3. Russell, "In Praise of Idleness," 2.
4. Russell, "In Praise of Idleness," 5.
5. Johan Huizinga, *Homo Ludens: A Study of the Play Element in Culture* (Boston, MA: Beacon Press, 1950); Josef Pieper, *Leisure, the Basis of Culture*. Tr. A. Dru (New York: Pantheon, 1952).
6. Bernard Suits, *The Grasshopper: Games, Life and Utopia* (2nd Ed.) (Peterborough, ON: Broadview, 2005), 21.
7. Huizinga, *Homo Ludens*, 13.
8. Huizinga, *Homo Ludens*, 13.
9. This illustrates what a colleague and I call "the prostitution trap." See Jason Holt and Robert Pitter, "The Prostitution Trap of Elite Sport in *He Got Game*," in Mark T. Conard (ed.), *The Philosophy of Spike Lee* (Lexington: University Press of Kentucky), 19–21.

10. Huizinga, *Homo Ludens*, 13.
11. Huizinga, *Homo Ludens*, 13.
12. Mike Myers, Bonnie Turner, and Terry Turner, *Wayne's World* (Hollywood: Paramount, 1992).
13. Ludwig Wittgenstein, *Philosophical Investigations*, ed. G.E.M. Anscombe and R. Rhees, trans. G.E.M. Anscombe (Oxford: Blackwell, 1953), section 66.
14. Suits, *The Grasshopper*, 54–55.
15. Suits, *The Grasshopper*, 55.
16. See for example Craig K. Lehman, "Can Cheaters Play the Game?" in Jason Holt (ed.), *Philosophy of Sport: Core Readings* (Peterborough, ON: Broadview, 2014), 231.
17. As variously reported online. See dictionary.com. Retrieved from www.dictionary.com/e/slang/thats-what-she-said/ on May 19, 2018.
18. Russell, "In Praise of Idleness," 5.
19. "Wayne's World: Aerosmith," in *Saturday Night Live: The Best of Mike Myers* (New York: NBC Home Video, 1999), original airdate: 17 February 1990.
20. Huizinga, *Homo Ludens*, 12.
21. Huizinga, *Homo Ludens*, 12.

12

Bulls, Bears, and Beers
Da Philosophy of Super Fandom

Robin Barrett

Hello my friends, welcome to "anudder edition" of the *Blackwell Philosophy and Pop Culture Series*. If you're reading this book then there's a good chance you're a fan of *Saturday Night Live*. Today's guests will be some deep thinkers who will help us answer the question, *what is a fan?* As the philosopher Erin Tarver notes, a fan is "a special type of spectator."[1] Simply watching a sporting event or artistic performance does not make you a fan. A fan is someone who, at minimum, has an interest in a thing to such a degree that they make it a recurring part of their life. Some people are fans of music, movies, or television, but we'll be focusing on sports fans. Specifically, we'll be concerned with partisan fans, the kind who watch football for the love of a particular team, not for pure love of the game.

The Spectrum of Fandom

There is one specific group of sports fans of particular interest to me, and if you're reading this chapter, I'll assume they are of interest to you as well. Of course, I'm referring to a certain group of guys who gather at Ditka's restaurant "in the heart of Chicago," known as "Bill Swerski's Super Fans." The sketch series starred, most notably, George Wendt, Chris Farley, Mike Myers, Robert Smigel, John Goodman, and of course, Joe Mantegna. The series also featured several guest appearances by Chicago sports figures like Mike Ditka (coach of da Bears) and Michael Jordan (star of da Bulls), both of whom were frequent subjects of the show's dialogue.

Saturday Night Live and Philosophy: Deep Thoughts Through the Decades, First Edition. Edited by Jason Southworth and Ruth Tallman.
© 2020 John Wiley & Sons Ltd. Published 2020 by John Wiley & Sons Ltd.

There is a whole spectrum of fandom, but Bill Swerski and his buddies are fans of the highest order, true fanatics, *Super Fans*. They are devoted to their teams and wildly optimistic about their chances of winning. Their love of da Bears and da Bulls is rivaled only by their love of eating Polish sausages, smoking cigars, and drinking beer. It's the kind of love that can give you "a couple" heart attacks in any given week.[2] By contrast, a person with a minimal commitment who can only seem to make time to watch their teams during the biggest games would be a *casual fan*. Casual fans might like a sports team because it's a local team, or some of their friends like the team. But it's unlikely that a casual fan will spend much – if any – money and energy on this low-level interest.

Some fans have more devotion than casual fans, but aren't nearly as committed as Super Fans. We'll call these *moderate fans*. Moderate fans are the type to occasionally go out of their way to invest time and energy in the team. They'll even give up a little enjoyment in a different area for the sake of supporting their team. For example, they'll perhaps miss the opening sketch of *Saturday Night Live* to watch the last two minutes of "da Bulls" game. Moderate fans will spend money, but they won't break the bank.

Super Fans are a whole different species of fan, who invest as much time and energy as they can in their team. Super Fans acquire memorabilia and will sometimes spend more than their budget permits. They might even have *forty* years' worth of season tickets, as the Super Fans do in the sketch titled, "Bill Swerski's Super Fans: Letter About the Firing of Mike Ditka."[3]

Identity

Fans identify with each other through their shared interest, becoming a community. They wave the same banners. They support the same teams emotionally, financially, and otherwise. They also support each other through camaraderie and conversation. People who don't otherwise have much in common can make an immediate connection when they realize they are fans of the same team. For example, you might not expect the characters in "Bill Swerski's Super Fans" to get along with the characters played by Mike Myers and Dana Carvey in "Wayne's World," but you'd be wrong. Wayne and Garth would be high fiving the Super Fans at Ditka's restaurant. In addition to being

Super Fans of Aerosmith, the boys from Aurora, Illinois are also Bulls and Bears fans (not to mention the Blackhawks). Next time you watch everyone's favorite cable access show, look closely at the pennants hanging on the stairs in the basement.

Fan groups share a common identity, but they are separated by degrees of interest and commitment. A casual fan might be interested enough to go online and watch the *SNL* sketches their coworkers are talking about on Monday morning. A moderate fan would probably watch the show when it airs if they're not too tired or busy. But a Super Fan will forsake other obligations in order to catch any and every show. Beyond that, a Super Fan would own all four decades of *SNL* on limited edition, collector's series Blu Rays. And if they don't yet exist, the Super Fan will petition NBC until they do (or at least until they get a cease and desist letter).

Mobility Along the Spectrum

So how does one become a Super Fan? No one is born a Super Fan. Newborns show little interest in anything outside of the necessities of existence: food, water, sleep, moderate comfort, and so forth. But, at some point, a person has to choose their allegiance. Some kids become fans of classic shows with traditional superheroes like the "Ambiguously Gay Duo" (sketch series written by Robert Smigel and starring Stephen Colbert and Steve Carell), even though their friends might be more into sports. Differences with friends can test the real allegiance of fans. Will these kids form bonds with other kids who prefer Ace and Gary, or will they form bonds over sports to fit in with their friends?

Depending on the level of fandom, there are different directions a fan can move. Casual and moderate fans can regress, grow, or stay the same, whereas Super Fans can only regress or stay the same. There is no greater level than Super Fandom, so there is no opportunity for increase. And, while the casual fan is the lowest level of fandom, it is also possible to leave fandom altogether. So, how do these transitions occur?

When something is such a low priority in a person's life that it's merely a casual interest, it is easy for that thing to fall by the wayside and be forgotten. Eventually, a casual fan may leave fandom altogether. Some may be bandwagon fans, who will switch their allegiance to a winning team – something a Super Fan would never do!

As mentioned, moderate fans also have room for growth or regression. The team is never the most important thing for the moderate fan. Over time, an increase in commitments and restructuring of priorities may lead to a loss of interest in the team to such a degree that a moderate fan becomes a casual fan. Sometimes a moderate fan will move in the other direction, diving deeper into fandom, no longer willing to miss a game. Once content to know a few facts about the team, now they have to know every fact. They start to spend more money, acquiring all kinds of memorabilia. They may even become alienated from friends and loved ones who do not share their devotion to the team. They may eventually surround themselves with the same few people every week, at the same restaurant in Chicago, talking about the same things. Beware: this is how a moderate fan becomes the kind of Super Fan who spends Thanksgiving with fellow fans rather than family.

But how does a Super Fan revert back to moderate fandom? Have you ever seen a coach who looked like he was one whistle away from an aneurysm? No, not Coach Ditka. But for mere mortals, coaching is stressful work, and many retire early due to the strain on their health.[4] Being a Super Fan has similar effects. It's stressful knowing your team needs you. Of course, it doesn't always have to be as serious as a health issue. Maybe a special someone wants to be taken out some Saturday nights instead of watching the game, and the Super Fan decides to comply for the sake of the relationship. Really, an aversion to any number of negative consequences could ultimately drive someone away from Super Fandom. Maybe that is a good thing, at least in some cases. To grasp this, we need to ask *what are the virtues and vices of fandom?* Or maybe, first and foremost, *what are virtues and vices?*

Virtues and Vices

According to the Greek philosopher Aristotle (384–322 BC), moral virtues are at the mean between two extreme vices, excesses or deficiencies.[5] As an example, courage is a virtue, the perfect midpoint between two vices, an excess called recklessness and a deficiency called cowardice.[6] Virtues and vices usually relate to desires, and Aristotle notes that some desires are common to all of humanity. These would include things like food and drink, since everybody not only desires but also requires them. With these types of desires, the only real danger is excess – think of the vice of gluttony displayed in that restaurant in the heart of Chicago. By contrast, there are also "idiosyncratic pleasures,"[7] which are unique to some people. These pleasures get us into the realm of fandom, since not everybody is a fan of the same things. Aristotle writes, "If they enjoy some of the sorts of things one ought to enjoy, they do so more than they ought or more than most people do. That the excess with respect to the pleasures is licentiousness and is blameworthy, then, is clear."[8] Aristotle describes the vice of excess in desire as "licentiousness." By contrast, he describes the virtuous, moderate position, saying, "A person is spoken of as moderate for not being pained by the absence of pleasure and for abstaining from pleasure."[9] In summary, desiring either too much or too little of a good thing is a vice, but moderation in pleasurable things is virtuous. With this in mind, let's look at a few of the virtues and vices of fandom.

Knowledge is a virtue of fandom; some fans are veritable encyclopedias. In fact, the term "fan" originated to describe people who were so full of trivial knowledge that it would spill out into all of their speech.[10] Nerdy, know-it-all fans are sometimes mocked on *SNL*. Think, for example, of the sketch "Trekkies,"[11] in which one Trekkie, played by Kevin Nealon, seeks to impress two other Trekkies, played by Dana Carvey and Jon Lovitz, with answers to their trivia questions, such as Khan's middle name. A few moments later, Carvey asks William Shatner a ridiculous piece of trivial minutiae, "What was the combination of the safe?" Shatner, of course, scoffs at the absurdity of such a question.

According to Aristotle, it is a virtue to love that which is noble.[12] And there is nobility in athletic competition. Nicholas Dixon, a philosopher who writes on fandom, would agree with Aristotle, as he argues persuasively that athletes and other artists are worthy of admiration because "their displays of physical excellence… mental qualities… and coolness under pressure…" are "ennobling of human nature."[13] In other words, it's good to be a fan! Failing to appreciate skilled performers is a deficiency of aesthetic judgment.

Dixon points out that a certain type of fan, which he labels *partisan* fans, are loyal to individuals or entities, as opposed to being fans of the sport or entertainment medium itself.[14] This appreciation or admiration of the excellence displayed by an individual can quickly turn into an unhealthy obsession. This is the primary vice of the Super Fan, an excess of admiration that becomes obsessive devotion. Athletes and stars are often disturbed and repulsed at the obsession of some fans. For instance, in the sketch, "7 Degrees Celsius: The Fruit on the Bottom Tour,"[15] Jimmy Fallon's character, Wade from 7 Degrees Celsius, turns down an offer to go to a young man's birthday party, even though, or especially because, this young man is the president of Wade's fan club.

Phil Hartman, playing the emcee of the Star Trek convention in the sketch, "Trekkies," makes the crowd aware of a rare piece of memorabilia from an earlier convention. Some Trekkies have traveled hundreds of miles to be there. Fed up with the nonsense, Shatner tells his fans to "Get a life!... For crying out loud, it's just a TV show... Look at you, look at the way you're dressed... You've turned an enjoyable little job that I did... into a colossal waste of time... Grow the hell up!"

Being attracted to the beauty of the arts and the excellence of athletic competition is a good thing. And favoring one entertainer over another is also good. But to disdain rivals without good cause is an excess in partisan loyalty. As Dixon says, "Some partisan supporters have a hostile attitude toward rival teams and their supporters, which is indefensible, even if it never leads to any tangible harm."[16] Just because your team is not in the Super Bowl, it's not appropriate to say "Both teams look like garbage, Dad," as Beth Cahill does in the "Quiz Masters" sketch.

In the sketch, "Phil and Ricky on Super Sunday,"[17] Billy Crystal and Christopher Guest sling spirited insults, each to defend their favorite team before the big game. Partisan fans are not, however, unique to the domain of sports. Think of how Team Edward and Team Jacob divided partisan fans of the vying male leads in the *Twilight* trilogy. In the parody, "Lab Partners: Team Edward vs. Team Jacob,"[18] the characters played by Taylor Lautner and Jenny Slate not only alienated each other but their classmates as well.

Aristotle recognizes that pleasure and pain are part of life. Indeed, pleasure and pain are directly related to our character: "The pleasure or pain that accompanies someone's deeds ought to be taken as a sign of his characteristics... For moral virtue is concerned with pleasures and pain... so as to enjoy as well as to be pained by what one ought."[19] That is to say, one should enjoy that which is good; in fact, some good things are worth an appropriate amount of pain. Remember, it's the licentious person who is "pained more than he ought to be because he does not attain his pleasures."[20]

Fans can relate to this in terms of the pain of a big loss. "Weekend Update: Matt Damon and Seth Meyers on Coping with Losing"[21] features two Red Sox fans who were more than happy to offer their advice to Yankees fans after losing the World Series, establishing their credentials as "Experts in heartbreaking failure." Damon claims to have been hospitalized for a week after the Red Sox big loss in 1986. "One thing not to do, is take all of your team's paraphernalia, put it in a big pile, and light it on fire," says Meyers. Such an action would indicate an excess of pain. It's good to be sad when your team loses; it shows commitment and loyalty! It shows you truly care. But to be heartbroken, hospitalized, or destructive shows that your priorities are severely misplaced.

What Hath Athens to do with Chicago?

For bandwagon fans, that form of casual fan that will switch allegiances whenever it seems popular to do so, their relationship to their team is like being romantically involved with someone you like but don't love. Without love, it's tough to be committed and loyal. Bandwagon fans suffer from a deficiency of virtues, primarily, a lack of commitment and love. They avoid pain, but the exchange is not noble.

By contrast, Super Fans suffer from excessive commitment. Their love for the team has consumed them, as they have forsaken more tangible sources of affection in their single-minded devotion to the object of their fandom. Super Fans are committed to a fault. Commitment is good, but utter devotion to sports or other entertainment is idolatry. Loyalty is good, but the people closest to you are the ones who deserve your loyalty the most. If you miss important events and gatherings (like Thanksgiving), or push virtuous people out of your life to make room for an idol, that is unhealthy.

Moderate fans have found an identity in a community of people who share the same interests and want some of the same things. Moderate fans love their teams enough to support them, but they don't love their teams more than life itself, or more than their own family and friends. They are committed to their favorite teams, players, and performers, but they won't ignore obligations to people in their lives for the sake of the team. Moderate fans are loyal, but they are loyal to other people ahead of their teams. They can rejoice when their teams win, and they can be sad when their teams lose, but they keep their emotions balanced.

It's Good to Be a Fan if ...

It's good to be a fan, especially of *SNL*. If somebody bought this book for you but you don't know why, you're probably just a casual fan of *SNL*. If you bought this book because you like *Saturday Night Live* just enough to watch it and read about it occasionally, then you're probably safely in the moderate fan zone. If you bought this book because *Saturday Night Live* is one of the most important things in your life, then you are a Super Fan. You may be taking things too far. And if you wrote a chapter in this book, then you're definitely a lost cause. Come back to reality, because your friends and family need you.[22]

Notes

1. Erin C. Tarver, *The I in Team: Sports Fandom and the Reproduction of Identity* (Chicago, IL: University of Chicago Press, 2017), 21.
2. "Bill Swerski's super fans: thanksgiving." Aired November 23, 1991. Chris Farley's character had "a couple" heart attacks that week.
3. Aired January 1, 1993.
4. Katie Moisse, "NFL Coaching Culture Boosts Heart Risk," ABC News, November 4, 2013. Retrieved from https://abcnews.go.com/Health/nfl-coaching-culture-boosts-heart-risk/story?id=20776373 on July 6, 2019.
5. Aristotle, *Nicomachean Ethics*. Tr. Robert C. Bartlett and Susan D. Collins (Chicago: University of Chicago Press, 2011), 35, 1107a.
6. Ibid., 1107a–1107b.
7. Ibid., 1118b.
8. Ibid.
9. Ibid.
10. Tarver, *The I in Team*, 13.
11. Aired December 20, 1996.
12. Aristotle, *Nicomachean Ethics*, 1179b.
13. Nicholas Dixon, "The ethics of supporting sports teams." *Journal of Applied Philosophy* 18.2 (2001), 156.
14. Ibid., 149.
15. Aired March 11, 2000.
16. Dixon, "Ethics of supporting teams," 154.
17. Aired January 19, 1985.
18. Aired December 12, 2009.
19. Aristotle, *Nicomachean Ethics*, 1140b.
20. Ibid., 1118b.
21. Aired October 5, 2002.
22 This chapter may or may not have been written "in a van down by the river."

Part IV
AND NOW FOR OUR MUSICAL GUEST

13

Liveness and Lip-Synching
Andy Kaufman and Eminem

Theodore Gracyk

In an age where most music is both created and consumed in a recorded format, live performances often serve as a test of a musician's chops: do they really have talent? Can they deliver live, without the manipulations and corrections of studio trickery? Sometimes they cannot, and *Saturday Night Live* has been a venue in which some of the biggest stars have delivered under-rehearsed, incompetent, or uninspired performances.

Many fans thought that Eminem's 2017 performance showed that he fell into this last category: he seemed to be "washed up and old," a mere "nostalgia act" who has run out of steam.[1] However, that line of criticism is very different from the complaints that greeted his previous *SNL* performances, in 2004 and 2013, when he was widely criticized for *failing to perform*. In 2004, many viewers accused him of lip-synching "Mosh" to a prerecorded vocal track (but viewers were divided about whether he genuinely performed "Just Lose It"). In 2013, The *Daily Mail* described his *SNL* performance of "Bezerk" as miming. "While the show is called *Saturday Night Live*, it seems this particular portion of the episode may not have entirely lived up to the name," wrote show business reporter Jona Kirby. "At certain parts of the performance Eminem's mouth movements were out of time with the music."[2] Not surprisingly, many fans reacted to the appearance of lip-synching with internet posts that expressed their anger and their sense of betrayal. In both 2004 and 2013, Eminem declined to make a personal comment on the brouhaha. Instead, a spokesman came forward to say that Eminem had employed a prerecorded vocal track, but Eminem was rapping along with that track,

Saturday Night Live and Philosophy: Deep Thoughts Through the Decades, First Edition. Edited by Jason Southworth and Ruth Tallman.

to give the effect of doubling his voice. This explanation did not fly with many fans who studied the broadcast. And, to be fair, it should be noted that a number of other *SNL* musical guests have very obviously lip-synched (and been ridiculed for it). One is not entirely surprised when a flash-in-the-pan pop star lip-synchs. But one does not expect it of Eminem, whose career is based on the authenticity of his art. Faking it in performance seems antithetical to the implicit promise he makes to his audience when he performs.

My purpose is not to determine whether, or to what extent, Eminem lip-synched on *SNL* in 2004 and 2013. Instead, I want to look at the deeper question of why it would matter. I want to focus on the idea that underlies his spokesman's explanation about doubling his voice. The key idea given in Eminem's defense is that viewers who were upset were simply not understanding the *nature* of his performance.[3] Implicitly, his defense admits that lip-synching would be a fraudulent performance. However, the defense reclassifies these performances as genuine but flawed, ones in which he sometimes went silent when he should have been "doubling" the prerecorded vocal. In short, we are asked to evaluate these performances in terms of what Eminem was attempting to achieve. If this is an essential criterion for evaluating performance – and I think it is – then we have uncovered an important rule about performances: we cannot evaluate a performance unless we know what the performer is trying to achieve.[4] And that, in turn, permits a surprising flexibility about live performance: lip-synching on *SNL* is not contrary to its identity as a live broadcast. That, in any case, is what I intend to demonstrate. However, to see why this is the case, we must examine what it is that makes for the "liveness" of live performance.

The Argument that *SNL* Is Not Live

What makes *Saturday Night Live* "live"?

Although not a radical programming innovation, the first seasons of *SNL* were noteworthy for their commitment to a renewal of live television. In the early, so-called "golden age" of television, live broadcasting was the norm. As late as 1964, America's introduction to Beatlemania was a live appearance on the Ed Sullivan Show. Dan Aykroyd remembers the thrill of the unexpected, real-time revelation: "'Oh man, I remember that Sunday night, we didn't know what had hit us – just sitting there watching Ed Sullivan's show. Up until then there were jugglers and comedians ... and, then, suddenly! The Beatles."[5] The first time I felt a similar frisson watching *SNL* itself was in December 1977, when Elvis Costello suddenly cut off "Less Than Zero," a tune familiar from his debut album. He apologized – "I'm sorry ladies and gentlemen, there's no reason for me to do this song here" – and then launched into a vitriolic new song, "Radio Radio." When he got to the line "I wanna bite the hand that feeds me," there was no mistaking his intention: *SNL* was live, and there was nothing they could do about his anti-commercial gesture unless they wanted to black out the broadcast. By that point in the 1970s, television was almost exclusively "canned" or prerecorded and such moments were almost unknown. As punishment for his open rebellion, Costello was not invited back for more than a decade.

Many claims are made about the special nature of live performance, and about special relationship it constructs between the performer and the real-time, face-to-face audience.[6] Consequently, there is an important strain of thought in the area of performance studies that contends that Aykroyd did not watch the Beatles perform in 1964, and that I did not see Costello perform on *SNL* in 1977. We did not see them perform, it is argued, because only the audience that is present in the room is experiencing the performance. A performance is a communicative interaction of performer and audience who are co-present to one another during the performance.[7] Aykroyd was not co-present in the room with the Beatles in 1964, so he was not a party to the performance. When we watch television and use other mass media as our mode of access, we interact with a piece of technology: the performers are not present to us. Consequently, we cannot intervene and change the course of the performance, as I once did with T-Bone Burnett in 1984 when he was opening for Elvis Costello. I called out a request from the balcony, to which Burnett responded by offering an alternative song that was not planned for that night's setlist. Calling out requests to a television set in the 1970s and 1980s had no such effect: they were not voice-activated. In short, because live performance requires co-presence, the standard account of performance tells us that *nothing* we see on television is a performance, much less a "live" one. The only Eminem fans who had a right to feel cheated by his *SNL* performances in 2004 and 2013 were those who were present in the studio audience, for they were the only ones to whom he delivered a performance.

According to the foregoing account of performance, the expectations of co-presence and simultaneity are related to the essential uniqueness, and hence unrepeatability and *ephemerality*, of live performance. Anyone can go on the internet and view recordings of Eminem's *SNL* performances, and I expect that when I get to my next example, Andy Kaufman, some readers will stop reading in order to view the video evidence. But here again, a traditional analysis of performance emphasizes that these will be viewings of playbacks of recordings and so not really viewings of performances at all.[8] Recordings do not let us view performances, and live broadcasts do not, either. They are merely simulations of "real events." On these grounds, it does not matter what Eminem did or did not do when appearing on *SNL* in relation to those who were watching their television screens: it's all just a simulation of performance, anyway.[9]

So, given these ideas about live performance, *SNL* never shows live performances when they broadcast live. Which just seems kooky to me! I am not of the opinion that it is only "live" in the limited sense that it is "filmed before a live audience." What adjustments should we make this analysis of performance?

What Is Required to View a Performance?

I do not think that someone has to be co-present with a performance in order to be part of the audience for that performance. When Charlie Chaplin stood in front of a movie camera and twirled his cane and did his comic, waddling walk, his audience was not the film director and the camera crew. His audience was the millions who would later pay a nickel each to see his projected image in the movie theater. Chaplin gave a performance-on-film, and the fact that the audience could not interact with him, as had the earlier audiences who saw him in vaudeville theater, does not mean he was not performing when he was before a movie camera. Two things matter here. First, what is required to view a performance, if co-presence is not part of the equation?[10] Second, and more fundamentally, what does it mean to perform, so that there is a performance to view?

Suppose I am sitting in an airport, waiting for my flight, and I notice that someone who is walking past me has a gait like Charlie Chaplin in his "Little Tramp" films. We are co-present and I am entertained. However, it does not follow that I am the audience for a performance. I am not viewing a performance unless the person I'm watching is walking that way intentionally and is doing so *in order to* entertain people who see it. In other words, I'm only viewing a performance if the person is putting on a "show" for me. Or, to use the language of Paul Thom, I am only viewing a performance if the person is doing what they are doing *for an audience*.[11] The action of the performer becomes a full-fledged performance when an audience attends to it. As Francis Sparshott puts it, "To be a performance is to be the object of an isolating act of attention."[12]

There is no good reason why the act of attention cannot be mediated by technology, such as a recording or a television broadcast. Before music concerts in large venues began to show close-ups of the performers on large screens flanking the stage, it was common for audience members to bring binoculars to rock concerts in sports stadiums. Before that, it was common for opera fans to own "opera glasses" (small binoculars), and cheap disposable ones were sold in the lobby at opera performances for audience members who did not own them. No one will say that looking through opera glasses during *Madame Butterfly* means that one is no longer viewing the opera performance. And, Kendall Walton argues, it makes no sense to deny that one is seeing it if one is viewing the unedited products of film technology.[13] Enhanced and delayed viewing does not cancel out the fact that we see and hear what has been recorded. And even if one adopts the more complex view that photographs and films and sound recordings are more like paintings and drawings, producing *representations* of what they show us, there is still a significant difference between camera-derived representations and hand-produced representations. Unless they are edited afterwards in some form of post-production, camera-derived representations have a degree of epistemic or evidential access that cannot be assumed to be present in hand-produced representations. There is no reason to think that Rembrandt's painting of the Holy Family resting while fleeing into Egypt looks anything like the reality of it. He interprets the episode in visual terms that will be familiar to his audience: his painting features northern Europeans in a European landscape. To use Rembrandt's painting as evidence of what they actually looked like, or what their journey looked like, would be a terrible blunder. However, had there been photography two thousand years ago and had someone snapped a photo of the Holy Family as they fled to Egypt, then that photo would certainly *allow us to see*, in a way that paintings do not, what was to be seen at that moment. And, of course, unedited video footage would be even better!

The upshot of accepting the legitimacy of technologically-mediated viewing is that being a member of the audience for a performance is not simply, nor even primarily, a matter of being present at the performance. It is mainly a matter of audience attention. (The term "audience," after all, derives from the Latin verb for hearing: the audience for music is restricted to those who actually hear the music.) We all know that physical attendance does not always correlate with attending to what is happening on stage. And this is not a recent phenomenon. Music historians tells us that early opera performances were largely social events, as attendees spent most of their time turned away from the stage, largely indifferent to the performance: "conversation, business dealings, political meetings, and amorous assignations constituted the normal activity of audience members, as did eating and drinking, circulating, gambling, and receiving acquaintances in one's boxes."[14] Most audience members only directed their attention to the opera sporadically, or when a star performer had a featured number. So, rather than physical presence, one becomes a member of the audience for a specific performance by giving ongoing attention to what is presented for attention.

On my view, technological enhancements change *how* we can attend to what is performed, not *whether* we attend to it. Technological mediation is a perfectly respectable method for attending to something. The fact that binoculars did not exist during the first two and a half centuries of opera does not imply that it's improper to view a Mozart opera with opera glasses. And if I am not disqualified from watching a performance of Mozart's *Così fan tutte* because I use opera glasses, there is no reason, in principle, to deny the use of other kinds of mediation. For pragmatic reasons, amateur astronomers will view the moon through a telescope during a lunar eclipse. No one denies that they have seen the eclipse. Likewise, technological mediation allowed televised viewing of Eminem's *SNL* performances of 2004 and 2013, and – provided that the videotape was not altered in the interim – technological mediation allowed viewers on the west coast to view the performance when it was later rebroadcast to the Pacific time zone. It is also consistent with the sense of "attending to a performance" that I am pursuing to say that I used the YouTube website to have another look at his performances of "Mosh" and "Bezerk." In fact, because the video was created in conjunction with its live television broadcasts, it is very likely that I have much better audio-visual access to it than did some of the people seated in the back row of the balcony in the New York studio on the night of the performances. *SNL* performances are designed to be viewed via the mediation of television, and their "live" status is a function of their initial broadcast to remote viewers in real time, rather than because there are people physically present where the performances take place.

Framing

There is an aspect of Sparshott's description of what it is to be a performance that requires further elaboration before we can return to the topic of lip-synching. One of the essential characteristics of performance is that performances *frame* human action for an audience.[15] To borrow a phrase from David Davies, the framed event or object is a "focus of appreciation," which is the relevant subset of perceivable aspects of artistic activity.[16] Consider the analogy of a painting's frame, where the frame is a physical enclosure that marks the limit of the object offered for appreciation. Suppose that I happen to be in New York's Museum of Modern Art at just the right time, and Henri Matisse's *The Piano Lesson* (1916) – one of my favorite artworks – is being taken off the wall for shipment, and I get an opportunity to look at the backside of the canvas. What I see there might be of considerable historical interest, but it is not a part of the painting intended for audience appreciation: it is (literally) not what has been framed for observation. Similarly, performance traditions have culturally-specific means of indicating what action the audience should take notice of, and when they should and should not do so.[17] Most obviously, there is the physical stage itself, as the place where the performance happens. However, the stage is not decisive. George Dickie offers the example of the presence of stagehands who appear on stage to move property and scenery during a performance of traditional Chinese theater. According to the operative conventions, these actions are observable by the audience and yet they are not presented to the audience for their attention.[18] Like an equipment "roadie" who runs onto the stage to hand a musician a different guitar, making possible the next stage of the performance, the observable action of the equipment crew member is not itself part of the performance. Neither one is framed *for the audience*. Furthermore, some of the onstage actions of *performers* do not count as performance. In a standard string quartet, there are short breaks between the four movements, during which members of the quartet often retune their instruments. Although onstage and visible and audible, this activity of tuning the instruments is not part of the performance.

We see, therefore, that onstage activity may contribute to a performance without counting as an aspect of that performance. And *offstage*
activity is sometimes part of the performance, too. Many traditions of
puppet theater keep all human action out of sight. Nonetheless, the
puppeteers are the performers. Similarly, the orchestra is hidden from
the audience at the Bayreuth *Festspielhaus*, the concert hall constructed
for presentation of Richard Wagner's "Ring" opera cycle. In this case,
the musicians are classified as performers of the music that they contribute during a performance of Wagner's *Götterdämmerung*. Yet the
stage manager, also unseen and making no less vital a contribution, is
not considered a performer.

Following Davies, the decision about which contributing activity
does and does not count as part of a particular performance depends
on audience awareness that real-time *framing* activity is itself a focus
of appreciation within performance practice.[19] It is not simply a matter of *which actions* are framed. Some of the performers' actions are
acts of framing that direct attention to other actions as content for
viewing. In short some actions undertaken by performers have the
function of signaling which performance activity does and does not
count *as* performance activity, as part of what the audience should
appreciate.

In other words, part of viewing a performance is attending to what
the performers do so that we, the audience, will attend to what is
important to attend to at any given point in the performance. For
example, when a performance involves two or more performers, their
activity of coordinating and adjusting their actions to one another is
a relevant focal point for audience attention. But there are times when
we should *not* attend to the actions of all the performers with equal
attention. In concerts and theater productions, lighting is frequently
used to spotlight one performer, "backgrounding" others who remain
on stage. Here, the framing is done by an offstage technician. But in
"traditional" presentations of older plays, this technology was not
available, and the performers had to take action to generate a parallel
framing of attention. For example, there is a key scene in Act 5 of
Shakespeare's *The Tragedy of King Lear* where the insane king tells
his daughter Cordelia that she should join him in prison. Shakespeare
does not give Cordelia any lines to say in response to the king's mad
interpretation of events. A director of *King Lear* has to make a decision about the silent presence of the character of Cordelia during
these twenty-some lines of dialogue. What should the actress who
plays Cordelia *do* during this time? Is she part of the action, or

removed from it? For example, does the actress turn her back to the audience, so that we cannot see her face, or does she move off to the side of the stage, or does she face the audience and convey an emotional response to Lear? If the latter, will it be pity? Will it be anguish? In just the same way that the subsequent exit of Lear and Cordelia reframes what happens next, the actress' physical orientation on stage just prior to that exit is an important bit of framing. It tells the audience whether to attend to Lear while ignoring Cordelia, or to attend to Lear but also to Cordelia's response to Lear.

In short, not everything that happens on stage during a performance has the same function in the performance, and some of it does not count as part of what is performed. Only some of the visible activity is placed "in the frame," while other activity contributes to the active process of framing other elements for the audience to appreciate as performed activity.[20]

Let us apply these observations to lip-synching. Building on his spokesman's admission that his performance included a prerecorded vocal track, there are two ways to evaluate Eminem's *SNL* performances of 2004 and 2013. One interpretation is the one that angered viewers: Eminem was *merely* lip-synching "Mosh" and "Bezerk." He was intentionally framing activity that did not take place on the *SNL* stage as taking place there and then, deceiving the audience about the relationship between what they saw and heard. He was creating a virtual performance while presenting it to the audience as a non-virtual performance.[21] Based on normal audience expectations about performance, together with the framing cues offered on that occasion, Eminem was aiming to deceive. A second interpretation of "Mosh" and "Bezerk" is more charitable: he was attempting to double his voice with a prerecorded vocal (as his spokesman claimed), but he did a bad job of it. He did a bad job of it in two distinct ways: he often failed to coordinate his "live" vocal with the prerecorded track, as intended, and he failed to frame what he was doing in a way that would allow his audience to understand and appreciate his performance intentions and the resulting focal point for audience attention. On the first interpretation, he did not perform "Mosh" and "Bezerk" on those occasions. On the second interpretation, he gave a bad performance.

Had he instead opted to present lip-synching *as* lip-synching, Eminem might have given a great performance. After all, it had been done during the very first broadcast of *SNL*, and it was done to great acclaim.

Andy Kaufman Lip-synchs

During the premier broadcast of *Saturday Night Live* (October 11, 1975), Andy Kaufman was introduced to the audience as a "musical guest," a crucial bit of framing. He then gave a brief performance in the persona of "Foreign Man."[22] Because it was his first performance on network television, few viewers knew what to expect.

Kaufman strides onto the stage and stands beside a small table that holds a phonograph. Looking at the audience, he freezes, his eyes widen, and he betrays near-panic. Taking control of himself, he turns to the phonograph and places the stylus on the record. For those of us who are old enough, we immediately recognize the theme song of the Mighty Mouse cartoon program. "Foreign Man" stands frozen as the song plays.[23] Suddenly, as the song reaches the triumphant line of "Here I come to save the day!", he raises one arm in a grand, sweeping gesture, and lip-synchs the one line. The audience bursts into laughter and then applauses, and he goes silent as the song continues into the next verse. The fingers of his left hand twitch nervously. As the song approaches the key line again, he opens his mouth prematurely, realizes his mistake, and hangs his head in shame. He shakes it off, and as the record approaches the line again, he repeats the arm gesture and successfully lip-synchs it. The song continues and he calms himself with a sip of water from a glass on the table beside the phonograph. The audience, now understanding the joke, laughs and applauds as he drinks. The third and final time that the song reaches "Here I come to save the day!", he lip-synchs again, and the audience goes wild with applause.

What is the performance here? It is essential to recognize that although it includes lip-synching, he is not *merely* lip-synching. By laughing and applauding, the studio audience is not merely responding, in Samuel Johnson's famous line, to a performance "not done well; but you are surprised that it is done at all."[24] After all, who would applaud a sip of water? It may have taken a few moments, but the audience recognized quickly that Kaufman was performing a character, and he did it well. He performed a character who is so lacking in talent that all he can do is lip-synch, and who barely gets that right due to his (performed) stage fright.[25] In the process, lip-synching is initially performed and mocked, but then ultimately transformed. The character is so determined, so earnest, that a performance that begins from the premise that lip-synching could never be a legitimate performance is transformed when the sketch suggests that it is harder than it looks: the very act of performing is an act of bravery. By the end, lip-synching is a triumphant entertainment.

Within the Mighty Mouse piece, Kaufman pretends to set the bar for his own performance at a ridiculously low level. Anyone can stand beside a phonograph and lip-synch, and such a "performance" is so lacking in originality that there is no point to doing it for an audience. That judgment is encouraged by the way that Kaufman sets things up, with faked ineptitude and nervousness. But then the piece invites the audience to reconsider. For example, when the audience was waiting for the performer to start the performance, hindsight recognizes that the performance had already begun. As it dawns on the audience that onstage actions that should be "out of frame" are actually being performed, as acts meriting audience attention, the baseline assumptions about what has been framed for appreciation is challenged, interrogated, and then reversed. Although the announcement that it is a musical performance frames the lip-syncing as the primary action of interest, the lip-syncing is not the only activity that satisfies Sparhsott's description of performance as "the object of an isolating act of attention." The *whole piece* is the true object of attention: Kaufman's other actions onstage (the bug-eyed look, the twitching hand, the pretense of shame) reframe our understanding of that action. In other words, onstage actions that would normally be framed as non-performance inessentials are actually framed as cues to the complex interpretation of a seemingly inane performance.

In an important respect, Kaufman was a philosophical performer, raising philosophical questions with his art. During the *SNL* premier, he was bringing the technique of Andy Warhol to the television-viewing masses. In 1964, Warhol famously confronted the artworld by filling an art gallery with his recreations of Brillo boxes – the cardboard cartons in which a commercial product was shipped to stores. The Warhol *Brillo Box* was a three-dimensional variation of the huge silkscreened canvasses of Campbell's soup can labels that he produced in 1962. In each case, Warhol straightforwardly copied a design that someone else had created. Since these unoriginal objects were nonetheless artworks, Warhol's apparent lack of creativity was a vehicle for questioning our expectations about creativity in art.[26] During the *SNL* premiere, Kaufman was similarly using live performance to question the very nature of live performance.

The genius of Kaufman's performance is, in large part, that it motivates the audience to laugh *with* him and not merely *at* him, a distinction that he raised directly in the persona of "Foreign Man" during his second appearance on *SNL*. To laugh with him, we have to understand that the sketch involves no deception. He intends to lip-synch, the sketch frames his lip-synching as his key intention, and then he successfully synchronizes his mouth and his arm gesture with the sounds coming from the phonograph. He has, in fact, given the live performance that he frames as the relevant object of focal attention. At the same time, the performance – and our scrutiny of it – is absurd in its (seeming) pointlessness. Thus, by presenting something that involves almost no skill, the sketch foregrounds the issue of what we, the audience, expect from a live performance. At the same time, the framing of the lip-synching as a performance-within-a-performance makes it clear that Kaufman (rather than the character he plays) wants to highlight its performativity and liveness. The additional measure of Kaufman's genius, then, is his ability to make us aware that we are an audience, and our attending to his actions is as important as his actions. If his action of lip-synching is absurd, then so is our action of attending to it. Unless, of course, you are one of the audience members who has not moved on from its misleading framing and who does not grasp his full intentions, in which case his lip-synching comes across as an embarrassing display: we can only laugh *at* him.

So, basically, Eminem's *SNL* presentations of "Mosh" and "Bezerk" are Kaufman's "Mighty Mouse" piece minus the frame that raises the philosophical issues. Offering no larger frame and no indication of more complex intentions, Eminem's *SNL* performances of "Mosh" and "Bezerk" offer the audience little or nothing to appreciate. Depending on what you think he intended to do, he either did not give a live performance, or he gave a bad live performance. Kaufman, in contrast, used lip-synching to give a great live performance.

Notes

1. James Draper, "'Washed up and old!': Eminem is SLAMMED on social media for bizarre *SNL* performance." *Mirror*, November 20, 2017. Retrieved from www.mirror.co.uk/3am/celebrity-news/washed-up-old-eminem-slammed-11553398 on July 28, 2018.
2. Joan Kirby, "Did Eminem lip-sync on *SNL*?" *Daily Mail*, November 4, 2013. Retrieved from www.dailymail.co.uk/tvshowbiz/article-2487366/Eminem-accused-miming-way-performance-Saturday-Night-Live.html on July 28, 2018.

3. This defense is independent of the point, frequently made, that almost every "live" event now incorporates some kind of mediating technology. See Philip Auslander, *Liveness* (London and New York: Routledge, 1999), 24.

4. For more on this point, see Stephen Davies, "So, you want to sing with the Beatles? Too Late!" *The Journal of Aesthetics and Art Criticism* 55 (1997), 129–137.

5. Quoted by Paul McCartney in The Beatles, *The Beatles Anthology* (San Francisco: Chronicle Books, 2000), 119.

6. For example, see Graham McFee, *Understanding Dance* (New York: Routledge, 1992), 88–89.

7. For example, Marco De Marinis, *The Semiotics of Performance, trans.* Áine O'Healy (Bloomington: Indiana University Press, 1993), 50, following Tadeusz Kowzan, *Literature et Spectacle* (Hague: Mouton, 1975). See also Peggy Phelan, *Unmarked: The Politics of Performance* (London and New York: Routledge, 1993), 146.

8. See David Osipovich, "What is a theatrical performance?" *The Journal of Aesthetics and Art Criticism* 64 (2006), 461–470, and Paul Thom, *For an Audience: A Philosophy of the Performing Arts* (Philadelphia, PA: Temple University Press, 1993), 3.

9. See Auslander, *Liveness*, 22.

10. When I say "view," it should be understood that much of the experience is auditory. We can hear a music performance we did not attend by listening to a recording of that performance.

11. Historically, Thom's directedness criterion was linked to a co-presence criterion, but I will argue below that these two features have no essential relationship to one another.

12. Francis Sparshott, *The Theory of the Arts* (Princeton, NJ: Princeton University Press, 1982), 41.

13. Kendall L. Walton, "Transparent pictures: on the nature of photographic realism." *Critical Inquiry* 11 (1984): 246–277. For a short, clear summary of Walton's position and the ensuing debate about it, see Katherine Thomson-Jones, *Aesthetics and Film* (London: Bloomsbury, 2008), ch. 2.

14. Georgia Cowart, "Audiences," in Helen M. Greenwald (ed.) *The Oxford Handbook of Opera* (Oxford: Oxford University Press, 2014), 666–684, at 668.

15. Framing of an event for an audience is explicit in the definition of theater offered by Paul Woodruff and in definitions of "performance" advanced by Elin Diamond and Richard Bauman. See Woodruff, *The Necessity of Theater: The Art of Watching and Being Watched* (Oxford: Oxford University Press, 2012), 38; Elin Diamond, *Performance and Cultural Politics* (New York: Routledge, 1996), 1; Richard Bauman, "Performance," in Richard Bauman (ed.), *Folklore, Cultural Performances, and Popular*

Entertainments (Oxford: Oxford University Press, 1992), 41. It also plays an important role for Richard Schechner, *Performance Theory* (London and New York: Routledge, 2003), 15–18, 105.

16. Davies, *Art as Performance*, 26 and 50.

17. See Hamilton, *The Art of Theater*, 201–204; see also the discussion of tuning versus playing within the scope of musicking in Theodore Gracyk, *On Music* (New York: Routledge 2013), 45–47.

18. George Dickie, *Art and the Aesthetic: An Institutional Analysis* (Ithaca, NY: Cornell University Press, 1974), 87–88.

19. Specifically, this framing activity is part of any artist's or performer's "intentionally guided generative performance," or, in other words, their creative activity of generative contextualized communication (Davies, *Art as Performance*, 98). I endorse a great deal of Davies's view, but stop short of the excessively revisionist conclusion that Matisse's generative performance *is* the work of art, rather than the completed canvas. See Amie L. Thomasson, "Debates about the Ontology of Art: What are We Doing Here?" *Philosophy Compass* 1 (2006): 245–255.

20. Based on the ideas I have advanced here, I offer the following set of features as the necessary and sufficient conditions for being a performance. A performance is (1) an individual or group action, (2) of some particular duration, during which (3) the intention-guided activity aims to generate an observable event, during which (4) the generative activity of framing the focus of appreciation for an audience is itself offered for observation and appreciation for the duration of the generative act, and (5) the observable generative activity exhibits an acquired skill.

21. A virtual performance is one that falsely depicts temporal relationships among perceptible generative acts. However, virtual performance is not a deceptive practice when its virtual status is not hidden or denied. A nice example of nondeceptive virtuality is Fred Astaire's "Bojangles of Harlem" dance at the end of the movie *Swing Time* (1936). The stage is lit so that Astaire casts three huge shadows on the stage background as he dances, but then the element of virtual performance is suddenly revealed when, 80 seconds along, Astaire throws out his arms and crouches, frozen for a few seconds, while the three shadows remain upright, tap dancing. He is dancing to prerecorded shadows, which alters audience appreciation when the synchronization resumes.

22. Kaufman's performance methods are discussed by Philip Auslander, "Comedy, mediatization, resistance: Andy Kaufman and Sandra Bernhard," *Presence and Resistance: Postmodernism and Cultural Politics in Contemporary Performance* (Ann Arbor: University of Michigan Press, 1994), 139–167.

23. Kaufman had performed this skit in his nightclub appearances. There, it was clearly within the context of a performance of "Foreign Man": he introduced it with the line "but right now I will like to do for you de

music record," setting up audience surprise that "music record" was what he actually meant, and not one of the characters' language errors. Kaufman performed a seven-minute skit as "Foreign Man" on *SNL* in November, 1975.

24. James Boswell, *The Life of Samuel Johnson, LL.D.* (London: John Sharpe, 1830), 140.

25. An obvious antecedent for what Kaufman has created is the play-within-a-play at the end of Shakespeare's *A Midsummer Night's Dream*.

26. For an extended reflection on Warhol's accomplishment, see Arthur C. Danto, *Beyond the Brillo Box: The Visual Arts in Post-Historical Perspective* (Berkeley and Los Angeles: University of California Press, 1992).

Part V
WEEKEND UPDATE

14

I Hate Applause
Norm Macdonald and Laughter

Jeremy Fried

I was tempted to write this introduction as though it were my opening monologue as host of an episode of *Saturday Night Live*, but that seemed like it might aim at laughter and end up in the realm of silence. That said, I think we have a great chapter prepared for you tonight and your favorite musical guest is here, as soon as you put on some reading music.

Many people who were *SNL* fans in the 1990s recall the firing of Norm Macdonald as a watershed moment. What exactly went down and why has been the subject of many a long-winded conversation. Sometimes, the best way to answer one question is to ask some others. In this case, we'll be asking some questions about humor. Why do we try to make each other laugh? What is our goal? What response are we trying to produce? In exploring theories about why we employ humor, we just might be able to discover the motivations behind Macdonald's firing.

Buh-Bye: The Firing of Norm Macdonald

Norm Macdonald's firing surprised the original "Update" anchor, Chevy Chase, who claims Macdonald as his favorite anchor other than himself. It surprised David Letterman, who had to confirm that Macdonald wasn't performing some Andy Kaufman-esque routine when Macdonald came on *Late Night with David Letterman* only a few days after the firing to discuss it with the host.[1] And it surprised me, an avid watcher of *Saturday Night Live* and fan of Macdonald's decidedly odd sense of humor with frequent, sometimes inexplicable,

Saturday Night Live and Philosophy: Deep Thoughts Through the Decades, First Edition. Edited by Jason Southworth and Ruth Tallman.

references to Sylvester Stallone's lesser-known brother, you guessed it – Frank Stallone, and Germans' love of *Baywatch* star, David Hasselhoff.

Speculation ran rampant, both at my school lunch table and in Hollywood entertainment circles, about what led to Macdonald's firing. During the interview with Letterman, Macdonald stated that Don Ohlmeyer, an NBC executive, had fired him because he "wasn't funny."[2] Macdonald said that was even worse news than finding out he'd been fired. Nonetheless, Norm said Ohlmeyer was a good man and refused to offer any more details. This account didn't sound right to many people, especially Macdonald's fans. He's hilarious, so there had to be another explanation.

One popular explanation was that Ohlmeyer fired Macdonald for frequently targeting O.J. Simpson, Ohlmeyer's personal friend. James Downey, the producer and co-writer of Macdonald's version of "Weekend Update" supported this explanation.[3] However, this account doesn't add up. Simpson was also a constant target for the hosts of NBC's weeknight comedy shows, Jay Leno and Conan O'Brien, and neither drew Ohlmeyer's ire. David Letterman's alternative explanation was blunt: Don Ohlmeyer is an idiot.[4]

Years later, Macdonald offered a different assessment of his firing in an oral history of *Saturday Night Live*, saying that it came down to a philosophical disagreement between NBC management and himself about the goal of "Weekend Update." From Macdonald's perspective, the management wanted audience approval.

> Ohlmeyer and his crew thought every joke in "Update" should kill, and the audience should be clapping and cheering and stuff. They thought Jay Leno did that every night with his monologues, so why couldn't we do it one night for five minutes, where it would just be wall-to-wall laughter and applause?[5]

Macdonald's own view of what "Weekend Update" should do was completely different.

> My response was, I hate applause. I don't like an audience applauding because to me that's like a cheap kind of high. They kind of control you. They're like, "Yeah, we agree." That's all they're doing, saying they agree with your viewpoint. And while you can applaud voluntarily, you can't laugh voluntarily – you have to laugh involuntarily – so I hate when an audience applauds. I don't want to say things that an audience will agree with. I don't want to say anything that an audience already thinks.[6]

NBC management wanted cheerleaders and instead they had a Debbie Downer on their hands. Macdonald thinks that it was ultimately these divergent visions about what "Update" should do that led to his removal from the anchor chair. "'Update' was never a big pep rally when I was there. It was never a big party. So I think the network started going, 'It doesn't seem like as much fun as it should be.'"[7] It turns out that David Letterman was wrong. Ohlmeyer wasn't an idiot; he just didn't agree with Macdonald's philosophy of comedy. From Ohlmeyer's perspective, the whole point of a joke is to make people happy, and on that count, Macdonald wasn't delivering, or at least wasn't delivering enough.

Yeah, That's the Ticket: The Goals of Comedy

Most discussion in philosophy of humor focuses on what makes something funny. There have been countless efforts to identify necessary and sufficient conditions for comedy, and thus far, all attempts to identify these magical ingredients that could turn someone from a mere featured player into a superstar have failed.

However, there's a lot more to humor than just WHAT makes something funny. There's also the question of WHY make something funny.[8] This why question is, in essence, asking what the goal of comedy is. Why create comedy? Part of the reason that less attention has been paid to this question is that on its face, the answer seems obvious. The kneejerk intuition is that the reason we tell jokes is to make people laugh.[9] Yet, things are not as simple as they appear to be on the surface. Even Macdonald's own answer is more nuanced than merely wanting to make people laugh, and Don Ohlmeyer certainly didn't think that "Weekend Update" shouldn't be making people laugh. Fully exploring the positions of the conflicting parties alongside some philosophical theories of humor should help answer a burning question: was Norm Macdonald right to hate applause as a response to his "Weekend Update" jokes?

No One Can Resist My Schweddy Balls: Involuntary Reactions

When Macdonald talks about the laughter he aims for with his comedy, he's actually talking about a distinct subset of laughter. To think about this more clearly, I want to offer some categories of laughter.[10] Macdonald's goal is *involuntary laughter*, that is, laughter that the person cannot help but respond with upon hearing the joke. A paradigm example of this kind of laughter occurs when the actors "break" character and laugh during the sketch in which they are performing. Jimmy Fallon was notorious for breaking, such that Will Ferrell and Rachel Dratch made it the goal of their "Love-Ahs" sketch.[11] However, some have accused Fallon of breaking intentionally, thus falling into *faux laughter*. Macdonald would have no use for this kind of faux laughter.

Macdonald doesn't just require that laughter be involuntary. He also implicitly identifies *approving laughter* or *knowing laughter* as outside the scope of his goals. He does not want to say anything that the audience already approves of or anything that the audience already thinks. Approving laughter is the kind that accompanies something that you tacitly endorse. Imagine, for example, the laughter coming from a group of teenagers as one of their peers spray paints their name on a building.

Ernie Kurtz, a contemporary American historian known especially for his work about Alcoholics Anonymous, identified *knowing laughter* as the kind that responds to a joke that you already know but still enjoy.[12] Imagine, for example, the type of laughs you might hear at an A.A. meeting when someone describes a difficult but comic experience that everyone in the room has personally endured in some form.

Macdonald associates these types of laughter with the applause that he hates because he views them as voluntary reactions to jokes. When people laugh approvingly or knowingly they are not having a purely involuntary response. By contrast, Macdonald sees the goal of "Weekend Update" as making the audience break into fits of laughter, whether they want to or not. For Norm, this meant taking risks and not pandering to expectations.

Party On! Voluntary Celebration

Ohlmeyer had a different view of laughter. For him, the goal of comedy is approval in the form of laughter or applause – voluntariness doesn't matter. Ohlmeyer says that one of the reasons he fired Macdonald is that he would watch the tapes of "Update" segments and "hear crickets."[13] Macdonald would rather be met with this silence than pander to the audience merely to avoid it. Ohlmeyer, by contrast, believed that giving the audience what they want is key.

> I think what you have there…is the quintessential issue. When *Saturday Night Live* is really good, they do care what the audience thinks. And when *Saturday Night Live* is not really good, they're kind of doing it for themselves and their pals. That was what I felt was the weakness of "Weekend Update" at that time, which is that they were doing it for themselves.[14]

As Ohlmeyer sees it, the goal of both the overall show and "Weekend Update" should be to please the audience. Indeed, Ohlmeyer characterizes Macdonald's insistence on genuine laughter as selfishness, an unwillingness to take the audience into consideration. Macdonald put his own priorities ahead of what was best for the show.

We can see what Ohlmeyer thought was best for *SNL* by considering how the show changed while he had a controlling hand. Recurring characters have always been a part of *Saturday Night Live*, but the frequency of their appearances increased under Ohlmeyer's influence. There was also a rise in instances where the celebrity being impersonated would appear alongside the performer doing the impersonation. Suddenly, Janet Reno, Alex Trebek, Bob Dole, and Robert De Niro were in the studio to confront their doppelgangers. These celebrity appearances and recurring characters guaranteed an audience reaction. When Molly Shannon appears in her Catholic schoolgirl costume as Mary Katherine Gallagher the crowd immediately erupts into raucous applause before she says her first line. The same outburst of approval occurs when the real Joe Pesci shows up to attack Jim Breuer as host of "The Joe Pesci Show." These sketches and appearances may or may not be funny, but there is no risk that they will induce audience silence. The audience celebration is a guarantee, but it is a voluntary reaction in the form of approving laughter or knowing laughter.

Ohlmeyer usually watched the show on TV rather than in person, and applause or voluntary laughter certainly plays much better than silence on TV. Ohlmeyer's approach captures the tendency of people to respond to guidance. There is a reason that many late night shows employ applause signs. Nobody wants a guest to enter to silence, as that makes for worse TV. Television shows are famous for using "canned laughter" or laugh tracks. Many critics cringe when they hear these pre-recorded laughs, yet the use of laugh tracks persists because average viewers at home respond to them. By contrast, Norm aimed for something more authentic. Macdonald could feel whether what was happening was genuine or not, and he refused to pander, preferring silence to forced laughter.

Get Mr. Peepers an Apple: Play Theory

Macdonald's requirement that laughter be involuntary tracks well with Max Eastman's philosophical theory of humor known as play theory. Eastman saw similarities between humans and chimpanzees at play, as well as other animals. Identifying behaviors such as tickling as a form of play common to both humans and animals, Eastman concludes that humans are born having an instinctive, biological tendency to laugh.[15] Philosophers have followed Eastman's lead, not necessarily by focusing on the similarities between human and animal play, but by focusing on the biological aspects of humor.

One of the ways that play theorists have attempted to extend Eastman's work is by explaining laughter in terms of natural selection, as a positive adaptation. Humor can have social benefits like helping form bonds between individuals, encouraging creative thinking, and improving people's moods. The kind of improv exercises that future *SNL* cast members practiced at Second City or The Groundlings are popular team building activities at corporate retreats. Think about the benefits that sharing jokes with a group of friends can have on your mood. There is also mounting evidence that humor and laughter have a positive effect on physical health, making it easier to tolerate pain or deal with stress.[16] While these theories do not argue that we consciously pursue humor for these goals, they do make claims that these functions explain why humor developed as a biological human characteristic.

Macdonald's view of comedy falls within the purview of play theories of humor because of its focus on involuntariness. What gives the laughter its meaning and its value is that it occurs spontaneously and uncontrollably. So, while Macdonald is not arguing directly for the positive effects of humor or that producing these effects should be the goal, he is arguing in favor of the type of humor most likely to produce these effects.

I'm Good Enough, I'm Smart Enough, and Doggone It, People Like Me: Relief Theory

Sigmund Freud's (1856–1939) Relief Theory suggests that the main goal of humor and laughter is to relieve pent up stresses and mental strain that people carry around with them.[17] The most important difference between humor-as-relief and play theory is that in play theory the release is a positive consequence, but not the intended goal. In relief theory, the point of humor is to allow the release of these built up pressures. To modernize relief theory, the goal of the humor would be stress relief. This modified modernized version of relief theory works well with NBC management's goals for "Weekend Update." According to Ohlmeyer and company, the audience watches not purely to laugh, but to feel good in a variety of ways. It can be just as relieving to see something familiar and comfortable as to be surprised by something unexpected. Interestingly, while Macdonald's view initially appears to align with play theory, the actual goals that laughter is said to help achieve might be more successfully accomplished by Ohlmeyer's more open-ended vision of what "Weekend Update" should be trying to achieve. For Ohlmeyer, the goal is to deliver guaranteed laughs for the audience. "Weekend Update" is for the audience, not for the writers and cast members.

We're Here to Pump -clap- You Up!: The Goal of *SNL* and "Weekend Update"

Before the goodbyes and cast hugs, I've promised to say who was right about "Weekend Update," Macdonald or Ohlmeyer. The answer depends, I'd argue, on what you think "Weekend Update" and *SNL* are. If you think that they are merely a platform for comedy, then it seems pretty clear that Norm Macdonald was right. At its heart, comedy is a creative art, and comedians perform to provoke involuntary laughter.

However, there is a lot to suggest that *Saturday Night Live* is more than just a platform for comedy. At the end of the updated version of *SNL*'s history, the authors describe the show with a gravitas that simply does not attach to an average stand-up set. "When *Saturday Night Live* is at its best, it...reflect[s] an artful vision of who and where we are at the moment...we all seem to have some kind of stake in it, and in its well being."[18] This gets at the idea that *Saturday Night Live* has become a unique cultural icon that serves a purpose beyond mere jokes. It has a history that generations of families can share. Indeed, some of the most memorable moments in the history of the show have been responses in the wake of tragedy or celebrations of greatness that have not been restricted to humor. This aspect of *SNL* might reasonably have comfort and happiness as goals that are just as important as laughter. It is this version of "Weekend Update" and the show as a whole that Macdonald did not seem to appreciate, and in failing to appreciate it Norm lost sight of part of what makes *Saturday Night Live* so special.

Notes

1. James Andrew Miller and Tom Shales, *Live from New York: The Complete, Uncensored History of Saturday Night Live as Told by its Stars, Writers, and Guests* (New York: Back Bay Books, 2015), 430–440.
2. S. (2005, December 20). Norm MacDonald – David Letterman – 01-07-1998. Retrieved from www.youtube.com/watch?v=tudRETrphxk on July 6, 2019.
3. M. Sacks (2014, June 24). "SNL's James Downey on Working with Norm Macdonald and Getting Fired for Making Fun of OJ Simpson." Retrieved from www.vulture.com/2014/06/snls-james-downey-on-working-with-norm-macdonald-and-getting-fired-for-making-fun-of-oj-simpson.html on July 6, 2019.
4. Ibid.
5. Miller and Shales, 432.
6. Ibid.
7. Ibid.
8. WHO, WHEN, and WHERE to make something funny are also fine questions that will not be addressed in this chapter.
9. There are some obvious other goals a joke might have like eliciting a groan or even to impress in the manner of a virtuoso, but these goals generally come in tandem with the goal of laughter.
10. These categories are my own, though they are inspired by Max Eastman, who notes the existence of the "gleeful laugh" but chooses not to try and elucidate what it is, merely claiming that it must not be the same as the comic laugh. Max Eastman, *Enjoyment of Laughter* (New York: Halcyon House, 1936), 34.
11. "'Saturday Night Live': Will Ferrell Says the Goal of the 'Love-ahs' Sketch Was to Make Jimmy Fallon Break" (n.d.). Retrieved from http://ew.com/tv/2017/06/29/will-ferrell-jimmy-fallon-snl-break-lovers/.
12. Ernie Kurtz, E. *The Collected Ernie Kurtz* (New York: Authors Choice Press, 2008).
13. Miller and Shales, 439.
14. Ibid., 430.
15. Eastman (1936).
16. John Morreall, *Humor Works* (Amherst, MA: Human Resource Development Press, 1997).
17. Sigmund Freud, *Jokes and their Relation to the Unconscious*. Tr. J. Strachey (New York: W. W. Norton, 1960).
18. Miller and Shales, 699.

15

Saturday Night Live's Citizen Journalists and the Nature of Democracy

Kati Sudnick and Erik Garrett

"Communication can alone create a great community. Our Babel is not one of tongues but of the signs and symbols without which shared experience is impossible."

(John Dewey[1])

"Well, Jane, it just goes to show you, it's always something – if it ain't one thing, it's another."

(Roseanne Roseannadanna)

From Emily Litella to Grumpy Old Man, from Joe Blow to Drunk Uncle, *SNL* has long employed guest characters as "citizen journalists" on its famous Weekend Update segment. These characters have provided a comic take on everyday issues impacting the life of citizens in the public sphere. The very first of these characters was Emily Litella, played by original cast member Gilda Radner. She went on Weekend Update to offer her editorial voice regarding misheard issues like "Canker [Cancer] Research," "Violins [Violence] on Television, or Endangered Feces [Species]." When the news anchor would point out her mistake, Litella's signature line was "Never mind."[2]

These citizen journalists spoof the everyday letters to the editor found in many print newspapers. They poke fun at the often misguided, uneducated, or otherwise problematic views expressed in some opinion pieces from the average person. Despite the humorous nature of these exchanges between the recurring Weekend Update characters and the anchors, they illustrate a central question in the operation of political philosophy and philosophy of education. How should a democratic

Saturday Night Live and Philosophy: Deep Thoughts Through the Decades, First Edition. Edited by Jason Southworth and Ruth Tallman.

government respond to an uneducated public? Should a democracy trust its citizens to know how to respond to complex issues, or should the public rely on experts to decide or guide public opinion?

These questions have been debated since before the founding of the of the United States. However, the invention of mass media and journalism provided a disruption to the debate about appropriate democratic forms. Now there is a public sphere where individuals can instantly be informed and can quickly disseminate information. Yet, as Weekend Update and its citizen journalists show, accuracy is not guaranteed. Therefore, we have a new phase in the debate about how to educate the average person to participate as a citizen in democratic institutions. Two of the first philosophers who take up the modern problems of participatory democracy in the public sphere are John Dewey (1859–1952) and Walter Lippmann (1889–1974).

"Weekend Update" provides us with a foundation to understand what Dewey and Lippmann argued about news, democracy, and the formation of public opinion. Lippmann argues that we need experts and a representative democracy that is more of a technocracy in which experts guide public opinion and decisions. Lippmann, though, didn't foresee the ways these experts could make things even more confusing. Just think of what it's like to rely on Stefon to decide the coolest spots in NYC. Dewey, by contrast, argued for more public education, participation, and a deliberative form of representative democracy that preserved the individual's ability to make more direct decisions. But we have to wonder if citizens like Tommy Flanagan, the pathological liar, are capable of being educated to know the truth and make decisions in the best interest of the general public.

"New York's Hottest Club Is…" Walter Lippmann, Public Opinion, and Weekend Update Correspondents

In *The Public and its Problems*, John Dewey acknowledges a debt to Walter Lippmann for helping him flesh out his understanding of "the public" and "public opinion." Lippmann was one of the founders of modern journalism, American media studies, and even the discipline and practice of public relations. Both Lippmann and Dewey agreed that one of democracy's major problems was that its practice requires a high level of knowledge, information, and expertise; yet many citizens do not have adequate levels of education, training, time, or even the will to achieve and exercise these skills.

In his 1922 book *Public Opinion,* Lippmann posited that the world was "altogether too big, too complex, and too fleeting for direct acquaintance"[3] with even major issues for the average citizen. Instead, people create "pseudo-environments" to make sense of their surroundings.[4] Pseudo-environments are the subjective biases and prejudices through which we view the world, often believing we are completely independent of others and their competing worldviews. With the fragmentation of news sources and social media outlets, Lippmann's pseudo-environment is alive and well in the form of the echo chamber; we only follow news sources and people on social media that fit within our personal narrative structures, leaving the rest out of sight and out of mind. This echo chamber mentality was foretold by Marshall McLuhan (1911–1980) when he spoke of electronic media's ability to retribalize people into particular groupings that ignore or screen out dissenting information.[5] In the echo chamber and the pseudo-environment, we only follow sources we agree with. As Lippmann theorized, these sources provide the maps that people rely on to generate opinions about the world. Problems arise when special interests infiltrate and propagandize the masses for nefarious purposes. Some of these propagandized people end up thinking they are experts on various topics.

Sadly, we are living through an epidemic in which a great many people think they're experts without really knowing anything. This is illustrated perfectly on Weekend Update by Drunk Uncle, portrayed by Bobby Moynihan, who believes he has the entire system figured out and lets everyone know about it. As an "informed" citizen lifestyle reporter, Drunk Uncle epitomizes someone who has been propagandized in a pseudo-environment that only increases his ignorance. Drunk Uncle consistently calls out millennial culture, using terms and brands incorrectly. For example, while commenting on Easter, Drunk Uncle veers off onto a tangent (as he usually does) about current culture:

> Kids today, they don't even stand when a woman comes into the room. All these kids care about is: Is this WiFi organic? Can I get some raw almonds on my yoga class? Netflix me! Netflix me! Netflix me![6]

Clearly, Drunk Uncle is hearing these terms via the news or online articles geared toward older groups who are certain that millennial culture is destroying the country. Drunk Uncle, while hilarious from afar, is Lippmann's worst nightmare. He relies on sound bites and listicles from his pseudo-environment, and he turns into a bitter drunkard who nags you around the holidays for owning a Prius.[7]

Lippmann was also concerned with the press itself. In 1922, the general public received their news information primarily from cheap newspapers. For the price to remain low, newspapers had to include a myriad of advertisements, but the ads affected the content of the newspapers. Consider the following: if a major corporation is investing advertising dollars into a newspaper, the newspaper would be less likely to report on any negative aspect of that corporation, lest they pull advertising support. According to Lippmann:

> The newspaper editor occupies a strange position. His enterprises depend upon indirect taxation levied by his advertisers upon his readers; the patronage of the advertisers depends upon the editor's skill in holding together an effective group of customers. These customers deliver judgment according to their private experiences and their stereotyped expectation, for in the nature of things they have no independent knowledge of most news they read.[8]

Lippmann saw the capitalist, for-profit requirements for newspaper survival as a major problem. The press serves the special interests of both its advertisers and their audiences, resulting in the commercialization of news that produces agreement whereas it should discover truth.[9] The line between propaganda and news becomes blurred, leaving less news-savvy individuals prey to misinformation.

While Drunk Uncle serves to represent the dangers of the press-illiterate citizen, another Weekend Update regular, Girl You Wish You Hadn't Started a Conversation with at a Party (shortened to Girl at Party), exemplifies Lippmann's overall wariness toward the formation of public opinion. Created and performed by Cecily Strong, Girl at Party comes armed with an array of information that gets crossed and convoluted as she berates others for not being as "woke" as she is.

In one segment concerning the 2016 election, Girl at Party says to anchor Michael Che, "do not manterrupt me when I'm womaning a point, Michael. This election is a misgrace; it's a colostomy Michael Che."[10] When Che tells her he's guessing she isn't happy with the election, Girl at Party responds, "maybe try being woke for a change because Kevin can wait but Syrian referees can't."[11] With her sentences littered with malaprops, Girl at Party represents someone completely overtaken by the propagandized news scene. Strong's character seems to believe she knows the truth about the reality around her and needs to shame others into falling in line. For instance, on another segment about Christmas, Girl at Party tells Seth Meyers "you don't care about Jesus 'cause you worship Hallmark,"[12] clearly parroting a blog.

Girl at Party serves as a cautionary tale about being overwhelmed and usurped by an unregulated press. She takes glimpses of information and spins them into her own weapons aimed at those who disagree with her, crossing wires and convoluting each factoid and turn of phrase along the way. Lippmann would see her as the result of an unchecked news cycle and a media-illiterate public. Girl at Party, while funny on screen, is a scary reality we face in social media comments and our day-to-day lives.

So, what is the solution? Long after Lippmann, the press is still flawed. With a seemingly unending list of news channels, syndicates, and blogs, the "manufacturing of consent" is alive and well. Lippmann's response to the uneducated electorate was to recommend a system of intelligent experts who would "audit" the news and provide the appropriate and needed information to understand decision makers and the public. This panel of experts, comprised of social scientists and political analysts, would constitute a "machinery of knowledge"[13] to filter the news and ensure credibility. Lippmann, alas, failed to foresee Stefon.

At first glance Stefon might seem completely goofy and funny, but he represents a type of expert thinking that Lippmann argued for. Stefon appeared on Weekend Update at times when New York City was bustling with tourists, such as holidays or special events. Instead of trying to read all the relevant travel guides, visitors could rely on Stefon for information such as "New York's hottest club is..."

Of course, in *SNL* style, it becomes apparent that only Stefon understands Stefon. Each time Stefon appeared on Weekend Update, the anchor had to stop him to say, "wait, what does X mean?" to which he would answer "oh you know, it's that thing where..." Stefon knows the ins and outs of every activity he describes, such as a hot club for St. Patrick's day that was a "former CVS, then became a Chase bank, then became a CVS again" and "has a troubling feel like when Larry King plays himself in a movie."[14] As viewers, we see Stefon as a fabulous alienesque club kid who uses hilarious terminology and imparts misinformation about what is "family friendly" for New York City. For Lippmann, however, he is something else entirely: an expert in his own field (despite mismatching his very specific expertise to a broader public).

In his unique way, Stefon illustrates the problem with the panel of experts that Dewey brings up in response to Lippmann: a manifestation of In groups and Out groups that control truth, creating an air of capitalistic class lines that those without power cannot cross. Stefon acted as a gatekeeper of knowledge for those unfamiliar with the New York party scene. Our inability to understand most of Stefon's terms illustrates how the public is at the mercy of these experts. For example, when we hear from economic forecasters predicting an economic slump, we trust them even when we don't understand them. Likewise, without the proper training to understand climate change science, citizens are forced to trust the experts and their data.

Point/Counterpoint: Dewey's *The Public and its Problems* as a Pragmatic Response

Ultimately Lippmann distrusted the public, because we have too many Girls at a Party and Drunk Uncles among us to make informed decisions. Instead, we should rely on experts to help opinion leaders "manufacture the consent." [15] Dewey wrote a review of Lippmann's *Public Opinion* and called the book "the most effective indictment of democracy as currently conceived ever penned."[16] However, Dewey was not ready to give up on democracy and instead wrote his own book *The Public and its Problems* as an attempt to take seriously the challenges to democracy that Lippmann noted. Whereas Lippmann suggested that societies need professional information experts who could accurately disseminate information, Dewey argued for more investment in public education to create a more critical citizenry, capable of making its own decisions. Dewey's bottom-up approach included citizen reporters, giving multiple standpoints to reach a more holistic truth.

Like Lippmann, Dewey was concerned with the role of propagandists, and he saw how quickly they could control public opinion. He wrote "the smoothest road to control of political conduct is by control of opinion."[17] Dewey realized that news sources in general can be co-opted by those with wealth and power, noting that "the assembling and reporting of news would be a very different thing if the genuine interests of reporters were permitted to work freely."[18] He argued for more participation and wider dissemination of information as an attempt to overcome corporate, business, and elite control of the information that was essential for citizens to make decisions in their democratic institutions.

Instead of defaulting to experts to make our decisions, Dewey pushed for supporting a free press that encouraged open communication and viewpoints that aid the public in making informed choices, rather than removing their power altogether. Dewey wanted increased communication and public access. He also argued that there should be "publicly funded" journalism like the BBC (in Great Britain) or NPR and PBS (in the United States) to help check corporate interest and control of the various communication media channels. If the public is not bombarded by corporate-owned news sources and special interest councils, then they may feel more empowered and vote on issues and policies that could move the country in a positive direction. We wouldn't have to default to Stefon-like experts to tell us where to go and what to do. Instead, we could make truly informed decisions by seeing events from multiple angles. The idea was to foster the "art" of debate and let individual citizens make their own decisions. Of course, we see this on the Weekend Update segment Point/Counterpoint.

During this segment, anchors Jane Curtin and Dan Aykroyd took on a hot button issue, providing (you guessed it) points and counterpoints. Besides giving us one of SNL's most recognizable catchphrases, "Jane, you ignorant slut," Point/Counterpoint demonstrates how one news source can cover competing viewpoints for the benefit of the consumer. A similar segment called "Really?!?" led by Seth Meyers and Amy Poehler follows a similar format in which they pull quotes and stories from the news and call them out for skirting around the issues. While these segments generally dissolve into insults as part of the punch line, "Point/Counterpoint" and "Really?!?" represent the kind of debate that can help members of the public to form their opinions.

Lippmann and Dewey pre-date television and the internet, but Dewey understood the technological distractions that kept people from seeking knowledge and participating in the public sphere. According to Dewey, "access to means of amusement has been rendered easy and cheap beyond anything known in the past" giving the public "too many ways of enjoyment...to give much thought to organization into an effective public."[19] While he does not offer any solutions to the problems of technological distraction, Dewey leaves us with a hope that we could eventually figure out how to use these technologies to increase political participation rather than merely distract. Having more Point/Counterpoint segments that allowed for a truly open public debate via all sorts of current media channels could foster a more educated public and engaged citizenry. Needless to say, such debates should feature more content and fewer personal attacks than a Weekend Update sketch.

We glimpse some hope in Cathy Ann, played by Cecily Strong, a citizen engaging in debate about public issues. In one exchange with anchor Michael Che she discussed the rise of the alt-right after the "pizzagate" incident. [20] Despite a few misspoken words and the gritty and brash nature of her character, Cathy Ann actually makes a good point about fake news and our public sphere. "I think everybody needs to get off the damn internet for a few days. ... including Donald Trump." Her prescription for a better democracy is "to go outside and meet people face-to-face and find your freedoms like the pilgrims and the cavemen all did." Cathy Ann is arguing for a public space where we can engage our fellow citizens in truly meaningful ways. She is correct that vitriol has increased via the anonymity of the web, and a return to face-to-face contact could spark more civilized debate. It's easy to hurl insults in cyberspace; it is a lot more difficult when you are looking the other person in the eye.

As Dewey sees it, a democracy will work best when it utilizes technology to increase public participation in a way that adds to public knowledge, debate, and discourse, instead of merely dumbing discourse down to the lowest possible denominator. Point/Counterpoint and Cathy Ann may be a little rough around the edges, but they represent the potential of an engaged citizenry participating in civil discourse.

Lippmann's response to Dewey's initial critique was anti-populist and anti-reform. In *The Phantom Public*, Lippmann argues that In and Out groups are inevitable and unavoidable within the current structure of democracy.[21] The only power the public has (and should have) is the ability to vote who is in and out. The rest we must trust to our representatives and experts. The public is a phantom, unable to create true change but able to make slight shifts in regard to who makes the rules. Lippmann argued that "the popular will does not direct continuously but that it intervenes occasionally."[22] This must be the case due to the general public not having "an insider's knowledge" of all events.[23] Having a panel of experts to explain what is going on is the only way, according to Lippmann, for the public to make informed decisions. Because we really don't know where New York's hottest clubs are, Stefon must stay.

A New Holiday Album: A Lesson Is in the Lyrics

Dewey's creative response to the problems of the public in democracy was not to rely on experts, but to rely on the arts and artists to help communicate important issues in the public sphere and foster more public participation.

> Artists have always been the real purveyors of news, for it is not the outward happening in itself which is new, but the kindling by it of emotion, perception and appreciation. ...It (democracy) will have its consummation when free social inquiry is indissolubly wedded to the art of full and moving communication.[24]

Art helps us make sense of the world, and also mobilizes the masses with an ability to play on our heartstrings with pathos and emotion. The citizen journalists of Weekend Update provide plenty of examples of artists and art critics delivering the news. From Adam Sandler's Opera Man[25] to Kristen Wiig and Fred Armisen's Garth and Kat,[26] artists are frequent guests, educating and stirring up the public. One of the most memorable Weekend Update visits was not from a character, but just Adam Sandler and his guitar. We remember the "Chanukah Song"[27] because it was funny and connected with audiences, Jewish and gentile alike. You might wonder, though, if Dewey puts too much responsibility on artists and if we are asking too much from *SNL*. In the words of Emily Litella, "Never mind."

Notes

1. John Dewey, *The Public and its Problems* (Athens: Ohio University Press, 1994), 142.
2. Bobby Moynihan's Anthony Crispino character who reported "secondhand" news is an homage to Radner's Litella.
3. Ibid., 19.
4. Ibid.
5. Marshall McLuhan, *Understanding Media: The Extensions of Man* (Cambridge, MA: MIT Press, 1994), xx.
6. Saturday Night Live, Season 37, Episode 18, 2012.
7. Ibid.
8. Lippmann, *Public Opinion*, 222.
9. Ibid., 237.
10. Saturday Night Live, Season 42, Episode 1708, 2016.
11. Ibid.

12. Saturday Night Live, Season 38, Episode 10, 2012
13. Lippmann, *Public Opinion*, end of news chapters
14. Saturday Night Live, Season 43, Episode 1741, 2017.
15. Walter Lippmann, *Public Opinion* (La Vergne, TN: BN Publishing, 2010), 171. The work was first published in 1922.
16. John Dewey, "Public Opinion," *New Republic* 30 (1922). Dewey: *The Middle Works* 13, 337
17. John Dewey, *The Public and Its Problems*, 182.
18. Ibid, 182.
19. Ibid., 138–139.
20. Saturday Night Live, Season 42, Episode 9.
21. Walter Lippmann, *The Phantom Public* (New Brunswick, NJ: Transaction Publishers, 2004), xxvi. The work was first published in 1927.
22. Ibid., 52.
23. Ibid., 54.
24. Dewey, 184.
25. Saturday Night Live, Season 17, Episode 18, 1992 first appearance.
26. Saturday Night Live, Season 35, Episode 10, 2009 first appearance.
27. Saturday Night Live, Season 20, Episode 7, 1994.

16

Fake News as Media Theory

SNL on TV Journalism

Gerald J. Erion

Longtime fans of *Saturday Night Live* know the routine. As the frantic first half hour winds down, the theme and title for our next must-see segment fades in: "Weekend Update." Built on the frame of the typical television newscast, this perennial feature targets prominent news subjects, news reporters and analysts, and even the sheer *form* of TV news. At its best, its incisive comedy functions as deep commentary on our most prominent authorities and social institutions.

These kinds of "fake news" bits on *SNL* become more meaningful when linked back to the work of media theorist Neil Postman (1931–2003). Postman's best-known book, *Amusing Ourselves to Death: Public Discourse in the Age of Show Business*, argues that TV journalism will inevitably reflect the influences and biases of television itself. The result is an entertaining but incoherent stream of "disinformation" in a "peek-a-boo world" of unfocused and shallow discussion.[1] Using Postman's arguments for structure and support here, we'll explore similar concerns reflected in the satirical news reporting of *Saturday Night Live*. We'll see that "Weekend Update" and other such pieces can ground key lessons that help us navigate our increasingly complex media environment, a point that Postman himself considers in his book's closing pages.

Saturday Night Live and Philosophy: Deep Thoughts Through the Decades, First Edition. Edited by Jason Southworth and Ruth Tallman.
© 2020 John Wiley & Sons Ltd. Published 2020 by John Wiley & Sons Ltd.

SNL and "Weekend Update"

Let's begin, then, with "Weekend Update." Co-created by *SNL* producer Lorne Michaels and writer Herb Sargent, then first anchored by
Chevy Chase in the October 1975 premiere, "Update" quickly became
an essential element of *SNL*.[2] In many ways it was also a precursor for
other shows more fully devoted to satirical news, like *The Daily Show
with Jon Stewart*, *The Colbert Report*, *Last Week Tonight*, and other
such programs.[3]

"Weekend Update's" basic structure was largely set in that first
episode; viewing the segment now, decades later, is a remarkably familiar experience for veteran *SNL* fans. The piece appears shortly (but not
immediately) after musical guest Janis Ian's performance, and amidst
advertising parodies of the sort that have become customary on *SNL*.
Adopting the anchor's position, Chase sits behind a news desk with a
stack of papers in his hands. As he delivers a series of gag stories,
several at the expense of then-U.S. President Gerald Ford, packaged
graphics appear over his shoulder in the style of a typical TV newscast.
Next, correspondent Laraine Newman reports live from the scene of a
string of (38!) ghastly murders at Manhattan's Blaine Hotel. ("The
motive again: murder, as it has been in the previous 37 slashings.")
And then just as we wonder whether Newman *really* intended to close
her grim account with a smile, Chase returns with a prank teaser
juxtaposing two horrific disasters against a much lighter lifestyle
report from a museum. Another ad and a short promotional announcement ("guests on NBC's *Saturday Night* stay at the fabulous Blaine
Hotel") set up the closing, a feel-good item on some newly-arrived
baby animals at the Washington Zoo. Alas, the story takes an unexpected but darkly humorous turn when we learn that Pip, a rare sand-
piper chick, has been crushed by a newborn hippo named Goggles.

In the years since *SNL* established this rough framework for
"Update," much has remained constant, even as the cast and set have
changed. Indeed, looking back, perhaps the only classic component
noticeably absent from that first "Weekend Update" segment is the
in-studio guest, such as Gilda Radner's all-purpose correspondent
Roseanne Roseannadanna, Colin Quinn's neighborhood reporter Joe
Blow, or Bill Hader's nightlife guide Stefon. It is thus likely that last
week's version of "Update" – not to mention next week's version –
will share the same basic structure as the original. And it is with
this basic structure in mind that we can begin our philosophical
discussion of TV news.

Medium Shapes the Message

Now, to make these philosophical links through "Weekend Update," it will help to bring in a few ideas from *Amusing Ourselves to Death*. Perhaps most fundamentally, Postman's book argues that our *forms* of communication can shape the *content* of the messages we share.[4] This is an idea that Postman borrows from the great Canadian media theorist Marshall McLuhan (1911–1980), whose catalog of famous lines includes his claim that "the medium is the message."[5]

Postman clarifies the point here with a thought experiment about smoke signals. Though an admittedly unusual media form, smoke signaling is nonetheless a great way to convey important messages beyond the range of the human voice. For example, we can tell an aerial search-and-rescue team that "My plane crashed over here" *far* more effectively by smoke signaling than by yelling. But of course, this benefit holds only for relatively simple messages. "Help!" is one thing, but more detailed items quickly become impractical. As Postman puts it:

> Puffs of smoke are insufficiently complex to express ideas on the nature of existence [or other philosophy topics, for example], and even if they were not, a Cherokee philosopher would run short of either wood or blankets long before he reached his second axiom. *You cannot use smoke to do philosophy. Its form excludes the content* (emphasis added).[6]

Postman thereby shows us that *the medium* of smoke signaling *shapes its messages*; in particular, smoke signals tend to be limited both in complexity and in length.

Moreover, the general point holds not just for smoke signals, but for other media as well, since any form of communication will have ways in which it influences its content. So, yes, smoke signaling shapes its messages. But so too does speech, and writing, and photography, and television. Indeed, Postman's particular interest in *Amusing Ourselves to Death* is TV, but we cannot forget that his argument is meant to apply more broadly. Adopting the spirit of Postman's work, we might even ask how social media shape their content. Consider the March 2014 cold open sketch in which President Obama, played by Jay Pharoah, struggles with a plan to use viral photos and video clips to foster discussion of complex health-care issues.[7] Social media platforms like Instagram and Twitter can of course convey powerful and concise messages, and they can certainly generate, as Pharoah's Obama puts it, "a lot of buzz." However, they are not great at carrying deeper conversations about politics, science, and so on. "Isn't it a little silly?" Obama asks in the sketch, just before giving in to dance with Pope Francis and canoodle with Justin Bieber. So, as our media environment continues to change, it becomes increasingly helpful to see Postman's thesis as a valuable philosophical insight, and one that *SNL*'s comedy can illustrate quite effectively.

Now, This: "Update," TV News, and Postman

To reconnect with "Weekend Update," let's move beyond Postman's smoke signaling example and dive a bit deeper into his arguments about *television*. As we noted above, TV – like any medium – will tend to shape its content in particular ways. In other words, there will be some messages that television is especially good at conveying, and some that it carries less effectively. Postman dubs this the medium's "bias," and he argues that *entertainment* is television's true strength. At the same time, though, television's entertainment bias tends to crowd out more serious journalism, political dialogue, religious discussion, and education. This is an important but often overlooked issue. As Postman sees it, "The problem is not that television presents us with entertaining subject matter, but that *all subject matter is presented as entertaining*" (emphasis added).[8] So, if we rely too much upon television to carry our most important messages and democratic conversations, we risk (as Postman famously puts it) "amusing ourselves to death." That is, we might lose our capacity to conduct serious, rational, and sustained public discussions to address our most pressing challenges.

The problem here seems especially acute in the case of TV news, a topic to which Postman devotes an entire chapter. The bulk of this section of the book has him documenting a range of reporting, commenting, and editing transgressions that are as common as they are disappointing. For example, he uses the familiar anchors' segue "Now…This" as the very title of his chapter on news. A throwaway phrase like this one has particular significance for Postman because it inadvertently exposes both the triviality of the individual news stories and the incoherence of the overall presentation. He writes, quite memorably:

> "Now…this" is commonly used on radio and television newscasts to indicate that what one has just heard or seen has no relevance to what one is about to hear or see, or possibly to anything one is ever likely to hear or see. [...] There is no murder so brutal, no earthquake so devas-

tating, no political blunder so costly – for that matter, no ball score so tantalizing or weather report so threatening – that it cannot be erased from our minds by a newscaster saying, "Now...this."[9]

So, we see that Postman's chapter title alone already expresses some of his deepest concerns about rendering journalism as televised entertainment. When television's entertainment bias leads the typical TV news program to be chopped up in short bits strung together incoherently and punctuated with ad breaks, we might wonder how it could ever hope to meet journalism's higher aims. This is a deep and serious point for Postman, and he devotes many pages to it in *Amusing Ourselves to Death*.[10]

But on *SNL, the same entertainment bias that so deeply concerns Postman is highlighted and then reframed as comedy*. Consider again our first "Weekend Update" segment from 1975, where Chase places together, on the same teaser graphic, two disaster stories and a lifestyle report. "Still to come: earthquake claims San Diego, 4 million die in Turkey, and Arlene visits an art museum." Could we ask for a better example of Postman's "Now...This" phenomenon in action? Here, though, the point is made with a joke instead of a logical argument, while Chase grins to make sure that we see the humor.

Indeed, even in just this first "Update" segment, close inspection can reveal other comic expressions of Postman's concerns. Consider again Newman's piece from the Blaine Hotel, for example. Such crime stories, still so common in much of our electronic news, are more like dark entertainment than deep journalism. Undoubtedly, they are genuine tragedies for victims and their families. But more broadly, they serve as gripping soap operas, or perhaps even horror stories, for viewers not directly connected with them. Likewise, Chase's closing piece on Goggles and Pip echoes the familiar, real-life versions of feel-good stories that so often round out the TV newscast. They add almost nothing of journalistic substance, of course. In an interview Chase himself even framed the Goggles-and-Pip bit as representing "one of those things I hated about the news back then."[11] So why do newscasters run these kinds of pieces? Producers can expect that audiences will find them compelling, and they are right: viewers have a hard time looking away. The goal is not information or education, then, but *entertainment*. "The result of all of this," Postman writes, "is that Americans are the best entertained and quite likely the least well-informed people in the Western world" (106).

The first "Weekend Update" segment contains one last element that we should discuss here: the now-classic parody advertisement. More recently, these bits have typically appeared elsewhere in the typical *SNL* episode, often after the monologue, or perhaps tossed into the last half hour. But in 1975, two such commercial messages appeared embedded *within* the "Update" segment itself. The first is a short spot for Triopenin, a pain relief drug that comes packaged in a frustratingly impossible-to-open bottle. (It's "childproof," though.) Then, just afterward, we see a promotional card for the aforementioned and yet still allegedly "fabulous" Blaine Hotel. (The late Don Pardo's inimitable voice attempts to reassure us: "The Blaine, a tradition for more than half a century.") Again, such ads within and around a real television newscast serve no journalistic purpose. And while some are surely entertaining, this isn't really their main function, either. Instead, they appear primarily for *financial* reasons; they pay the bills, in other words. But merely by being present in this way, they contribute to the newscast's incoherence. Indeed, an anchor might just as well invoke a "Now...this" before cutting to a commercial break, because the news stories are as disconnected from the ads as they are from each other. Another dimension of Postman's argument thus emerges here, as the constant interruption of commercial messaging further distracts us from the TV newscast's supposedly journalistic goals. Without question, then, "Update" jokes can echo Postman's critique, and they have done so since the show's debut nearly a decade before the publication of *Amusing Ourselves to Death*.

This, Now: More Recent "Updates"

Enough about *SNL*'s series premiere, though. Veteran viewers and newcomers both will recognize that many, *many* additional sketches over the years have expressed this same kind of comic attack. Indeed, even a theoretical first-time viewer tuning in for the 2017–2018 season finale could see echoes of Postman's critique still present in Colin Jost and Michael Che's *Update* segment. For starters, the mere fact that "Update" is *still there*, still using the form of the TV newscast as a vessel for comedy, suggests that the deep critique reflected by that comedy has remained perennially, and perhaps even *increasingly*, relevant.[12]

That night, for example, Jost delivered a story on a *New York* magazine report that President Trump and Fox News host Sean Hannity enjoy talking to one another on the phone before bedtime.[13] "I just think Hannity loses a lot of integrity as a journalist if he ends his night saying, 'No, Mr. President, you hang up,'" Jost quipped.

The point, of course, is that this seems at the very least a question-able relationship for a journalist to maintain with a major news figure. Nonetheless, such relationships are no longer remarkable in our era of pervasive, partisan, 24-hour cable news channels deliver-ing entertainment-influenced journalism.

And as it turned out, the 2017–2018 season finale included several different sketches on TV news. In the first half hour, for example, Kate McKinnon and Alex Moffat offered a hilarious spoof of MSNBC's daily program *Morning Joe*. In his role as Joe Scarborough, Moffat asks and then answers his own questions in the self-important man-ner of a narcissistic star host. Meanwhile, McKinnon (as Mika Brzezinski) offers a variety of nonsensical expressive interjections, as if providing an emotional soundtrack to the discussion. The two then engage in a peculiar flirtation that alternatively transfixes and horri-fies their colleagues and guests. It is a silly sketch, for sure, but also one that can lead us to again ask deep questions about the true aims of the show it parodies. Is *Morning Joe* journalism? Entertainment? Journalistic entertainment? Entertaining journalism? What do we really learn from such supposedly informative shows? How do they deepen our understanding of the world, if they do so at all? We might also ask the same kinds of philosophical questions of *Morning Joe*'s peer programs – *Fox and Friends, New Day, Today, CBS This Morning*, and *Good Morning America* – which provide so much daily news to so many people.

Then, a bit later in this same *SNL* episode, guest host Tina Fey (playing NBC's Dana Millbrook) introduces a *Dateline* hidden camera-type series called *Pervert Hunters*. As the sketch unfolds, Beck Bennett's prospective offender is coached through a series of increasingly polished acting per-formances by Fey's reporter character and her director Mitch, played by Mikey Day. (At one point Mitch remarks, "Oh my God, I love that energy, I love it; save that, but let's get that entrance again, and then we can talk about how you're not guilty, OK?") The sketch thus caricatures such true crime "investigations" and the conventions of their production, thereby drawing attention to important concerns about how television shapes the content of the supposed news reports it carries.

Given *SNL*'s long history, how many more examples might we discuss here? Arguably, there are just *too many to count*. Among the early highlights, consider Jane Curtin and Dan Aykroyd's classic "Point/Counterpoint" segment, which parodied the exaggerated but dramatic TV conflict – "Dan, you pompous ass" and so on – of a CBS *60 Minutes* feature. Kevin Nealon, as correspondent for *Update* anchor Dennis

Miller, introduced a series of absurd nearby live remotes called "News from 10 Feet Away" that lampooned TV's often useless field reporting. Nealon's later run at the anchor's desk opened with the ridiculous image of a rotating Earth dissolving into his own rotating head. He also incorporated a string of remarkable correspondent parodies: Robert Smigel delivered Hank Fielding's "moron's perspective," Chris Farley gave us Bennett Brauer (who might not have been "handsome," or even "presentable"), and David Spade developed *Hollywood Minute* as a searing sendup of entertainment news. Chris Kattan's "Terrible Reenactments" series poked fun at, well, terrible TV news reenactment techniques. More recently, Cecily Strong also anchored a hilarious spoof of *CNN Newsroom*'s *animated* reenactments. "So that's what it would look like if someone couldn't open a door," Strong's Brooke Baldwin character remarks after watching a crude computer-generated cartoon loop. "Amazing."[14] In his first stint as guest host, Kevin Hart's Hal Sumner anchored a program called *360° News*. The joke angle: "Eight cameras! One newsman! Eighty stories! One sentence each!" And finally, in a kind of meta-role poking fun at journalism in the age of sketchy sources, former cast member Fred Armisen returned to *SNL* to play writer Michael Wolff. When asked if his astonishing reports from the halls of the White House were true, Armisen's character shrugs and says "Yeah, sure, whatever" with a smirk. ("Even the stuff that's not true: it's true," he adds in another appearance.)

Note that each of these pieces focuses upon some element of TV reporting's entertainment bias, then lays out its absurdity for comic ends. Feuding commentators, sometimes not so different from those played by Curtin and Aykroyd, can be *entertaining*, but they are not especially enlightening. The same goes for engaging visual effects and camera tricks, to say nothing of the spectacular stories reporters can gather from unreliable sources. Through the years *SNL* has managed to target virtually every one of the cable news networks for such satirical treatment, from CNN to Fox to MSNBC. In these and many other ways, then, *SNL* brings up important philosophical issues as its jokes prompt us to ask deep questions about the nature and value of journalism.

Lorne Michaels and Philosophy?

Once we begin to see the parallels between *SNL*'s critique of television news and Postman's argument in *Amusing Ourselves to Death*, we might wonder if these similarities are coincidental or deliberate.

The truth seems likely to be a bit of both. According to Aaron Reincheld, "Weekend Update" had been from the very start an important element of *SNL* creator Lorne Michaels' vision for the program. In his history of "Update's" development, Reincheld notes that a newscasting parody had been part of an earlier Canadian TV program in which Michaels co-starred, *The Hart and Lorne Terrific Hour*. There was also an "Update"-like segment in the original *SNL* pitch to NBC, and Michaels himself had initially planned to serve as anchor for "Weekend Update."[15]

So, Michaels might well have sensed the potential significance of a TV news parody from *SNL*'s earliest days. Indeed, Reincheld argues that "Michaels intended *SNL*, and *Weekend Update* especially, to be considered a serious voice in the American political landscape and to serve an informational purpose."[16] Perhaps writers and performers could stay more-or-less focused on the entertainment dimension of the show; as Herb Sargent put it, "you just wanted to get some laughs."[17] But as Michaels joked during his interview with Reincheld, if it were impossible to learn while laughing, "my life would be meaningless, wouldn't it?"[18]

And as the story has progressed, *SNL* and "Weekend Update" both seem to have had lasting impacts within our wider culture. The show has by some measures become one of the most successful in television history, garnering dozens of awards – including multiple Peabody Awards – during its decades on the air. (Accepting his own Individual Peabody in 2012, Michaels joked with a straight face, "I can't tell you how happy I am to finally be among serious people.") *SNL*'s style of fake news, vital to the program through all of those decades, has itself influenced American society in some important ways, too. For instance, in a remarkable political example that unfolded just a few months after *SNL*'s premiere, President Ford's press secretary Ron Nessen appeared as guest host.[19] The administration's hope seemed to have been that doing so would help reduce the impact of Chase's stinging jokes about Ford; the president himself even pre-recorded that episode's iconic "Live from New York" opening line to show that he was a good sport, and in on the joke. Ford lost the election to Jimmy Carter later that year, of course, but his strategy established what has become a familiar pattern to us today, where presidential candidates from both parties treat guest appearances on *SNL* as all but mandatory campaign stops.[20] We have, then, good reason to suppose that *SNL*'s treatment of television news reflects a deeper, more significant philosophical perspective, perhaps in its design, and certainly in its effects.

That's the News. Good Night and Have a Pleasant Tomorrow

To close, let's note that Postman himself actually raises the issue of whether shows like *Saturday Night Live* could help us to see the dangers of television news. This prospect appears in the final pages of *Amusing Ourselves to Death*. After Postman's nearly 200-page case has established the lousy state of our electronic media environment, readers see that we are clearly in a bind. How, then, might we save ourselves here?

Postman briefly considers, and then soundly rejects, the possibility of passing laws that would regulate content producers and providers. Could we then instead somehow *harness* the tremendous power of television to help us better understand the entertainment bias and its effects? In other words, could we design a series of truly *educational* TV programs to show viewers how TV systematically weakens journalism, political discussion, and other forms of public discourse? Postman takes up this idea, too, adding:

> I imagine such demonstrations would of necessity take the form of parodies, along the lines of *Saturday Night Live* and *Monty Python*, the idea being to induce a national horse laugh over television's control of the public discourse.[21]

Such anti-television television programming is at least conceivable. But in the end, Postman doesn't see much cause for optimism here, either. "Television would have the last laugh," he writes, for "[i]n order to command an audience large enough to make a difference, one would have to make the programs vastly amusing"; "[t]hus the act of criticism itself would, in the end, be co-opted by television."[22] Perhaps Postman is right about this, though with hundreds of channels, streaming services, and other such TV providers now available, the odds may have shifted a bit since the release of his book.

In any case, Professor Postman does introduce one last possibility here, "desperate" though it seems to him: *education*, and in particular, education that can help its students to think more critically about our media environment.[23] In such a setting, driven by the deep questions we've considered in this chapter, there is evidently still hope that we might gain a proper understanding of entertainment-driven public discourse. Maybe the right *SNL* sketches or *Update* bits, carefully selected and surrounded with appropriate reflection and discussion, could play a role here, too. Consider again Jay Pharoah's President Obama, sighing at the farce of conducting a serious healthcare discussion through silly viral videos. Whether we laugh or cry at the scene – featuring the man often described as our first social media president no less – the philosophical lesson is clear: more than ever, effective communication demands that we carefully consider the strengths and weaknesses of our communication forms.[24] "We are in a race between education and disaster,"[25] Postman writes, and so we have little choice but to try.[26]

Notes

1. Neil Postman, *Amusing Ourselves to Death: Public Discourse in the Age of Show Business* (New York: Viking, 1985), 77–78 and 106–108.
2. Aaron Reincheld, "*Saturday Night Live* and *Weekend Update*: The Formative Years of Comedy News Dissemination." *Journalism History* 31 (2006), 190–197. See also Douglas Martin, "Herb Sargent, TV Writer, Is Dead at 81." *New York Times*, May 7, 2005, B7.
3. There are others, too, and for readers who enjoy these kinds of programs I would also suggest an under-appreciated 1994 BBC show called *The Day Today*, which offered an especially absurd TV news parody. Among other things, *The Day Today* covered the goings-on of an embedded parody soap opera, *The Bureau*, set in the rather cramped quarters of a currency exchange booth (or as its manager preferred to think of it, "a high-class *bureau de change*").
4. See Postman, 31: "the form in which ideas are expressed affects what those ideas will be."
5. Marshall McLuhan, *Understanding Media: The Extensions of Man* (New York: McGraw-Hill, 1964); see especially 7–21, and also Postman, 10.
6. Postman, 7.
7. Other recent sketches have joked about the effects of social media on their content, too. For instance, just before the 2012 US Presidential election, Aidy Bryant's social media expert Kourtney Barnes joined Seth Myers on *Update* to share examples of the superficial and off-topic comments that abound on these platforms. Likewise, the 2017 music video "Thank You, Scott" featured Kenan Thompson, Cecily Strong, and Sasheer Zamata mocking the limits of armchair activism via social media.
8. Postman, 87.

9. Postman, 99.

10. Lance Strate, a student and colleague of Postman's and now a Fordham University professor himself, provides a notable update to Postman's arguments about TV news in his book *Amazing Ourselves to Death: Neil Postman's Brave New World Revisited* (New York: Peter Lang, 2014).

11. Michael Cader ed., *Saturday Night Live: The First Twenty Years* (Boston, MA: Houghton Mifflin, 1994), 13.

12. *Weekend Update* has in fact been one of the few show elements to have lasted all these years, though it went through a series of name changes (including *SNL NewsBreak* and *Saturday Night News*) during the time that Lorne Michaels was away from the show (1981–1985).

13. Olivia Nuzzi, "Donald Trump and Sean Hannity Like to Talk Before Bedtime." *New York*, May 18, 2018, 34–38 and 108.

14. The computer-generated animations were followed soon after by a puppet show depicting closed-door negotiations for an international nuclear deal and the CNN Reenactment Dance Troupe interpreting key elements of a controversy over religious freedom laws.

15. Reincheld, 191.

16. Ibid.

17. Reincheld, 193.

18. Reincheld, 190.

19. Doug Hill and Jeff Weingrad share the story of Nessen's visit in their *Saturday Night: A Backstage History of Saturday Night Live* (New York: Beech Tree Books, 1986), 178–189.

20. See Mark Leibovich, "Chevy Chase as the Klutz in Chief, and a President Who Was in on the Joke." *New York Times*, December 29, 2006, A.21.

21. Postman, 161–162.

22. Postman, 162.

23. Postman, 162–163.

24. For instance, see Juliet Eilperin's "Here's How the First President of the Social Media Age Has Chosen to Connect with Americans." *The Washington Post*, May 26, 2015. Retrieved from https://wapo.st/2MbqpYD on July 6, 2019.

25. Postman, 163.

26. Thanks especially to my parents, Janice and Gerry Erion, who woke me up laughing at *Saturday Night Live* and then let me watch when it was *way* past my bedtime. Becca Palmer has also stayed up late with me to catch the show, hanging on even through the roughest 5-to-1 sketches. My editor and friend Bill Irwin first encouraged me to consider writing here, and Ruth Tallman and Jason Southworth kept me on track throughout the process. My students at Medaille College also helped workshop these ideas; Jill Baszczynski, Colleen Voigt, Kayleigh Slazyk, and Jess Helm were even generous enough to read drafts and offer comments. Thank you, each of you.

17

"Look, Children, It's a Falling Star"

David Spade and *SNL* Family Disloyalty

Jason Southworth and Ruth Tallman

During a controversial Weekend Update, David Spade made the following joke with an image of Eddie Murphy behind him: "Look, children, it's a falling star – make a wish."[1] The crack came at a time when Murphy's career was hurting (1995), and he took offense, refusing to return to the show for twenty years. But really, what's the big deal? Taking shots at stars – falling or otherwise – is sort of *SNL*'s bread and butter, right? Murphy argued that a shot at him was different, and inappropriate, because he was a member of the *SNL* family. He said, "I'm one of you guys. How many people have come off this show whose careers really are fucked up, and you guys are shitting on me?"[2] Murphy, a veteran of the show, knew that the joke must have passed through a lengthy approval chain – right up to Lorne Michaels himself – before making it to air. This amounted, in Murphy's eyes, to a family betrayal.

But why would we think of *SNL* as a family? Well, for one thing, *SNL* alums do have a history of defending their own, even in the face of bad behavior. When Tracey Morgan made violently homophobic comments during a stand-up show in 2011, former cast mates Tina Fey and Chris Rock both defended him (while condemning the content of his message). When Al Franken was accused of sexual misconduct in 2017, thirty-six women who worked with him on the show signed a letter in his defense.

Perhaps more compellingly, *SNL* alums regularly use familial language when speaking about the show. In describing his decision to leave *SNL*, Bill Hader said, "I'm not graduating, I'm actually leaving

Saturday Night Live and Philosophy: Deep Thoughts Through the Decades, First Edition. Edited by Jason Southworth and Ruth Tallman.
© 2020 John Wiley & Sons Ltd. Published 2020 by John Wiley & Sons Ltd.

my home. You know that's what this is – my family."[3] Andy Samberg echoed that sentiment, calling his decision to leave the show "one of the hardest things I've ever done in my life, because at that point, it's more than just a job, it's family."[4] Of course, families are not all sunshine and warm hugs. Describing her experience with the show, Cheri Oteri said, "it's almost like a family, even with its dysfunction."[5] So, even those who felt excluded used the familial language. Producer Jean Doumanian explained, "I was never part of the family. I didn't do drugs and I had a life outside of the show."[6] Abby Elliott recalled learning she would not be asked to return to the show the following season in familial terms as well, saying, "I felt as if that was my family – and then it wasn't."[7]

Because members of the *SNL* community think of it as a family, we can do so as well. But we can't automatically draw any particular conclusions regarding what types of behaviors would or would not be appropriate between *SNL* family members (in other words, was Murphy's twenty-year temper tantrum justified?). Like most areas of philosophy, there are a plurality of views when it comes to familial ethics. Let's take this opportunity to consider some of them, and to figure out what each view would say about the Spade-Murphy family feud. Who knows, we may even gain some insight into our own family squabbles.

Kissing Family: The Just Because View

The common, unreflective view is that our familial obligations are quite a bit different – more extensive – than our obligations to the general public. *SNL*'s most affectionate family, the Vogelchecks, seem to understand this view very well – so much so that they just can't stop kissing each other (and that's ok). On this view, known in Confucian ethics as filial piety, you owe your mom, your brother, your aunt (and so on) *just because* you exist in a particular familial relationship with those people. It's your role (rather than anyone's behavior) that determines your obligation. So even if you have (as most of us do) a relative who is – how should we put it? – a hot mess – you're never justified in writing them off. The particulars of what you owe your family are open for debate – perhaps money if you have it and they need it, maybe your time and attention, or maybe just love. Perhaps, the right thing to do would be to give Matt Foley a call for an intervention, because no one should allow a family member to end up eating government cheese in a van down by the river. At bare minimum, this Confucian view holds that you owe respect, or *xiao*, to your elder family members. It doesn't matter if they deserve your respect or not; you still have an unconditional obligation to be respectful toward them.

The Just Because View would certainly agree with Murphy's position regarding the wrongness of Spade's joke. Owing to his impact on the show in the early 1980s, Murphy is one of the elder fathers of *SNL*, and for a snot-nosed kid brother like Spade, relatively new to the show at the time, to poke fun at his comedic ancestor is simply not okay. The level of disrespect considered acceptable for a jokester to show toward regular people needs to be reined in for a member of the comedic family. It doesn't matter if Murphy and Spade had a good relationship, a close relationship, or any relationship at all. What matters is the role. Like it or not, Murphy and Spade both belong to the *SNL* family, and a family member isn't allowed to make a joke at another family member's expense, particularly one that is shared with those outside the family (you know, like on national television). This view would hold that Murphy was right to take offense, but his decision to basically divorce himself from the family – in refusing to return to the show for two decades – would not be considered acceptable. On the Just Because View, family is permanent and unconditional, and so, even though Murphy was wronged by the actions of his family, he still has his own filial obligations to fulfill.

Interestingly, the Just Because View implies that if someone *becomes* your family, you incur new obligations to that person. So, when Stefon married Seth Meyers, he gained much more than a new last name – he also gained a whole new set of responsibilities – to Seth as well as to the entire Meyers brood. And Seth incurred those same obligations regarding Stefon...and Stefon's family...can you imagine Stefon having parents and grandparents?

"Ya'll Want the Hose Again or Ya'll Gonna Be Good Boys?" – The Reciprocity View

There are many possible objections to the Just Because View. One is that in claiming we owe our families "just because" we fail to capture important reasons *why* we owe our families. According to the Reciprocity View, we do have special obligations to our families, but those obligations are not unconditional, and they are not derived from anything intrinsic to the familial relationship. Stemming from contractarian understandings of ethics, the Reciprocity View says that our obligations to others are determined by past interactions. If you invited me over to watch *SNL* at your place when my television broke, then I should return the favor when you're similarly in need of a comfortable venue for our favorite Saturday night activity. Likewise, if you didn't invite me to your last *SNL* watch party, I should feel no qualms about not inviting you to mine. It's pretty simple – you get based on what you give.

When all goes well, our families form our most long-lasting and reliable support systems. If you have the unshakable feeling that you owe your family – particularly your parental units – a lot, it just might be because of all they've done for you. If they were by your side through the ups and downs of childhood, providing for your needs, celebrating your triumphs, and consoling you through your heartbreaks, there's something very intuitive in feeling that you owe them for all they've done. Because of the extent of what they've done for you, you might feel that your obligations to them are unconditional – there's no possible way you could actually reciprocate for all your family has done for you, so it must be boundless. This might make you feel as if you accept the Just Because View.

To test your intuitions, consider what you think about the familial obligations of people who do not have loving, supportive families. Do you think a neglectful or absent parent is owed the same as a nurturing parent is? What about an abusive parent? Are they owed anything at all? Those who accept the Just Because View will have to say yes, on all counts, because, remember, that position is based on roles, not actions, and is unconditional. There can be no more or less. If this feels wrong to you, it might be that you accept the Reciprocity View, thinking that sure, good families deserve good treatment, but that bad families deserve, well, bad treatment. Or at least not good treatment. The family in the Brothers sketch from Season 44 exemplifies this view. When Jared (Beck Bennett) and Spencer (Kyle Mooney) misbehave, their father (Liev Schreiber) sprays them with a garden hose (kept right in the living room for quick access). The brothers seem to have picked up this tit-for-tat strategy from their dad. Spencer breaks a dish over Jared's head, so Jared throws Spencer through a wall. What you give is what you get, indeed.[8]

Because it's based on past actions, the Reciprocity View will never say that you owe family *just because* they're family. But that's precisely what Murphy seems to have expected of Spade. Murphy was on *SNL* from 1980 to 1984, and Spade didn't join the cast until 1990.

Like a big brother who had already left the house before the little one came along, Murphy, though part of the *SNL* family, wouldn't have had the opportunity to develop a familial relationship with Spade, and thus didn't accrue any reciprocal credit that Spade would need to pay off. The Reciprocity View would look at Spade's obligations to someone like Dennis Miller (baba ghanoush) quite differently. Miller, already an experienced and successful cast member, helped Spade land a spot on the show. Owing to Miller's role in helping Spade join the family, the Reciprocity View would argue that Spade owes a debt of reciprocity to Miller in a way that he does not owe one to Murphy.

Or does he? It's possible that Murphy didn't actually accept the Just Because View after all. According to Spade, in the midst of an epic telling-off phone call shortly after the incident, Murphy told Spade that he wouldn't have a job if it weren't for him (Murphy).[9] The reasoning, here, is that Murphy basically saved *SNL* when it was struggling back in the early 1980s. So, just as the hard work our parents or grandparents did before we were even born could put us in a situation of privilege, Murphy's hard work resulted in Spade being able to be on a really great and well respected show – stepping into a privileged situation that certainly couldn't have existed were it not for his familial *SNL* predecessors. Thinking about it like this, someone accepting the Reciprocity View might still argue that Spade was in the wrong. He did owe Murphy – not just because he's family, but for his actions within that familial role, and the positive impact they had on Spade's own comedic opportunities and career.

To throw another complication into the mix, we need to consider an objection that has been raised against Murphy's outrage. Fourteen years before Spade committed his familial transgression, Murphy, a relative newcomer to *SNL* himself, told a very similar joke at the expense of another *SNL* alum. The set-up is that, as a 19 year-old male, Murphy had to register with the Selective Service, a fact he is not happy about. He's invited onto Weekend Update, where he pleads his case to Uncle Sam as to why he shouldn't be drafted. In short, he argues, *SNL* needs him to fulfill the role of "token black." Given that he's busy filling that position, Murphy suggests that Garrett Morris, who left the show a year earlier, would be a better draft pick. Why Morris? Well, Murphy explains, "Word has it he has a lot of free time right now."[10]

This zinger has an awful lot in common with Spade's dig. In both cases, a rising *SNL* cast member throws shade on a former cast member whose current career seems to be lacking. If the treatment someone deserves is based at least in part on the way that person treats others, then Murphy's complaint is on shaky ground. After all, Murphy saw his *SNL* family member as fair game not only for a joke but for this particular kind of joke (targeting the state of Morris' career). So, Murphy has opened himself up to be the butt of that kind of joke as well. The Just Because View would say that both comedians (Murphy and Spade) behaved inappropriately, but that Murphy having done so first does not justify Spade's later behavior. Adherents of the Reciprocity View, however, might say that the acceptability of Spade's joke was determined by Murphy's earlier joke, such that, had Murphy not told his joke, Spade's own joke would have been less acceptable – turn about is fair play.

The problem with the Reciprocity View as an explanation of familial ethics, however, is that when you boil it down, it's not really about family at all. Sure, reciprocity tends to track family relations – most parents raise their kids well, or at least well enough, so most parents will have incurred a fair amount of reciprocal credit by the time the big job of getting those kids to adulthood has been accomplished. Same goes for other relatives. Grandparents, siblings, aunts, and uncles tend to help out when their young relatives need it, so, generally, there tends to be a relationship among family members in which reciprocity is owed. But the same is true of many teachers, coaches, helpful bosses, and friends. For many of us, once we're adults, the number of non-family members who have really helped us get where we are in life will begin to outnumber the familial influences.

Dysfunctional Family Feud: The No Special Obligations View

Good news for the Rileys and the Combs, the two families from Dysfunctional Family Feud who can't get through a sentence without being nasty to each other, there is a view of familial ethics that might excuse their behavior.[11] It's known as the No Special Obligations View. Popularized by contemporary philosopher Jane English, this view simply denies that we owe our family anything special.[12] English argues that people cannot possibly incur a debt by being born into a family that supports them, because debts are the kind of things that we must agree to and be able to opt out of.[13] If I ask you to bring me back a sandwich as you head out on your lunch break, I am aware that I'm incurring a debt. I will either need to give you money when you return with my sandwich, or at the very least be prepared to buy you a sandwich in the future. But if instead, you simply show up with an unsolicited sandwich for me, English would say that you've given me a gift, and gifts do not require repayment.

English argues that the decision to parent a child is a voluntary sacrifice, made not because a child has asked to be born and raised, but because someone has decided to be a parent. Our offspring do not move through their childhood racking up debt by taking the unsolicited love and support their parents have chosen to give them.[14] Rather, being raised is more like receiving a spontaneous sandwich – it's a gift, and does not require repayment. Sure, an entire upbringing is a more significant gift than an office lunch, but in both cases the recipient of the good thing didn't ask for it, and thus doesn't owe anything in return.

Additionally, English asks us to think about the motivation for why we do things for other people, familial and otherwise. Think about the sandwich again. If you bring me a sandwich that I didn't ask for, you're either trying to sneakily accrue some reciprocal credit in a backhanded way, or, you like me. There's nothing particularly strange or surprising about someone doing something nice for a person they have affection for. We even have a name for this – we call it friendship. English points out that we're not friends with people because we expect a return on the investment (and if we do have that kind of attitude, the relationship isn't actually a friendship, even if we call it that).[15] Friendships arise out of mutual affection, and when you care about someone, you want to help them when they need it, not out of obligation, but simply out of love. Think of the friendship shared between Wayne Campbell (Mike Myers) and Garth Algar (Dana Carvey). When Garth would get over-excited, Wayne would kindly remind him to take his Ritalin – not because it was his duty to do so, but because he cared about his friend.

English argues that our understanding of familial relationships should model that of friend relationships, rather than transactional ones. So, just as friendships are built on love and a desire to care for and be there for each other, and are decidedly *not* built out of obligations, family should be understood the same way. If you love a family member, you will treat that person well – not because they're family, but because you love them – just like friendship. English acknowledges that this is the ideal – it's great when family members love each other. However, there is no obligation. If you don't have feelings that compel you to treat a family member as a friend, you are under no obligation to do so. English sees nothing morally problematic about family members not having close relationships, and as a result there is nothing morally problematic about some family members treating each other no differently than they treat strangers.

On this view, Spade did not wrong Murphy by telling the joke. Spade and Murphy, though both part of the *SNL* family, did not have a friendship – they didn't even know each other. As long as the joke would be considered appropriate for Spade to make about a stranger, it would be appropriate for him to make it about Murphy. Of course, Murphy also expressed unhappiness with the greater *SNL* family that signed off on the joke, including Lorne Michaels. To the extent that any of those individuals did have a friend relationship with Murphy, then they could have been in the wrong to green light the joke. But again, the wrongness wouldn't have been because of an obligation to treat Murphy differently due to his membership in the *SNL* family, but rather because friends shouldn't treat friends in ways that hurt them. So, if Murphy had friends on the show who could have stopped the joke from happening, they should have done so.

Whatever your view on familial ethics – whether you skew Confucian and think the *SNL* cast, writers, and other extended family members owe their patriarch Lorne respect no matter what – or if you lean toward English and think what matters is friendship and the emotions (or lack thereof) it inspires, thinking through these views of family obligations can be helpful. Not only does it shed some light on different perspectives regarding the Spade-Murphy debacle, but it can help us think more clearly about our own families as well.

Notes

1. *Saturday Night Live*, Season 21, Episode 8, 1995.
2. Brian Hiatt, "Eddie Murphy Speaks: The Rolling Stone Interview," *Rolling Stone*, November 9, 2011.
3. James Andrew Miller and Tom Shales, *Live From New York: The Complete, Uncensored History of Saturday Night Live as Told by Its Stars, Writers, and Guests, Kindle edition* (New York: Little, Brown and Company, 2014).
4. Ibid.
5. Ibid.
6. Ibid.
7. Ibid.
8. Saturday Night Live, Season 44, Episode 5, 2018.
9. David Spade, "David Spade: This is why Eddie Murphy hated me, wouldn't come back to 'Saturday Night Live.'" *Salon*, October 21, 2015.

10. *Saturday Night Live*, Season 6, Episode 6, 1981.
11. *Saturday Night Live*, Season 17, Episode 4, 1991.
12. Jane English, "What do grown children owe their parents?" in Jecker (ed), *Aging and Ethics: Contemporary Issues in Biomedicine, Ethics, and Society* (Totowa, NJ: Humana Press, 1992), pp. 147–154.
13. Ibid., pp. 147–148.
14. Ibid.
15. Ibid.

Part VI
THE ABSURD STUFF THAT HAPPENS NEAR THE END

Part VI

18

The Simulated Reality of *Saturday Night Live*

Edwardo Pérez

One of the pleasures of watching *SNL* comes from knowing the show is live. The not-ready-for-prime-time-players, their guest hosts, the unannounced walk-on cameos, the house band, and the guest musicians are all in New York at the very moment the show airs, offering us a mocking, postmodern representation of reality through absurd (and sometimes very juvenile) humor. And, because it's live, there's always a chance anyone on stage might drop an F-bomb or break character and laugh uncontrollably. More than forty years in, we are familiar with *SNL*'s format, but we never know what's going to happen in any given show or how *SNL* will comment on whatever issues occupy the current moment. From guest hosts spoofing themselves in sketches, to the various impersonations of cultural figures, to the parody commercials to the pseudo-news of "Weekend Update," *SNL* humorously captures the present and reflects it back to us, satirically revealing the hidden realities we all experience.

The live element is perhaps the most significant aspect of *SNL*, not just in the performance and broadcasting of the show, but in the way each episode exists in its own timely moment, depicting a skewed, but still recognizable, version of reality. "Live from New York it's Saturday Night!" isn't just the declaration that opens each episode. It's an invitation (a verbal White Rabbit) to enter the altered reality of Studio 8H. We may watch *SNL* in reruns (or DVR playbacks or YouTube clips) but these viewings aren't the same as watching it happen in a live broadcast – which is why people living on the West Coast don't experience *SNL* the same way as the rest of us. (In fact, the West Coast broadcasts include edits and bleeps when something

Saturday Night Live and Philosophy: Deep Thoughts Through the Decades, First Edition. Edited by Jason Southworth and Ruth Tallman.
© 2020 John Wiley & Sons Ltd. Published 2020 by John Wiley & Sons Ltd.

unexpected happens). The first live broadcast in Mountain and Pacific time zones happened on April 15, 2017, about forty-two years into *SNL*'s run. This raises some interesting philosophical questions regarding *SNL*'s relationship to reality. What is *SNL*'s reality? Does *SNL* only exist in the live moment? What does "Live from New York" really mean?

One way to address these questions is to consider how reality is presented on *SNL*, and how we perceive it. Does *SNL* reflect reality, simulate reality, create reality, re-create reality, blend reality, alter reality, or delay reality? Does anything on *SNL* resemble or relate to reality in any meaningful way? Let's see if Plato (427–347 BCE) and his Cave Myth, and Jean Baudrillard (1929–2007) and his conception of simulacra, can help us better understand the nature of *SNL*'s reality.

God I Love a Scalding Hot Vodka

The Cave Myth in Plato's *Republic* describes a group of chained men watching shadows projected onto a wall. In the myth, the shadows are the men's perception of reality, a mere reflection of what's truly real. There are many ways to interpret the Cave Myth, but for our purposes it's enough to understand one of the myth's main points: that reality and perception are not always the same, because what we see and what we think is real may only be a reflection of what's actually real. Does this resemble *SNL*'s reality? Is *SNL*'s reality a reflection of the larger reality we experience?

We know the reality *SNL* depicts isn't real, yet the show's humor reveals that there might not be much of a difference between appearance and reality when the reality is reflected. After all, don't *SNL*'s sketches often depict what we're already feeling and reflect what we already know? Isn't that what makes them funny? Doesn't the humor allow reality to be both reflected and revealed more profoundly than the social commentary that occurs on cable news and talk shows?

Whether it's the simulated game shows and talk shows, mock presidential debates, or fake commercials, *SNL* utilizes reflections of reality as a way to critique reality. For sketches like Black Jeopardy and ads like Swiftamine, *SNL* constructs a fake reality to reflect the actual reality we're experiencing in the moment (such as racial inequality and the nauseous feeling we get when we realize that Taylor Swift might be cool). For sketches like the October 18, 2008 Cold Open, where Sarah Palin met Sarah Palin (Tina Fey), or "Bar Talk" from the October 3, 2015 episode, where Hillary Clinton (Kate McKinnon) talks to a bartender name Val

(Hillary Clinton), appearance and reality are blurred and reflected in a profound way (especially when Alec Baldwin address Sarah Palin as "Tina" and Bill Clinton (Darrel Hammond) runs when he sees two Hillarys). Indeed, these sketches allowed the real Sarah Palin and the real Hillary Clinton to engage in endearing, self-effacing (and very postmodern) self-reflection, while the audience was able to consider the reflective picture of the actual world contemporary to the sketches airings (the possibility of the first female vice president and first female president).

In the Cave Myth, Plato suggests that many of us would not want to leave the cave's simulated reality, that if we were to be made aware of the true nature of reality we'd become bewildered and seek to return to the simulation. There's a sense of security and familiarity within the cave. After all, in Plato's account, the men have been chained to the wall since they were children, the cave is all they know (and for those of us who are in our forties and have watched *SNL* since the show first aired, it's marked almost every stage of our lives). Yet, as Plato suggests, the only way to gain knowledge about reality is to leave the cave (or turn off the television). This is what makes *SNL* philosophically interesting; it allows us to gain knowledge while remaining in the cave (or coming back to it willingly every Saturday night), as the blended reality *SNL* presents functions beyond a mere reflection, offering humorous critical reflection on the issues of the day. To examine this further, let's turn to Baudrillard.

Well, Isn't That Special?

In his 1981 philosophical treatise *Simulacra and Simulation*, Baudrillard argues that symbols and signs have essentially replaced reality and meaning throughout society (and this was before the internet, Facebook, Laptops, and Smartphones became ubiquitous). While Plato observed that the reality we perceive is a reflection of reality, Baudrillard suggests it's a copy of reality – what he calls *simulacra*, which he organizes into different phases and orders while recognizing several phenomena contributing to the creation of simulacra, such as media, language, ideology, and socio-economic structures. Throughout all of this, Baudrillard emphasizes that we aren't just unaware reality is a façade (like in Plato's Cave Myth), we can't tell the difference between what's real and what's not.

For *SNL*, Weekend Update (like many aspects of the show) presents a facsimile of reality, mixing actual news stories with blunt commentary delivered by sarcastic anchors and original characters. For example, in the November 5, 2016 episode (which aired the weekend before the 2016 Presidential Election) *SNL* Weekend Update Co-Anchor (and *SNL* writer) Colin Jost begins by stating an actual fact, that "A Catholic Church in San Diego has warned parishioners that they will go to hell if they vote for Democrats" in the 2016 election.[1] Jost then blends this reality with a constructed reality by adding, "Here to comment on the state of the election is Church Lady," who offers in a mock-serious tone, "Jesus is not on the ballot, Colin."

While viewers know The Church Lady (Dana Carvey) isn't real, her commentary on the 2016 election and her presence in the skit provides an appealing blend of realities, especially to viewers familiar with The Church Lady's history on *SNL*. Indeed, the culmination of the sketch has The Church Lady singing Louis Armstrong's "What A Wonderful World" while a montage of actual politically-oriented photos plays behind her. The photos feature images of Hillary Clinton and Donald Trump (both looking like they're shouting at political rallies), Hillary and Bill Clinton (looking hopeful on the night of the DNC convention), Rudy Giuliani (looking like he's screaming angrily), Anthony Weiner (shirtless, taking a selfie), and Vladimir Putin (shirtless on horseback) – all serving as an ironic contrast to the lyrics of the song. But, what's paramount is that the simulated reality created by the sketch seems real.

Indeed, while the piece is funny, offering some pointed, contemporary social commentary, it does exactly what Baudrillard observes in a simulated reality, with The Church Lady functioning as if she were a real religious leader serving as some sort of moral compass for the nation – she's a sign of the real substituting for the real. For some, The Church Lady might've seemed more real than the actual news story Jost referenced. In fact, we see this throughout *SNL*'s history where characters become so real that they seem to exist in their own simulated reality, not just as a reflection of it. As Baudrillard might say, the imaginary becomes real and the real becomes imaginary because everything is simulated. To examine this further, let's see how some of Baudrillard's conceptions of simulacra are illustrated on *SNL*.

Justin Bieber for Calvin Klein

As Baudrillard explains, the first phase of simulacra reflects reality. Typically, this type of simulacra is merely an image of something, like a photograph. Yet, when we consider how impersonations function, as a copy of the person being impersonated, perhaps impersonations are simulacra, too. For example, Kate McKinnon's parody of Justin Bieber's Calvin Klein advertisement seems like a first phase simulacrum. Visually, McKinnon's hair, body pose, and tattooed arms are a close resemblance of Bieber's actual Calvin Klein ad and thus convey a decent reflection. Even McKinnon's characterization of Bieber in sketches largely remains a first phase simulacrum, as McKinnon relies mainly on the visual similarities between her and Bieber (especially through McKinnon's facial expressions) to make the impersonation a humorous reflection of Justin Bieber, but not a replacement.

Indeed, as good of an actress as McKinnon is, her portrayal would never be mistaken for the real Justin Bieber. Given that her Bieber essentially functions as an artificial replication, we can also describe McKinnon's impersonation as a first-order simulacrum. It's not a mass-produced copy (which would characterize a second-order simulacrum), nor is the distinction between the real Bieber and McKinnon so blurred that we can't tell the difference (which would characterize a third-order simulacrum).

Of course, McKinnon's Bieber follows a long line of impersonation simulacra that don't really move beyond the surface of the original character, using a resemblance related to physical traits and mannerisms or vocal accents and speech patterns to create a recognizable image. They're humorous and often spot-on simulacra, yet they don't really supplant the original in any significant way. Let's see what we can find when we look at the next phase of simulacra.

Don't Test When I'm Crazy On That Airplane Glue

For Baudrillard, when an image moves toward a masking and denaturing of reality it's in the second phase of simulacra. Natalie Portman's Raps (*Natalie's Rap*, which aired in 2006, and *Natalie's Rap 2.0*, which aired in 2018) seem to function in this way, as the combination of the rap video visuals and explicit lyrics (and Portman's commitment in both performances) work to convey a different image of the Oscar winning actress. Thus, both of Portman's rap videos move beyond the first phase of simulacra, as their representations of Portman reveal a side of Portman that denatures her personality, from a serious actress to a foul-mouthed, disaffected, self-absorbed gangsta rapper. She may not be a real rap artist, but her relative ease with the performance and the pointed nature of the lyrics seem to mask part of her real self. It's a farce, but it's done well enough to make the audience wonder if Portman really feels the way the lyrics of her raps suggest she feels (or if she could beat Eminem or Cardi B in a rap battle). Certainly, there's humor in watching her rap lyrics, such as "Don't test when I'm crazy on that airplane glue, put my foot down your throat 'til you shit in my shoe, leave you screaming, pay for my dry cleaning, fuck your man, it's my name that he's screaming"[2] in her first rap or "Xannies dissolving in my Pinot, my man dance, but he's not a ballerina, yeah, he twinkle his toes, but he give me good D, though, wrap a good burrito"[3] in her second rap.

While both of Portman's raps fit the second phase of simulacra outlined by Baudrillard, they remain first-order simulacra in the sense that they convey an artificial representation of Natalie Portman. She's not copying herself as one would do in a second-order simulacrum (she's never become a musician like Jennifer Lopez or Hailee Steinfeld did), nor is Portman replacing herself as one would in a third-order simulacrum (like Garth Brooks did through his rock star alter-ego Chris Gaines when he hosted *SNL* on the November 13, 1999 Season 25 episode). Rather, Portman's rap artist impersonation of herself fits with various other second phase, first-order simulacra from *SNL*, especially by guest hosts who typically present a version of themselves on *SNL* that slightly shifts the original image, conveying something different yet still recognizable (to Garth Brooks' credit, Chris Gaines looked and sounded completely different, which is why Gaines is an example of a third-order simulacrum).

Of course, second phase simulacra on *SNL* are not limited to guest hosts or cast members poking fun at themselves (or trying out new personalities). Kristen Wiig's Kathie Lee Gifford, Will Ferrell's George W. Bush, and Darrell Hammond's Sean Connery all create an impression of their respective original characters that goes beyond the first phase, impressions that mask and denature the original to the point that a variation of the original character is created. Wiig, Hammond, and Ferrell exaggerated Gifford's, Connery's, and Bush's respective personalities while retaining a familiar core. However, these three impersonations seem to straddle the philosophical bridge linking first-order and second-order simulacra.

On one hand, each of these impressions is an artificial replication, making them first-order simulacra. But, each impersonation can also be seen as a copy of the original, making them second-order simulacra. Ferrell's Bush, especially, creates an impression that can be mass produced and commodified, which, for Baudrillard, is what second-order simulacra do. Indeed, Will Ferrell capitalized on his Bush impersonation in his post-*SNL* career, touring the country in his self-written play, *You're Welcome America. A Final Night with George W. Bush*, which ran on Broadway from February 5 to March 15, 2009, was broadcast live on HBO, and was released on DVD.

Certainly, the commodification of *SNL* characters is nothing new. Every *SNL*-related film is essentially a second-order, commodified simulacrum. Accordingly, many *SNL* alums have traded on their *SNL* fame in film and television, effectively functioning as second-order simulacra in the sense that their post-*SNL* careers represent a different version of their *SNL* personality. Certainly, Al Franken (his sexual misconduct scandal notwithstanding) worked hard to craft a public persona vastly different from his daily affirming *SNL* character Stuart Smalley. This brings us to the third phase of simulacra.

Versace Pockets

The third phase of simulacra marks an absence of reality. This is where a simulacrum begins to take on its own reality. In this sense, reality is absent because it's altered. Maya Rudolph's Donatella Versace provides a humorous example of this, as Rudolph's portrayal of Versace (which was both praised and criticized by the real Donatella Versace) was essentially fictional – there's a connection to reality (because Donatella Versace is real) but, since Rudolph's version is largely original, there's an absence of reality, too.

In Rudolph's conception, Donatella was a rude, drunk, and not very intelligent Diva, masking the actual personality of the real Donatella. As Versace explained to Rudolph in a conversation with *Andy Warhol's Interview Magazine* in February 2013, "Maya, the diamonds you wear when you imitate me on Saturday Night Live are nothing compared to mine. [...] You can't do that to me, darling. You can't wear fake jewelry. I'm allergic to it. I get a rash all over my body." Versace goes on to school Rudolph in the rules of being a proper Diva (don't scream at guests, don't wear a dress in the tub, and get better-looking men to dance around you). What's significant is that Versace knows Rudolph is only doing an imitation, yet, Versace wants the imitation to be as real as possible. Certainly, Versace seems to fear that the audience will get a false impression – and unless a viewer was familiar with Versace's actual persona, they likely did.

Thus, at least for Versace, Rudolph's impersonation conveyed an absence of reality. After all, if Versace wouldn't wear fake jewelry, she'd never try to hawk her own brand of Hot Pockets, even if they did come with a $75,000 diamond tote (and it's doubtful her favorite flavor of hot pocket would be Cheesy Chili Cheeseburger). But, that's where the element of humor adds to the illusion, blending a perception of reality (Versace's Diva personality) with an interpretation of reality (Rudolph's inebriated Versace, shouting and slurring her speech at anyone who annoys her, even kids trick-or-treating at Halloween). This leads us to Baudrillard's conception of a hyperreality, which is a reality that seamlessly blends actual reality with simulated reality.

To understand Baudrillard's conception of hyperreality, let's consider the Cold Open sketch from the May 5, 2018 episode from Season 43, which blends reflected reality with actual reality to offer a revealing, critical take on the political storm surrounding President Trump, relying on an array of impersonations (and one "real" personality) as it depicts an interpretation of actual events in one of the most daring political sketches ever seen on *SNL*.

A Storm's A-comin', Baby

The May 5, 2018 Cold Open begins with a text that reads: "The following is based on real events." The sketch then satirically overlaps several scandals involving President Trump and various people in his orbit. The humor comes not just from being familiar with every scandal and every personality (and the actors portraying them), but also from experiencing the way the sketch blends realities, especially when the real Stormy Daniels plays herself at the end of the sketch. Daniels' presence is a reflection of reality (as we can imagine what an actual Daniels/Trump conversation might sound like) and a blending of the reflection with actual reality, as Daniels' candid comments toward Trump (Alec Baldwin) seem to represent her real feelings (and the feelings of some viewers and audience members, who cheered her on). This is where things truly become hyperreal.

As Baudrillard observes, in a hyperreality "there is neither fiction nor reality anymore – hyperreality abolishes both."[4] Viewing *SNL* this way means that the fiction and reality are so blended we don't really see either. Instead, we see the hyperreality that not only abolishes both but blends them into something else. Certainly, the May 5, 2018 Cold Open can be seen operating this way. Consider the following excerpt of dialogue between Trump and Daniels:

TRUMP:	Just tell me what do you need for all this to go away?
DANIELS:	A resignation.
TRUMP:	Yeah right. Being president is like doing porn, once you do it, it's hard to do anything else. Besides, my poll numbers are finally up. And speaking of "polls" being up.
DANIELS:	Oh, come on.
TRUMP:	Well, we'll always have Shark Week. I solved North Korea and South Korea, why can't I solve us?
DANIELS:	Sorry Donald, it's too late for that. I know you don't believe in climate change, but, a storm's a-comin', baby.
TRUMP:	I've never been so scared and so horny at the same time, and ...
TRUMP AND DANIELS:	Live from New York, it's Saturday Night!

Adding to the hyperreality, *SNL*'s twitter account (@nbcsnl) sent several tweets in real time during the May 5 live broadcast, intensifying the layers of blurred realities. The most provocative tweet was a photo of Stormy Daniels and Alec Baldwin (still in character as Trump) accompanied by a caption that echoed Stormy's admonition from the skit: "I know you don't believe in climate change, but a storm's a-coming!" – Stormy Daniels #*SNL*. The tweets captured the moment perfectly, encapsulating the spirit of the Cold Open sketch while enhancing its hyperreality.

Indeed, the May 5, 2018 Cold Open sketch is groundbreaking in its ability to juggle thirteen characters involved in at least thirteen overlapping political scandals and in its willingness to confront the prurient nature of Trump's presidency by allowing an actual porn star (who's accused the President of the United States of having an affair) to participate in the sketch, redefining the scope of *SNL*'s satirical abilities in the process. Moreover, the sketch marks a pivotal moment in our nation's history, a moment so surreal (and at times incomprehensible) it has to be reflected back to us through a comical hyperreality, one that allows us to laugh at the profound insight *SNL* conveys through its satirical, simulated reality.

Live From New York

On a final note, it's worth considering the fact that *SNL* exists as a live show, meant to be seen in real time, as if Studio 8H were a modern version of Plato's Cave, with audience members watching a reflected, simulated, hyperreality. Does this enhance the reality we experience as viewers? Does seeing *SNL* the moment it airs make its version of reality seem more real? Once an episode airs, can it ever really exist again? Does every episode of *SNL* simply fade into history, becoming a humorous ninety-minute snapshot that once seen, loses its relevance? Is meaning abolished through an endless cycle of simulacra or is it constantly (re)created? As we asked at the beginning of the chapter, what does "Live from New York" really mean?

For Baudrillard, it might mean that *SNL* functions as a microcosm of our society, representing an imaginary world and our actual world – which are both simulations, because, for Baudrillard, the imaginary becomes real and the real becomes imaginary. Like our world, *SNL* is live and yet it isn't. It exists and yet it doesn't. It captures contemporaneous moments but then they fade. From this perspective, every aspect of *SNL* is nothing more than a reflection of what's real, as Plato observes, or a simulation of what's real, like Baudrillard suggests – just like our world. On one hand we know that the array of original characters, impersonations, sketches, commercials, and Weekend Update news reports are fictional. They don't exist and yet they do, becoming real not just in the portrayals and in the airings of episodes but in the way we interact with them, marking every moment they portray and creating reality while reflecting it and simulating it back to us.

Thus, as a reflection, a simulacrum, and as a microcosm, *SNL* continuously copies itself, duplicating the well-known format in endless variation from week to week and season to season, adding and subtracting characters and sketches along the way to match the contemporaneous moments it simultaneously (re)creates and reflects – just as our world does every day. What *SNL* ultimately reveals, then, is that the most important aspect of reality is the experience of the (real/simulated) moment occurring right now. If you don't tune in, you've missed it.

Notes

1. Joshua Stewart, "Catholic parish's bulletin says Democratic voters are doomed to hell, Clinton is satanic." The *San Diego Union-Tribune*, November 2, 2016. As Joshua Stewart reported, the Immaculate

Conception Catholic Church claimed in a bilingual bulletin claimed, "It is a mortal sin to vote Democrat," citing legislative policies on abortion, same-sex marriage, euthanasia, human cloning, and embryonic stem-cell research as proof that Democrats (politicians and those who support them) will go straight to hell when they die.

2. Natalie's Rap.
3. Natalie's Rap 2.0.
4. Jean Baudrillard, *Simulacra and Simulation*. Tr. Sheila Faria Glaser (Ann Arbor: University of Michigan Press, 1994, 125). To be clear, Baudrillard is describing the hyperreal nature of J.G. Ballard's novel *Crash*. Nevertheless, his description explains how a hyperreality functions, which seems appropriate to apply to *SNL*.

19

Deep Thoughts about Deep Thoughts
The Existentialism of Jack Handey

John Scott Gray

"It takes a big man to cry, but it takes a bigger man to laugh at that man."[1] Wisdom such as this, whether you are a laugher or a crier, sets the work of Jack Handey apart from other fare on *Saturday Night Live*. "Deep Thoughts" and "Fuzzy Memories" were fan favorites as transitional pieces between larger set pieces on *SNL* in the 1990s. Delivered over soothing music and serene images, Handey's bits never showed his face on screen, calling to mind his observation that "the face of a child can say it all, especially the mouth part of the face." Handey was no child, and so perhaps we didn't need to see his face.

Classic Handey thoughts include "sometimes I think I'd be better off dead. No, wait. Not me, you,"[2] and "Mom used to warn me that I could lose an eye playing with BB guns. But she never warned me that I could also lose my BB gun, which I did."[3] These dark and offbeat takes on the human condition often have an existentialist feel. Existentialism is a philosophy concerned with "the individual, the experience of choice, and the absence of rational understanding of the universe with a consequent dread or sense of absurdity in human life."[4] In other words, human beings find themselves trying to live meaningful lives without truly comprehending the nature of what that meaning may be, or whether or not true meaning could even exist. Sounds funny, right?

Saturday Night Live and Philosophy: Deep Thoughts Through the Decades, First Edition. Edited by Jason Southworth and Ruth Tallman.
© 2020 John Wiley & Sons Ltd. Published 2020 by John Wiley & Sons Ltd.

The Absurdity of Finding Fun in the Absurd

For French philosopher Jean-Paul Sartre (1905–1980), human existence boils down to moments when we recognize our responsibility to make a choice within a context that may make our choices meaningless. The only meaning that exists in the world is the meaning that we give it. As Sartre famously said, "existence precedes essence."[5] We are not born with a pre-established essence that makes us who we are. Instead, we make ourselves who we are via the choices we make and the lives we live. If we choose a life of crime, we can still, within the context of that choice, decide the degree of seriousness or humor we bring to our experiences. In Handey's opinion, "if you're robbing a bank, and your pants suddenly fall down, I think it's okay to laugh, and to let the hostages laugh too, because come on, life is funny."

Still, we can sometimes find ourselves paralyzed by concerns about whether or not anything that we do will make a difference. Does life really have meaning if we are doomed to die, if all the people we know are doomed to die, and if our sun and planet are doomed to perish in a fiery supernova? Our options may change with time as we become aware of more exciting possibilities, but then we may find ourselves falling for the illusion that the grass is greener on the other side of the fence. As Handey reminds us, "whether they live in an igloo or a grass shack or a mud hut, people around the world all want the same thing: a better house!" While a new house might temporarily satisfy a desire, it would not lead to lasting happiness or meaning.

Albert Camus (1913–1960) notes that, "a man wants to earn money in order to be happy, and his whole effort and the best of a life are devoted to the earning of that money. Happiness is forgotten; the means are taken for the end."[6] In a materialistic society, many people are obsessed with wealth and status, thinking those things will make us happy. When success fails to deliver what we hope and expect, we find ourselves adrift. Life, like the humor of Jack Handey, is absurd, defying our hopes and expectations. Camus compares the human condition to the story of Sisyphus, the mythological figure doomed to push a boulder up a hill for all eternity, only to watch it fall down the other side. Like Handey, Camus manages to find a silver lining in a very gray cloud, "the struggle itself toward the heights is enough to fill a man's heart."[7] Sisyphus' efforts may be futile, but he can nonetheless be happy. What matters is the way he acknowledges this absurdity and yet perseveres. Handey likewise advocates perseverance in the face of meaninglessness, musing that "sometimes I think the world has gone completely mad. And then I think, 'Aw, who cares?' And then I think, 'Hey, what's for supper?"

What to Do When Clowns Kill Your Father

Despite the heroic example of Sisyphus, existentialists do not ignore the difficulties brought on by circumstances. Some paths are easier to follow than others. For example, many people find clowns more scary than funny, but not everyone can get over the fear of clowns with equal ease. Thinking about it, Handey says, "I've wondered where this started, and I think it goes back to the time I went to the circus and a clown killed my dad." While the common fear of clowns may arise from any number of places, having one actually kill your father in your presence might lead you to see them as less than hilarious, whether you want to laugh or not.

The ease of certain paths over others was a central part of Simone de Beauvoir's (1908–1986) groundbreaking book, *The Second Sex*. In that text, she talks about the ruts that certain mindsets create that lead toward sexist worldviews. Those closed-minded, rutted attitudes then infuse the minds of women, programming them to fill the roles that the ruts dictate. Think, for example, of how certain jobs are often seen as being men's work or women's work. When we picture a nurse, we tend to think of a woman. There is nothing wrong with being a nurse, but there is something wrong if a woman cannot picture becoming a doctor. As de Beauvoir said, "the vicious circle is met with in all analogous circumstances; when an individual (or a group of individuals) is kept in a situation of inferiority, the fact is that he *is* inferior."[8] It is indeed difficult to resist society's programming and to make substantial changes in one's life. As Handey sees it, "It's easy to sit there and say you'd like to have more money. And I guess that's what I like about it. It's easy. Just sitting there, rocking back and forth, wanting that money." De Beauvoir counsels against just sitting there. We need to take action, and we need other people to support us in pursuing our dreams and fighting stereotypes. Otherwise, we find ourselves stuck in the rocking chair, doing what is easy and going nowhere.

Still, we need to recognize that our dreams may not match our realities, and talking about our dreams can get us in trouble. As Handey observes, "Sometimes it's hard to tell if something is actually a memory, or you just dreamed it. So, I asked my boss if I called him a lying, stinking thief, or I just dreamed it, and he said I just dreamed it. Whew, that was close." A dream may not be reality, but it is a perception of reality that opens doors, including fears, which may not have been open before.

When You Die Laughing

In keeping with his existentialist vibe, Jack Handey has numerous deep thoughts about death. He observes, for example, that you, "Better not take a dog on the Space Shuttle, because if he sticks his head out when you're coming home his face might burn up." He also offers us sound advice on surviving a perilous situation when he counsels that, "If you ever fall off the Sears Tower, just go real limp, because maybe you'll look like a dummy and people will try to catch you because, hey, free dummy."

For the philosopher Martin Heidegger (1889–1976), awareness of our mortality is a defining characteristic of humanity. As humans, we must come to terms with the fact that we are going to die, and that awareness can allow us to live an authentic life. In the existential sense, "authentic" means to possess, "that attitude in which I engage in my projects as my own."[9] Digging deeper, this means that I must do things not because I think others think I should, but because I think I should. The weight of our mortality, however, can be addressed by looking at death less as something to dread and more as a fact that we can acknowledge and even laugh at. As Handey muses, "Dad always thought laughter was the best medicine, which I guess was why several of us died of tuberculosis." For Heidegger, we must accept our mortality in a way that other species can never even comprehend. We know the clock is ticking. We know that our days are numbered. We know that our parents sometimes make awful decisions that only serve to speed along our moment of demise (like treating tuberculosis with laughter). But we must authentically face our mortality and take responsibility for our lives. As Handey says, "If you go parachuting and your parachute doesn't open, and your friends are all watching you fall, I think a funny gag would be to pretend you were swimming." While we may not be able to stop the inevitable fall (something that is true for all of us, whether our parachute opens or not), we can control our response. We can face our fate with resolve. Even if we must die, we can do so while laughing in the face of death itself. That, jokes aside, is what one can glean from Handey's suggestion.

Handey turns to discussions of death in his Fuzzy Memories as well, remarking on how he'd, "never forget the time we were at the beach and we buried Uncle Joe in the sand. Boy, did we get in trouble! In fact, we got arrested. It turns out you can't bury people at the beach. Only at the cemetery." While this joke plays on our experience of days at the beach, its humor hinges on a misdirection of attention. Indeed, attention creates significance in the world. You may spend years in a room, unaware of where the power outlet is, until the day when you find yourself needing to plug in a dying laptop. At that time, the outlet becomes the most significant thing in the room. In Handey's beach joke, we picture kids playfully placing sand over their uncle, perhaps covering him from neck to toe. Then, the swerve comes, and as the joke reveals the arrest, our brains quickly turn toward a more somber state of being.

Another example of this kind of swerve in our attention comes from the Fuzzy Memory in which Handey recalls: "Once, when I got lost in the woods, I was afraid that eventually I might have to eat Tippy. But finally I found my way home, and I was able to put Tippy back in the refrigerator with my other sandwiches." Our attention is led in one direction, as the fear of eating Tippy makes us wonder what kinds of things one might fear eating if desperately lost in the forest. Perhaps a beloved dog? Maybe a sister? Quickly, however, that tension is released as our attention is drawn toward the refrigerator and the absurd notion that Tippy was not a pet or a person, but a sandwich all along.

Making the Funny: Why Delivery Matters

When reading Handey's Deep Thoughts in his various books, one loses much of what really made the original bits so funny on television. Phil Hartman's calming meditative voice announces, "And now...deep thoughts...by Jack Handey..." With peaceful music playing and images of streams or trees or clouds moving in the background, the words begin to scroll on the screen. Handey himself reads the words with a deadpan delivery that makes the most absurd claims infinitely funnier. Fuzzy Memories detoured from that formula, showing re-enactments of the familial scenes described by Handey. The deadpan delivery and the peaceful music remained, but the visual depictions of those stories may have undermined their success. Something that is funny in the abstract may be less funny when depicted in reality. The punchline still sneaks up on you, but it is obscured behind a curtain of audio/visual stimulation.

Delivery is particularly significant in political humor. Regardless of your political leanings, there have probably been presidents in the past forty years whom you have not liked. Handey provides a humorous outlet for those frustrations when he says, "I wish a robot would get elected President. That way, when he came to town, we could all take a shot at him and not feel too bad." This fantasy is all the funnier because of the incongruous video of a rocky stream with waterfalls. The same is true of Handey's suggestion that, "I think a good gift for the President would be a chocolate revolver. And since he's so busy, you'd probably have to run up to him real quick and hand it to him." In both cases our minds are free to imagine whichever President we chose.

More serious in light of contemporary politics is Handey's remark that "to me, truth is not some vague, foggy notion. Truth is real. And, at the same time, unreal. Fiction and fact and everything in between, plus some things I can't remember, all rolled into one big 'thing.' This is truth, to me." While spin has always been a part of the political process, the use of more and more advanced forms of communication technology has led to greater confusion and concern for what is or is not true. Truly, it is much more difficult to make authentic choices in an environment in which truth itself is rejected as a legitimate possibility.

Getting the Joke

Jack Handey may not actually be an existentialist philosopher, but as Handey himself said in a particularly positive thought, "perhaps, if I am very lucky, the feeble efforts of my lifetime will someday be noticed, and maybe, in some small way, they will be acknowledged as the greatest works of genius ever created by man." On the flip side, he also opined that, "I hope life isn't a big joke, because I don't get it." This may be the most brilliant point of all, because Handey's Deep Thoughts are actually deep thoughts, disguised as comedy, disguised as deep thoughts. Thanks to Handey, we can all be in on the joke together, and be wiser for it.

Notes

1. Jack Handey, *Deep Thoughts: Inspiration for the Uninspired* (New York: Berkeley Publishing Group), 1992. This book does not have page numbers, and so quotes are given in the text without attribution.
2. Jack Handey, *Deeper Thoughts: All New! All Crispy!* (New York: Hyperion, 1993).

3. Jack Handey, *Fuzzy Memories* (Kansas City: Andrews and McMeel, 1996).
4. Simon Blackburn, *The Oxford Dictionary of Philosophy* (Oxford: Oxford University Press, 1994), 129.
5. Jean-Paul Sartre, *Existentialism is a Humanism* (New Haven, CT: Yale University Press, 2007), 20.
6. Albert Camus, *The Myth of Sisyphus and Other Essays* (New York: Vintage Books, 1983), 103.
7. Ibid., 123.
8. Simone de Beauvoir, *The Second Sex* (New York: Vintage Books, 1989), xxx.
9. "Existentialism," *Stanford Encyclopedia of Philosophy*. Retrieved from https://plato.stanford.edu/entries/existentialism/#AnxNotAbs on July 6, 2019.

20

The Ladies Man and "President Bush"

Can Someone Be Too Stupid for Moral Responsibility?

Jason Southworth

Saturday Night Live is populated with wildly ill-behaved characters. Leon Phelps, the Ladies Man (Tim Meadows) is more interested in sexually exploiting his female callers than he is in helping them with their problems. In Celebrity Jeopardy, Burt Reynolds (Norm Macdonald) is far more interested in psychologically torturing Alex Trebek (Will Ferrell) than in playing the game. *SNL*'s incarnation of George W. Bush (Will Ferrell) is blatantly self-interested, racist, and crass. But we have deep affection for these characters, even when they behave in ways that we would typically find objectionable. Why is this? Why are we willing to let them off the hook? Well, one thing these characters have in common is they're all dumb – dumb as hell. So dumb, in fact, we might question the appropriateness of saying it, if they were real people. We're left to wonder whether it's possible to be too stupid for moral responsibility.

Moral Responsibility: Well Isn't That Special?

As we go about our lives, we make choices and take actions (or fail to do so). These actions then result in people judging us. If we behave appropriately, others might want to praise us, something Stuart Smalley (Al Franken) is very good at. When we act inappropriately, they might want to blame us, as poor Gilly (Kristen Wiig) knows all too well. For it to be correct to attribute praise or blame to someone, that person

Saturday Night Live and Philosophy: Deep Thoughts Through the Decades, First Edition. Edited by Jason Southworth and Ruth Tallman.
© 2020 John Wiley & Sons Ltd. Published 2020 by John Wiley & Sons Ltd.

needs to be "morally responsible" for their actions. So, on a base level, we might say that to be morally responsible means that a person is the type of being deserving of moral praise or blame. Philosophers call this moral agency. Things lacking moral agency don't deserve praise or blame. But how do you tell if something has moral agency? Sometimes, it's pretty clear. No matter what's going on with Blue Öyster Cult, you can't blame the cowbell. But when dealing with beings that can reason, it can be trickier to determine moral agency.

The first philosopher to offer an account of moral responsibility was Aristotle (384–322 BCE). In the *Nicomachean Ethics,* Aristotle recognized that not all individuals qualify as moral agents. To be a moral agent, one must possess a capacity for decision-making. For Aristotle, something counts as a decision only if the decision-maker has thought about it and come to their answer after being motivated by their moral values. Just because someone is a moral agent, however, doesn't mean they act *as a moral agent* all of the time. To act as an agent, the action or disposition must be voluntary, which means the action must be uncoerced, and the agent needs to be aware of what they are doing and the consequences of doing it.

Subsequent philosophers have disagreed regarding how to understand Aristotle's account. Some believe praise and blame are appropriate responses whenever the agent deserves the praise or blame. This view is known as the Merit View. Others believe that praise and blame should be directed at the agent if and only if it would increase the likelihood of the agent changing or improving their behavior in the future. This view is known as the Consequentialist View. Let's consider these views in more detail, to see what they can tell us about characters like the Ladies Man.

The Merit View: I'm Good Enough, I'm Smart Enough

Merit-based accounts of moral responsibility argue that, for someone to be held morally responsible, they must deserve it. One reason a person might deserve to be held morally responsible is because of their actions. If they did something good, they deserve to be praised, and if they did something bad, they deserve to be blamed. This seems pretty easy to apply to our characters. When the Ladies Man gives bad advice, or makes misogynistic comments, or when Bush stereotypes and belittles the people it's his job to protect, they've done something bad, and thus deserve to be blamed. But is it really that simple?

Typically, people who accept the Merit View argue that praise and blame are only merited for actions that are within the agent's control. This is known as the Control Principle, and the philosopher Bernard Williams (1929–2003) framed it in terms moral luck.[1] Elements of moral luck are those that violate the Control Principle such that someone ends up getting praised or blamed for actions that weren't entirely within their control. Here, we're focusing only on a tiny segment of the problem of moral luck, that of Constitutive Luck. Constitutive Luck involves elements of our characters that fall outside of our control, factors such as genetic predispositions and early environmental influences that contribute to the type of people we become. There's disagreement regarding how much we are able to control the way we respond to these factors, but there's no debate regarding the fact that no one has any control over the hand they've been dealt by the genetic lottery, or what kind of influences they had early in life – these were just matters of moral luck.

The concept of Constitutive Luck can help us evaluate the behavior of Burt Reynolds and Sean Connery on Celebrity Jeopardy. Reynolds (Norm Macdonald) has low-brow taste and is easily distracted. These aspects of his character seem to be facts, rather than choices. When he disappears to get his Big Hat and, upon returning, can't shut up about the Big Hat, he's not trying to upset Trebek. He's trying to be entertaining, but is in fact annoying. The Control Principle requires that we not blame Reynolds for an inability to be funny. Ferrell's Connery, on the other hand, seems to be entirely in control of his nastiness. He is deliberately insulting. There's no reason he couldn't be nice if he tried, so the Merit View will blame Connery for his mother-based insults.

The Consequentialist View: No One Can Resist My Schweddy Balls

Remember, the Consequentialist View of moral responsibility holds that praise and blame are only appropriate when their application would reasonably result in a change in the agent's future behavior. In *A System of Logic*, John Stuart Mill (1806–1873) claims that being a moral agent is all about deliberation and reflection. We need to think and reflect on our desires so that we only act on them when it is appropriate to do so, and in appropriate ways. When we think and reflect this way, we act in our capacity as "progressive beings."

Mill doesn't mean anything political in this phrasing. He just means that, through deliberation and reflection, we will improve or progress as moral agents (although it's worth noting that Mill would also agree with virtually all policies typically associated with political progressives).[2]

Given his emphasis on open deliberation and reflection, it should be clear why Mill is seen as a proponent of the Consequentialist View of moral responsibility. Praise and blame can do wonders to influence the future actions of a reflective and deliberative person. When we receive feedback from those around us regarding our actions, we're able to reflect and incorporate the results of our reflection into our deliberations regarding future actions. Each piece of praise or blame we receive serves as a nudge, making us a little more likely to behave well in the future (by reinforcing good behavior with praise and discouraging bad behavior with blame). For instance, if Pete Schweddy (Alec Baldwin) had received some negative feedback regarding the phrasing of his signature treats, he would most likely have been mortified, and modified his phrasing immediately.[3]

Perhaps the greatest *SNL* example of a character who has taken the Consequentialist View to heart is Stuart Smalley. Stuart praises the people who come on his show if they take even the smallest of baby steps. He sees praising a person who has decided to make an affirmation as the best way to encourage them to do it again in the future. On the flip side, when her teachers scold Gilly for her outrageous behavior, they're also employing the Consequentialist View, hoping to make her less likely to behave in mischievous ways in the future by giving her negative feedback regarding her actions.

Of course, for any of this to be effective, the agents receiving the feedback need to be willing and able to engage in the steps of reflection and deliberation. Gilly appears unwilling to modify her behavior, and seems unmoved by negative feedback (or perhaps even to crave it). Leon Phelps, the Ladies Man, also appears unchangeable. He seems unable to recognize that his behavior is inappropriate. Callers react with shock and dismay, frequently hanging up on him, but he blusters on, seeming not to notice that people react badly to his suggestions. The Consequentialist View is built on the idea that praise and blame are only appropriate when it will have a positive effect on the recipient's future actions, so there would seem to be no point in blaming Leon or Gilly. If the negative attention motivates Gilly to continue misbehaving, there might be a moral imperative to remain silent in the face of her antics.

Strawson's View: Yeah, That's the Ticket

Maybe you're feeling as if neither the Merit View nor the Consequentialist View quite capture what we want when we think about moral responsibility. Philosopher P.F. Strawson (1919–2006) accused both views of over-intellectualizing the process of attributing praise and blame. Each of those views measures praise and blame against an objective standard of responsibility (merit and consequences, respectively). Strawson argues that our impulse to judge and hold people responsible is really a matter of attitudes and emotional states regarding our interpersonal relationships. In blaming and praising, Strawson says, we express facts about ourselves, "how much we actually mind, how much it matters to us" and "whether the actions of others…reflect attitudes towards us of good will, affection, or esteem on the one hand or contempt, indifference or malevolence on the other."[4] Strawson calls these factors "participant reactive attitudes." They are (a) natural attitudinal reactions to another's good will, ill will, or indifference, and (b) they are made from a position of engagement in a social world composed of interpersonal relationships, including a relationship with the person being praised or blamed. These interpersonal relationships don't require that we have a direct relationship with the person being held morally responsible, however. We might be in a more general relationship, like fellow citizens, or sentient beings. Because reactive attitudes are expressed naturally as a part of life, they aren't rational in the way the Merit View and Consequentialist View claim. As Strawson puts it, the practice "neither calls for nor permits, an external 'rational justification.'"[5]

Just because, on Strawson's view, our impulse to hold others morally responsible is immediate and natural, this does not mean that all reactive attitudes are appropriate in all cases. We might have to revise our reactive attitude or reject it completely in some circumstances. Strawson sees two obvious ways this could happen. First, upon further investigation, we might determine that while it initially seemed like the person was coming from a place of ill will, we misjudged the situation. Think, for instance, of State Department Attache Jacob Silj (Will Ferrell). People are initially upset by his loud voice, taking him to be aggressive and hostile. But after learning that he suffers from a voice-related medical condition known as voice immodulation, their reactive attitude changes from one of judgment to apology. We could make a similar mistake in misattributing praise, as well. For instance, we might first want to praise third party presidential candidate Senator Tim

Calhoun (Will Forte) for being dependable, forthright, and smelling good, but once he reveals that he's a crystal meth enthusiast who can't wait to push the button, our evaluation might change to blame.[6]

The second way in which our reactive attitudes might change is by determining that the individual under evaluation is not truly capable of participating in genuine interpersonal relationships. This could be for a limited time, because of something like a brain injury or drug use (we see you, Senator Calhoun), or it could be permanent, due to an impairment, cognitive or otherwise, that undermines the individual's ability to act as a moral agent. Such individuals, Strawson says, are not appropriate targets of moral praise and blame. Instead, we should simply ask: is this person likely to cause harm to others, or to be harmed by others? And might we prevent that harm? Typically, we reserve this disposition for young children, animals, and non-sentient objects. Think about how people sometimes anthropomorphize disease or natural disasters and express reactive attitudes. This was done to comic effect with the Chris Farley El Niño sketch.[7] Upon reflection, we can see that such a reaction is nonsensical (which is precisely why Farley as Force of Nature is funny).

Though Strawson rejects both the Merit View and the Consequentialist View, his position captures part of the inclinations that lead people to each of these views. We're attracted to the Merit View because there's something intuitive in the feeling that people deserve praise and blame based on their actions. The Consequentialist View is attractive because it seems unfair to praise and blame someone if they can't do anything about it. Strawson's view can account for both of those impulses.

Now let's apply Strawson's view to *SNL*. Bush, in particular, is an interesting case, because the character is a fictionalized version of an actual person. Bush the character is profoundly stupid. He knows this, is self-conscious about it, and wants to overcome it. We see him psyching himself up for a conversation with Dick Cheney (Darrell Hammond) and Condoleezza Rice (Maya Rudolph), determined not to embarrass himself.[8] This character is dumb to the point of being pitiable – he is not an appropriate object of praise or blame. Thus, we're free to find the character likable, even though he's riddled with morally despicable traits. The real-life Bush, is not the brightest bulb, but he's nowhere near as dumb as his *SNL* counterpart. And herein lies the problem that has garnered criticism of that character. In presenting a version of Bush that is not blameworthy, Ferrell might have inadvertently contributed to a conflation of the fictional with the real, such that viewers failed to hold the real-life Bush accountable for his actions as well, a factor some have argued contributed to his reelection.[9]

In thinking about the Ladies Man, the Consequentialist View left us at a bit of a loss. Upon realizing that negative feedback wouldn't result in behavior modification, there was no clear guidance regarding what to do about Phelps. Strawson's view gives us some direction. Once we recognize that Phelps isn't an appropriate target for our reactive attitudes, we also recognize that he more appropriately belongs in the category of someone whom we need to either protect from harm or prevent from harming others, without ascribing praise or blame. Phelps doesn't seem to be in danger of being harmed, but he is in a position where he can harm others. We probably need to take away his talk show.

Where Do We Go from Here? – Buh-Bye!

For starters, after having learned how to apply these categories to our most lovably incorrigible *SNL* favorites, we're now in a position to apply this standard to real people. It's unlikely that there will be a large number of people with whom we have interpersonal relationships that fall outside the scope of our reactive attitudes, and when we do encounter such individuals it's far less likely to be humorous. Recognizing, however, that an individual might simply fall outside of the parameters under which praise and blame are appropriate, we might realize that such individuals instead deserve our compassion. Thinking through these ideas can also help us to be cognizant of times when we ought to modify our reactive attitudes based on the situations that we find ourselves in. As we discovered with Jacob Silj, just because a behavior strikes us as outrageous in the moment, this doesn't mean we should stand by our initial evaluation if presented with further evidence, either about the situation or about the person.

Past that, we can also think about how this standard of responsibility could be applied to other, non-moral instances of responsibility, such as managerial, epistemic, and aesthetic responsibility. For instance, we might find Alec Baldwin not to be aesthetically blameworthy for his terrible impersonation of President Trump. It isn't his fault, after all, that he has a very limited range as an actor. We might, however, hold Lorne Michaels managerially responsible for approving the stunt casting, since there are other more skilled options that he could have chosen (such as Anthony Atamanuik, whose impersonation of President Trump you can see on *The President Show*). But this is just one example. Go forth and judge responsibly![10]

Notes

1. Bernard Williams, *Moral Luck* (Cambridge: Cambridge University Press, 1981).
2. John Stuart Mill, *A System of Logic*, Book 1, ch. 2, sections 1–4, 1843 (earlymoderntexts.com).
3. *Saturday Night Live*, Season 24, Episode 9, 1998.
4. P.F. Strawson, "Freedom and Resentment," *Proceedings of the British Academy* 48 (1962), 5.
5. Ibid., 23.
6. *Saturday Night Live*, Season 33, Episode 7, 2008.
7. *Saturday Night Live*, Season 23, Episode 4, 1997.
8. *Saturday Night Live*, Season 27, Episode 19, 2002.
9. *THR* Staff. "Horatio Sanz: "Conservative" 'SNL' May Have Helped George W. Bush Get Elected," *The Hollywood Reporter*, March 20, 2015.
10. I would like to thank my partner, Ruth Tallman, for her invaluable support and advice.

Index

Saturday Night Live and Philosophy: Deep Thoughts Through the Decades, First Edition. Edited by Jason Southworth and Ruth Tallman.
© 2020 John Wiley & Sons Ltd. Published 2020 by John Wiley & Sons Ltd.